FOR LOVE OF THE IMAGINATION

I have entitled this book *For Love of the Imagination*. Long ago, I fell in love with the imagination. It was love at first sight. I have had a lifelong love affair with the imagination. I would love for others, through this book, to fall in love, as I once did, with the imagination.

Michael Vannoy Adams

For Love of the Imagination is a book about the imagination – about what and how images mean. Jungian psychoanalysis is an imaginal psychology – or what Michael Vannoy Adams calls "imaginology," the study of the imagination. What is so distinctive – and so valuable – about Jungian psychoanalysis is that it emphasizes images.

For Love of the Imagination is also a book about interdisciplinary applications of Jungian psychoanalysis. What enables these applications is that all disciplines include images of which they are more or less unconscious. Jungian psychoanalysis is in an enviable position to render these images conscious, to specify what and how they mean.

On the contemporary scene, as a result of the digital revolution, there is no trendier word than "applications" – except, perhaps, the abbreviation "apps." In psychoanalysis, there is a "Freudian app" and a "Jungian app." The "Jungian app" is a technology of the imagination. This book applies Jungian psychoanalysis to images in a variety of disciplines. *For Love of the Imagination* also includes the 2011 Moscow lectures on Jungian psychoanalysis. It will be essential reading for psychoanalysts, psychotherapists, students, and those with an interest in Jung.

Photograph by Rose Callahan

Michael Vannoy Adams is an internationally prominent Jungian psychoanalyst in New York City. He is a clinical associate professor at the New York University Postdoctoral Program in Psychotherapy and Psychoanalysis. He is also a faculty member at the Jungian Psychoanalytic Association, the Object Relations Institute for Psychotherapy and Psychoanalysis, and the New School, where he was previously associate provost. He is the author of *The Fantasy Principle: Psychoanalysis of the Imagination* (Routledge, 2004) and *The Multicultural Imagination: "Race," Color, and the Unconscious* (Routledge, 1996). He is the recipient of three Gradiva Awards from the National Association for the Advancement of Psychoanalysis. He has been a Marshall scholar in England and a Fulbright senior lecturer in India.

For information about Jungian psychoanalysis, visit Michael Vannoy Adams's Web site: www.jungnewyork.com.

FOR LOVE OF THE IMAGINATION

Interdisciplinary Applications of
Jungian Psychoanalysis

Michael Vannoy Adams

Routledge
Taylor & Francis Group

LONDON AND NEW YORK

First published 2014
by Routledge
27 Church Road, Hove, East Sussex, BN3 2FA

Simultaneously published in the USA and Canada
by Routledge
711 Third Avenue, New York, NY 10017

Routledge is an imprint of the Taylor & Francis Group, an informa business

British Library Cataloguing in Publication Data
A catalogue record for this book is available from the British Library

Library of Congress Cataloging in Publication Data
Adams, Michael Vannoy, 1947-
For love of the imagination : interdisciplinary applications of Jungian psychoanalysis /
Michael Vannoy Adams.
pages cm
Includes index.
1. Jungian psychology. 2. Imagination. I. Title.
BF173.J85A333 2013
150.19'54--dc23
2013002593

ISBN: 978-0-415-64408-2 (hbk)
ISBN: 978-0-415-64409-9 (pbk)
ISBN: 978-0-203-74298-3 (ebk)

Typeset in Garamond
by Saxon Graphics Ltd, Derby

MIX
Paper from
responsible sources
FSC
www.fsc.org   FSC® C013604

Printed and bound by CPI Group (UK) Ltd, Croydon, CR0 4YY

IN LOVING MEMORY OF JAMES HILLMAN

CONTENTS

PERMISSIONS

Permission to reprint or reproduce the following material is gratefully acknowledged.

Approximately 1,590 words from the *Collected Works* of C.G. Jung. Jung, C.G., *Collected Works of C.G. Jung*, © 1977, Princeton University Press; reprinted by permission of Princeton University Press.

Adams, M.V. (1998) "For Love of the Imagination," in J. Reppen (ed.), *Why I Became a Psychotherapist*, Northvale, NJ, and London: Jason Aronson: 1–14; reprinted by permission of Jason Aronson, Rowman & Littlefield.

Adams, M.V. (2006) "The Islamic Cultural Unconscious in the Dreams of a Contemporary Muslim Man," *Journal of Jungian Theory and Practice*, 8,1: 31–40; reprinted by permission of *Journal of Jungian Theory and Practice*.

Adams, M.V. (2008) "Imaginology: The Jungian Study of the Imagination," in S. Marlan (ed.), *Archetypal Psychologies: Reflections in Honor of James Hillman*, New Orleans: Spring Journal Books: 225–42; reprinted by permission of Spring Journal Books: www.springjournalbooks.com.

Adams, M.V. (2009) "The Sable Venus on the Middle Passage: Images of the Transatlantic Slave Trade," in P. Bennett (ed.), *Cape Town 2007: Journeys, Encounters: Clinical, Communal, Cultural: Proceedings of the Seventeenth International Congress for Analytical Psychology*, Einsiedeln: Daimon Verlag: 161–6; reprinted by permission of Daimon Verlag.

Adams, M.V. (2009) "Obama and Icarus: Political Heroism, 'Newspaper Mythology,' and the Economic Crisis of 2008," *Spring: A Journal of Archetype and Culture*, 81: 291–318; reprinted by permission of Spring Journal Books: www.springjournalbooks.com.

Adams, M.V. (2012) "Golden Calf Psychology: James Hillman Alone in Pursuit of the Imagination," *Quadrant*, 42,2: 58–69; reprinted by permission of *Quadrant*.

Adams, M.V. (2012) "The Invisible Hand and the Economic Unconscious: The Most Important Image of the Last 250 Years," in P. Bennett (ed.), *Montreal 2010: Facing Multiplicity: Psyche, Nature, Culture: Proceedings of the Eighteenth Congress of the International Association for Analytical Psychology*, Einsiedeln: Daimon Verlag: 547–58; reprinted by permission of Daimon Verlag.

The Voyage of the Sable Venus, engraving by William Grainger, 1801, after painting by Thomas Stothard, Image ID 1252460, Manuscripts, Archives and Rare Books Division, Schomburg Center for Research in Black Culture, the New York Public Library, Astor, Lenox and Tilden Foundations; reproduced by permission of the New York Public Library: www.nypl.org.

Push/Jump!, painting by Michael P. Jenkins, 2008, © Michael P. Jenkins; reproduced by permission of Michael P. Jenkins.

Postcards from C.G. Jung to Ernest Jones, November 25, 1913, and December 2, 1913, © 2007 Foundation of the Works of C.G. Jung, Zürich; reproduced by permission of Foundation of the Works of C.G. Jung, Zürich.

The Arlington Court Picture, painting by William Blake, 1821, the Chichester Collection (the National Trust), NTPL 46894, © National Trust Images/John Hammond; reproduced by permission of the National Trust.

Baal with Lightning Spear, limestone stele, 1600–1400 BCE, Louvre, Paris, Art Resource, ART131886, © Erich Lessing/Art Resource, New York; reproduced by permission of Art Resource, New York.

Ghosts of Birds, appliqué by Chris Roberts-Antieau, © Chris Roberts-Antieau; reproduced by permission of Chris Roberts-Antieau.

The artist of the "Critic" drawings (Figures 14.1 and 14.2) has granted permission for them to be reproduced in this book.

PREFACE

Jungian psychoanalysis is an imaginal psychology. It is an example of what I call "imaginology" – which I define as the study of the imagination. In contrast to the words "imaginary" (which means "unreal") and "imaginative" (which means "creative"), the word "imaginal" merely means a relation to images. What is so distinctive – and so valuable – about Jungian psychoanalysis is that it emphasizes images.

What is the relation of Jungian psychoanalysis to images? Jungian psychoanalysis either interprets through "amplification" or experiences through "active imagination" both what and how images mean. Amplification is an interpretative method. It is a comparative and contrastive method. When an image in the psyche (for example, in a dream) is amplified, it is not only compared to but also contrasted with that image in other sources (for example, in myths) to identify similarities and differences. Active imagination is an experiential method. It is a dialogical method. It is a conversation between the ego and the unconscious – or, more specifically, between the ego-image and non-ego images that emerge spontaneously, autonomously, and purposively from the unconscious. It is not a dictation by non-ego images to the ego-image but a negotiation between the ego-image and non-ego images. The ego-image talks to and listens to non-ego images, and non-ego images talk to and listen to the ego-image.

There are also Jungian interdisciplinary applications. Among them are cultural, economic, political, literary, and artistic applications. What enables this application of Jungian psychoanalysis is that all disciplines include images. Disciplines are more or less unconscious of these images and the influence that they exert. As an imaginal psychology, Jungian psychoanalysis is in an enviable position to engage these images effectively, interpret them accurately, and experience not only what they mean but also how they mean, and, in the process, to render conscious what has previously been unconscious.

On the contemporary scene, there is no trendier word than "applications" – except, perhaps, the abbreviation "apps." This popularity is the result of the digital revolution. With incredible rapidity, the software industry develops and introduces applications for hardware devices such as computers, tablets, cell phones, music players, and video games.

Psychoanalysis is an application that has applications. There is a "Jungian app" as well as a "Freudian app." The "Jungian app" is a theory that, as a practice, is a technology of the imagination.

Psychoanalysis is not only a "pure" science but also an "applied" science. Jean Laplanche utters a proper caution about the term "applied psychoanalysis." The term implies, he says, that a theory and a method "are abstracted from a privileged domain, namely that of clinical psychoanalysis," and then applied to other domains. Laplanche repudiates that notion, as I do. "When psychoanalysis moves away from the clinical context," he insists, "it does not do so as an afterthought, or to take up side-issues" (1989: 11). To Laplanche – and to me – clinical psychoanalysis is a domain with a status no more privileged than any other domain. Other contexts are at least as psychoanalytically important as the clinical context. Psychoanalysts are not just "clinicians."

The conventional definition of "applied psychoanalysis" is that it is the application of psychoanalysis to disciplines other than the clinical. For Freud, however, the distinction between clinical psychoanalysis and applied psychoanalysis is "not a logical distinction" (1927, *SE* 20: 257). He regards clinical psychoanalysis as one among many applications of psychoanalysis, and he does not privilege the clinical application over other applications.

Historically, the most immediate application of psychoanalysis was clinical. Freud applied psychoanalysis to increase consciousness and cure illness – which he defined as nervousness. Before Freud became a psychoanalyst, he was a neurologist. In that capacity, he attempted to reduce neurosis to neurons, as contemporary neurologists (or "neuroscientists") attempt to do, but, ultimately, he repudiated that effort as an exercise in futility. After Freud became a psychoanalyst, he argued that individuals were nervous because they were unconscious and that, if they were to become more conscious, they would become less nervous. This radical proposition remains the fundamental principle of psychoanalysis. The purpose of both the "Freudian app" and the "Jungian app" is to increase consciousness.

Freud says that the clinical application of psychoanalysis, valuable as it is, is "only one of its applications." He even entertains the possibility that "the future will perhaps show that it is not the most important one." For Freud, psychoanalysis is much more than a clinical application. "In any case," he declares, "it would be wrong to sacrifice all the other applications to this single one" (1926, *SE* 20: 248).

Freud says of the clinical application that "for a long time it was our only purpose." Eventually, however, psychoanalysis was applied, he notes, "to numerous fields of knowledge." That is, there were interdisciplinary applications of psychoanalysis. Initially, such applications were problematic. "An application of this kind," Freud says, "presupposes specialized knowledge which an analyst does not possess, while those who possess it, the specialists, know nothing of analysis and perhaps want to know nothing." As a result, he says, "analysts, as amateurs with an equipment of greater or less adequacy, often hastily scraped together, have made excursions into such fields of knowledge as mythology, the history of civilization, ethnology, the science of religion and so on." Specialists in other disciplines tended to regard analysts as ignorant interlopers and to dismiss them. Analysts, Freud says, "were no better treated by the experts resident in those fields than are trespassers in general: their methods and their findings, in so far as they attracted attention, were in the first instance rejected." He says optimistically, however, that "these conditions are constantly improving, and in every region there is a growing number of people who study psycho-analysis in order to make use of it in their special subject" (1933 [1932], *SE* 22: 145).

What, however, of analysts, Freudian or Jungian, who have the audacity to apply psychoanalysis to other disciplines? If analysts have no expertise in those disciplines are the results inevitably superficial, even incompetent? Do those analysts deserve the contempt of specialists? Are such efforts mere effrontery?

More personally, what qualifies me to apply Jungian psychoanalysis to other disciplines? Forty years ago, as a graduate student, I deliberately pursued an interdisciplinary education – I studied intellectual and cultural history, political and economic history, the history of ideas, literature, the philosophy of science, and psychology. Eventually, I also studied clinical social work and Jungian psychoanalysis. Over the years, I have taught at eight different universities or colleges and five different psychoanalytic institutes. I am now a clinical associate professor at the New York University Postdoctoral Program in Psychotherapy and Psychoanalysis, and, for the past twenty-five years, I have been a faculty member at the New School, where I have had the opportunity to teach interdisciplinary courses from a psychoanalytic perspective. I have written three previous books, as well as numerous articles on various topics. That cumulative experience is the basis of the Jungian interdisciplinary applications in this book about Jungian psychoanalysis as an imaginal psychology.

I have entitled this book *For Love of the Imagination*. Long ago, I fell in love with the imagination. It was love at first sight. I have had a lifelong love affair with the imagination. I would love for others, through this book, to fall in love, as I once did, with the imagination.

This book also includes the 2011 Moscow lectures on Jungian psychoanalysis. These are three lectures that I delivered as the keynote speaker at the Fifth Conference of the Moscow Association for Analytical Psychology, June 10–12, 2011. I wrote them specially for that occasion and have now revised them for publication. The conference was held at the International University in Moscow – the first private university in Russia – which was founded in 1991 by Mikhail Gorbachev and George H.W. Bush. The theme of the conference was "The Mythological Unconscious," the title of one of the books that I have written. Two Jungian colleagues, both dear friends, Sylvester Wojtkowski from New York and Henry Abramovitch from Jerusalem, also spoke at the conference. It was a special pleasure to be on the program with them. I thank Elena Pourtova, Stanislav Raevsky, and Lev Khegay, who also spoke at the conference, for inviting me to Moscow, and I thank Natalia Pavlikova for translating into Russian the lectures that I delivered in English at the conference. Over the years, I have spoken to many Jungian organizations. None has impressed me as much as the Moscow Association for Analytical Psychology. It was an honor to meet the members of that organization and a joy to witness the vitality of Jungian psychoanalysis in contemporary Russia.

Finally, I especially thank Kate Hawes, Publisher, and Kirsten Buchanan, Senior Editorial Assistant, for commissioning and producing this book for Routledge.

Michael Vannoy Adams
New York City, 2013

References

Freud, S. (1926) "The Question of Lay Analysis: Conversations with an Impartial Person," *SE* 20: 183–250.

Freud, S. (1927) "Postscript," *SE* 20: 251–8.

Freud, S. (1933 [1932]) *New Introductory Lectures on Psycho-Analysis*, *SE* 22: 1–182.

Laplanche, J. (1989) *New Foundations for Psychoanalysis*, trans. D. Macey, Oxford: Basil Blackwell.

Part I

IMAGINAL PSYCHOLOGY

1

FOR LOVE OF THE IMAGINATION

Why I Became a Psychotherapist

I became a psychotherapist because I so love the imagination. William Blake says: "The Imagination is not a State: it is the Human Existence itself" (1976a: 522). That is exactly how I regard the imagination. For me, psychotherapy is essentially an affair of images – of how we imagine and, more important, reimagine ourselves. This process of imagining and reimagining ourselves I call the *fantasy principle* (Adams 2004). I consider the fantasy principle more fundamental than either the "pleasure principle" or the "reality principle."

Why I became a psychotherapist is inseparable from what kind of psychotherapist I became. Although I esteem all of the different schools of psychoanalysis, I have a particular interest in the Jungian school and in the "Hillmanian" school of imaginal (or archetypal) psychology that James Hillman has elaborated (Adams 2008). Jungian analysis interests me because it emphasizes the imagination more than the other schools do.

Psychoanalysis – especially Jungian analysis – has enabled me to return to the imagination. To "return" to something, one must, of course, have "left" something. In a certain sense, I left the imagination. In another sense, however, it was not I who left the imagination (nor was it the imagination that left me). Rather, the imagination was left – left behind me for several years. According to Richard Kearney, the imagination may be leaving us all, not temporarily but permanently. In the postmodern period, Kearney says, we may be witnessing the death of imagination and attending, if not the funeral, at least a wake (1988). There may be such a general trend, but it is a quite particular experience that I wish to emphasize. Mary Watkins, who has described the many varieties of imaginal techniques in use historically in European and American psychology (1984) and who has championed the importance of what she calls "imaginal dialogues" (1986), criticizes certain psychologists (among them, Jean Piaget, Lev Vygotsky, and George Herbert Mead) for undervaluing or even devaluing the imagination. For such psychologists, the imagination is a developmental stage that we should grow out of as we grow into adulthood. For them, the imagination is merely a "phase" of childhood.

I grew up as a child in a small town in Texas. I was an only child until the age of nine when my father and mother – 56 and 50 years old at the time –

adopted my brother and sister, two Korean-American war orphans, ages four and five. For my parents, for my family, that was a supreme example of what I call the "multicultural imagination" (Adams 1996b). Before that, however, as an only child, I had experienced nine years of what a Jungian might call introversion. I do not mean that I was oblivious to external reality in some schizoid sense or that, like Jung, I had in any radically dichotomous sense a public "No. 1" personality and a private "No. 2" personality (1963: 45). Nor do I mean that I had an imaginary companion or an imaginary world – what David Cohen and Stephen A. MacKeith call, after Robert Silvey, who collected many elaborate examples of such worlds, a "paracosm" (1991). I merely had an opportunity to develop an internal, imaginal reality in relation to external reality. Others have had the same or a similar experience. I was hardly unique. As an only child, I was sometimes a lonely child, but I also developed the capacity to be alone without feeling lonely, as well as a respect for the necessity of privacy, even secrecy, and I appreciated what Anthony Storr calls the virtues of solitude (1988), for it provided me with an occasion to imagine.

I had time and space as a child to indulge in what Gaston Bachelard calls "reverie" (1969). My father and mother had moved to a big, old house on ten acres where one of my grandfathers earlier in the century had once had a business that he advertised, true or not, as the largest nursery in northeast Texas. On either side of that land were streets with houses in 1950s suburban style, but those ten acres were, for me, a quite separate reality, which I called "the field." Other children had yards; I had a field. In a sense, it was a field of daydreams, a field for my imagination – a field with black soil, red and yellow roses, purple irises, and white gardenias (that most fragrant flower, my father's favorite), and apple, pear, and peach trees. In that field I played for hours on end by myself, alone with my imagination.

If nature was outside, art was inside. In the house, I played in a room next to my mother's studio, where she drew in charcoal and pastel and painted in oil, where she glazed clay and enameled metal and fired her creations in a kiln. There was also the farm of my other grandfather – eighty acres that a railroad and a highway divided into three parts, a house with two fireplaces (one a hearth in the kitchen, where my six-foot, four-inch grandfather would warm his back while he ate his cornbread after he had dipped it in his buttermilk), a barn (where I learned to handle the udders of cows and to squirt a stream straight into the mouths of cats at a considerable distance), horses, hogs, chickens, and dogs. Jung says that "the chthonic portion of the psyche" – the aspect "through which the psyche is attached to nature, or in which its link with the earth and the world appears at its most tangible" (1927/1931, *CW* 10: par. 53) – grounds life in the most transparent way in archetypal images. In my experience as a child, it was not only nature – earth, plants, and animals – but also art that "archetypalized" my imagination. My imaginal reality was a combination of the chthonic and the aesthetic dimensions – my grandfathers' and father's world and my mother's world.

4

For me, the imagination was not left behind abruptly. If I were to attempt to date the experience, I would say that it occurred over the years between the ages of 13 and 21. In a sense, the process seems to me to have been quite normal – it just happened. I do not believe, however, that it was inevitable, nor do I believe that it was developmentally desirable, as if the imagination was merely one of those childish things that I needed to put behind me. Someone else might simply regard those years as a period of extraversion necessary for socialization. It is difficult for me to do so, however, because I sensed that I missed something. I intuited that I had lost something, perhaps irretrievably. What exactly I had lost, what precisely I missed, I would have been hard put to say, but I now know that it was the imagination.

School and university did not, at least for me, validate the imagination. Educationally, the imagination was not of much visible value. In that context, I resorted to journalism. I edited school and university newspapers, I majored in journalism, and I worked as a summer intern reporter on the *Washington Post* and the *Atlanta Constitution*. I became preoccupied with the external political reality of current events, especially civil rights and the Vietnam War. Then something happened that was to transform me irreversibly. I discovered psychoanalysis, I discovered Freud – I began to rediscover the imagination. In retrospect, I realize that an interest in external political reality can also be a very serious expression of the imagination. As Andrew Samuels notes, there is not only political imagery but also a *politics of imagery* (1993: 14) – but at the time I did not experience it as such. The year was that year of years, 1968. As a Flower Powerist and New Leftist, I read Herbert Marcuse's *Eros and Civilization: A Philosophical Inquiry into Freud* (1955) and Norman O. Brown's *Life Against Death: The Psychoanalytical Meaning of History* (1959). Marcuse and Brown impressed me because they both, although in different ways, called for an end to repression.

My girlfriend at the time was majoring in psychology. She had a special interest in psychoanalysis and Freud. She was writing a senior honors essay on Freud and the scientific method, attempting to demonstrate that, methodologically, Freud had been a scientist. We engaged in intense discussions about psychoanalysis – I citing Marcuse and Brown, she citing Freud. She was extremely critical of the way that Marcuse and Brown used the word "repression" and insisted that they were not using it in the same technical sense that Freud used it. She challenged me to read Freud in the original, in the James Strachey translation, as she had already done. I began to do so. Reading Freud was a revelation. I had never before encountered a system of ideas of such vast imaginative proportions. Freud so impressed me that a year later, when my girlfriend and I flew to England to backpack across Europe, our very first stop in London was the Hogarth Press, where, with my meager undergraduate savings, I proudly ordered a set of the *Standard Edition*, to be shipped to America to await my return at the end of our travels. Since then, I have never been without those twenty-four volumes; they have accompanied me to England for three years and to India for a year.

5

At the time, I was still seriously contemplating a career in journalism. While working as a summer intern reporter on newspapers, however, I had gradually begun to feel that journalism was not the life for me. The emphasis on current events began to seem superficial – too much surface and not enough depth. I now know that it was not journalism that was superficial. It was I who was superficial. I needed more depth. My recent experience with psychoanalysis had led me to believe that ideas were deeper than events. I decided to go to graduate school – I enrolled in the American Civilization program at the University of Texas at Austin.

In my very first semester in that program, I took two courses – "Freud in America" and "Herman Melville" – that profoundly influenced me. The courses were a fortuitous combination. I had never read any of Melville's works, but as I began to do so I discovered that there was a great deal of psychoanalytic literary criticism on his works – especially on *Moby-Dick* and on *Pierre*, the novel in which Melville, like Freud, emphasizes "the two most horrible crimes … possible to civilized humanity – incest and parricide" (1971: 351). I also discovered that one of those who had written psychoanalytic literary criticism on Melville was Henry A. Murray, the Harvard psychologist who (in collaboration with Christiana Morgan) had developed the Thematic Apperception Test, or "TAT." One of the inspirations for the TAT was evidently Murray's reading of "The Doubloon" chapter in *Moby-Dick*, where Melville describes the various interpretations of the gold coin by Captain Ahab and the other sailors as, in effect, a projective test. As one of the sailors says of the attempts to interpret the doubloon: "There's another rendering now; but still one text" (1988: 434). Another, equally important source for the TAT was Morgan's artistic renditions of her fantasies, or "visions," which Jung employed in seminars to illustrate the technique of "active imagination" (Douglas 1993; Jung 1997).

The immediate consequence, for me, was that I began to entertain the possibility that I might become a psychoanalytic literary critic. I also began to perceive (or, more accurately, to project) sexual symbolism everywhere in Melville's works. This interest of mine made a certain impression on Jay Leyda, the eminent literary, music, and film scholar. Leyda, who had edited *The Melville Log* (1969), two magnificent volumes of biographical documents, visited the University of Texas while I was a graduate student there. We had lunch, during which I waxed enthusiastic about my interest in Melville and in sexual symbolism.

The next year, Leyda published an essay, "Herman Melville, 1972," in which he reflected on the then current state of scholarly and critical work on Melville. He lamented that "the art of Herman Melville has been reduced from discovery to a reading assignment" (1973: 163). According to Leyda, the study of Melville was now merely an academic exercise:

> What we once read for joy has been transformed into a "subject," or rather an object for criticism and interpretation. The man who wrote

these works has been pushed aside (again!) by well-meaning persons who tell us what the words really mean – so that there's not much room for either man or works. Critical microscopes are brought into play, but I'm no longer sure for what purpose.

(1973: 163)

Whom, exactly, did Leyda have in mind? As I read the essay, I was chagrined to realize that he had me in mind. Leyda wondered what the purpose was of "a close, a very close hunt for the sexual puns" in Melville's works (1973: 163). He asked: "Is it to learn more about its author than we knew before? or to draw attention to the ingenuity of the interpreter?" (1973: 163–4). Leyda even gave me a funny name: "the hunting inspector" (1973: 164). My critical microscope was, of course, psychoanalysis.

In the meantime, I was awarded a Marshall scholarship (comparable to a Rhodes scholarship but funded by the British Parliament in commemoration of the Marshall Aid Plan for Europe after World War II) to pursue doctoral research in American Studies at the University of Sussex in England. I proposed to write a psychoanalytic dissertation on – what else? – the sexual symbolism in Melville's works. I spent much of the next three years in the library of the British Museum, at a desk under the dome of the Reading Room (I felt as if I were sitting inside a beautiful blue eggshell). I tried to read every book on symbolism that Melville might have read. Many of these books were late-eighteenth- and early-nineteenth-century works in what we would now call comparative mythology. The more I read, the more I began to suspect that my psychoanalytic approach to Melville was woefully naïve.

As I discovered in those works of comparative mythology the sources of much of Melville's symbolism in *Moby-Dick*, I realized that the symbolism was not, in any psychoanalytic sense, unconscious. I began to appreciate Melville as a literary "psychologist" who had imaginatively adapted symbolism from works in comparative mythology to serve his own, quite conscious purposes. I finally decided that psychoanalysis had less to say about Melville than Melville had to say about psychoanalysis. In the process, I also inadvertently became less Freudian and more Jungian. I did not conclude that the source of Melville's symbolism was the collective unconscious, but I did believe that the source was comparative mythology of the sort that so fascinated Jung in, for example, *Symbols of Transformation* (1911–12/1952, *CW* 5). Methodologically, Melville was a Jungian – or Jung was a Melvillian.

One morning while reading the London *Times*, I came across an article on the poet and Blake scholar Kathleen Raine. I had never heard of her, but something about the article made me feel that her own work on William Blake might have something to do with my work on Melville. I wrote a letter to the author of the article, and he forwarded my letter to Raine. Shortly, I received an invitation to visit her in London. Raine served me tea and scones with clotted cream and jam. In her I discovered a kindred spirit who graciously befriended me. On the walls of her house were wonderful engravings by Blake. She showed me other possessions – Yeats's fountain pen, his ESP cards, and his poltergeist photographs. Then and on a number of occasions afterward, we talked about Blake and Melville and the fact that they had both used many of the same sources in comparative mythology. Raine's psychoanalytic sympathies were, as mine had become, Jungian, although, like me, she did not regard either Blake or Melville as unconscious in any psychoanalytic sense. In her major work, *Blake and Tradition* (1968), she had demonstrated that Blake had imaginatively adapted traditional symbolism. My own research had become, in effect, a study of Melville and tradition – and the mythological symbolism in *Moby-Dick*.

On one of my visits to Raine, she suddenly said to me that on my return to America I must meet a Jungian analyst by the name of James Hillman. I had never heard of Hillman, and it was several years before I met him. By then, I had begun to read the books that he had written – among them, the two that have always most impressed me, *Re-Visioning Psychology* (1975) and *The Dream and the Underworld* (1979). What so interested me about Hillman was his emphasis on the imagination and his effort to elaborate "a psychology of image" (1975: xi). Here, finally, was a psychoanalyst for whom the imagination was primary and constitutive of internal reality, not secondary and derivative from external reality.

Through the cumulative influence of Marcuse, Brown, Freud, Melville, Jung, Raine, Blake, and Hillman, I finally returned to the imagination. After graduate school, I did become a psychoanalytic literary critic for ten years. Then I moved to New York, where I accepted a position as associate provost of the New School and entered psychotherapy with a Jungian analyst, the first of three with whom I have worked over the years. Eventually, I earned a degree in clinical social work and a certificate in psychoanalysis. I now have a private practice as a psychoanalyst with a special interest in Jungian theories and methods.

I consider it a great privilege to be a psychotherapist. To be a psychotherapist is to be privy to the imagination of others. I feel honored and humbled to be in the presence of someone who shares with me, confides in me, what he or she imagines. I am fascinated by the imagination, whether it be beautiful or ugly, happy or sad, complex or simple, comic or tragic – or, from the perspective of psychopathology, healthy or sick. To me, the discovery that internal reality, psychic reality – or imaginal reality – is just as real as any external reality is the most important discovery of psychoanalysis. Psychoanalysis does not quite assert that, as Blake insists, "Mental Things are alone Real" (1976b: 617), but it does contend that what I call the psychic construction of reality (or the imaginal construction of reality) is the basic issue in psychotherapy. "The psyche creates reality every day," Jung says. "The only expression I can use for this activity is *fantasy*" (1921, *CW* 6: par. 78). How does someone construct reality imaginally? What images does someone employ, consciously or unconsciously? What is the internal, imaginal experience of external events? These are the questions that I, as a psychotherapist, ask and attempt to answer. When Jung first began to work as a young psychiatrist at the Burghölzli Hospital in Zürich, what astonished him was that nobody "concerned himself with the meaning of fantasies, or thought to ask why this patient had one kind of fantasy, another an altogether different one" (1963: 127).

The reason that I am a Jungian rather than a Freudian is that it seems to me that Freud wants to rectify the imagination – to require what I call the fantasy principle to conform to what he calls the reality principle. For me, Freud is ultimately too much of a realist and not enough of an imagist. He proposes a distortion theory of the imagination. According to Freud, the function of fantasy is to distort reality. The images in a dream, for example, are mere manifest appearances, distortive derivatives of a latent reality. These images are not what they seem to be or seem to mean. From this perspective, the purpose of psychoanalysis is to expose the distortion, identify the derivation, and provide a rectification of the fantasy in strict accordance with reality.

In contrast, it seems to me that Jung wants to explore the imagination without prejudice. As Jung says:

> It is true that there are unprofitable, futile, morbid, and unsatisfying fantasies whose sterile nature is immediately recognized by every person endowed with common sense; but the faulty performance proves nothing against the normal performance. All the works of man have their origin in creative imagination. What right, then, have we to disparage fantasy?
>
> (1931, *CW* 16: par. 98)

For Jung, the purpose of psychoanalysis is, as Blake says, "Conversing with Eternal Realities as they Exist in the Human Imagination" (1976b: 613) – or, in Jungian terminology, dialoguing with archetypal realities as they exist in fantasy. According to Jung, the images in a dream – or in active imagination – are exactly what they seem to be or seem to mean. He proposes a precision theory of the imagination. "Precision means whatever is actually presented," Hillman says. "Simply: the actual qualities of the image" (1977: 69). The unconscious, Jung argues, is incredibly precise in the selection of qualitatively apt images to epitomize psychic reality. It is difficult to interpret psychic reality not because some censor distorts, or encrypts, reality in a code that we then have to decipher but simply because the unconscious, like some poet, communicates in images with which we are only more or less familiar. We do not have to translate these images – we have to define them. We have to explicate all that a specific image implies.

The imagination is, in this sense, what the philosopher of science Michael Polanyi (who also befriended me in Texas and later in England) calls a "tacit dimension" (1966), or what the physicist David Bohm calls an "implicate order" (1981). Jungian analysis employs a phenomenological (or "essentialist") method. It inquires into the essential being or meaning of images, the fundamental phenomena of psychic reality. From a Jungian perspective, the unconscious does not so much conceal as it reveals. What an image is or means is not hidden from us, as if there were some deceptive intent – it is simply unknown to us, because we have not mastered the poetic, or imagistic, language that the unconscious employs.

I marvel at the compositional autonomy of the imagination. When and how does this compositional process occur? Are our dreams gradually composed during the day while we are awake, or are they instantaneously composed during the night while we are asleep? Are our dreams born, like Athena, full-blown from our heads? In a sense, we do not dream – we are dreamed. We do not compose our dreams. Some autonomous process, which for lack of a better word we call the imagination or the unconscious (we used to call it "God"), composes our dreams. Rather than a supernaturalistic, metaphysical account of this process, psychoanalysis offers a naturalistic, metapsychological account – as if that were an adequate, scientific explanation. Similarly, do we fantasize, or are we fantasized?

The ingenuity of the imagination – or the unconscious – never ceases to amaze me. Someone – for example, a woman – tells me a dream, and that dream tells me precisely (and often incredibly concisely) who she imagines she is. "Someone shoots the president," the dreamer reports. "Then there is chaos." Immediately, I know that there exists in the psychic reality of the dreamer a would-be assassin who shoots the president. Who is this president? Or, phenomenologically, what is a president, what is the essence of "president"? A president is not a dictator who dictates in an authoritarian mode; a president presides in a democratic mode. A president is the head of the executive branch of a government. What the dreamer imagines – or what the unconscious of the dreamer images to her – is an assassination attempt on the executive function of the psyche. The imaginal assassin shoots (the dream does not say that he kills) an imaginal president. The psyche experiences the attempt as chaotic – and potentially fatal to the executive function.

What does this dream have to do with the dreamer? In this instance, the dream has to do with what I might call the mind–body politic of the dreamer. It has to do not only with her psychic reality but also with her physical reality. The images in this dream immediately evoked in the dreamer a spontaneous association to an injury that she had previously suffered to her spinal column in an automobile accident. A physician had prescribed a brace, but for reasons of vanity (or, if one prefers, narcissism) the dreamer had ignored or neglected – one might justifiably say "repressed" – the prescription, with the result that her condition had deteriorated. The images in the dream enabled the dreamer to appreciate that one aspect of her psyche, a vanity function, was, in effect, attempting to assassinate another aspect, the executive function, the central nervous system in the spinal column. The dream was not a distortive image of this psychophysical "political" reality; on the contrary, it was a very precise image of it.

Although it is true that the dream did not literally image the condition of the dreamer, this fact does not mean that the imagination distorted that reality, as if it intended to deceive the dreamer. The dream metaphorically imaged the mind–body state of the dreamer, and it did so accurately, with scrupulously elegant exactitude. Jung says that the "obscurity" of the dream is not a distortion but "is really only a projection of our own lack of understanding." If a dream seems "unintelligible," he says, it seems so "simply because we cannot read it." According to Jung, we must "learn to read it" (1934, *CW* 16: par. 319). In order to do so, we must, Jung says, "stick as close as possible to the dream images" (1934, *CW* 16: par. 320). It is apparently from this specific passage that the Jungian analyst Rafael López-Pedraza derives inspiration for the dictum "stick to the image," which Hillman emphasizes as the basic principle of imaginal psychology. Hillman admonishes us to "'stick to the image' in its precise presentation" (1977: 68). From this perspective, the language of the unconscious consists of exquisitely precise images that serve a metaphorical purpose (Adams 1996a; Adams 1997). Not only Jungians but also at least some contemporary Freudians appreciate that, as Arnold H. Modell says, metaphor is the very "currency" of the psyche (1990: 64). In short, as psychotherapists, we must learn the language of metaphor.

I practice what I call psychoanalysis of the imagination. Whether images emerge in dreams, in active imagination, or in the psychotherapeutic dialogue, I address them in one and the same way. (Even reports of experiences of real external events are what I would call "the imagination of everyday life," for what is ultimately important is not the literal, objective event but the subjective, metaphorical experience of that event.) I believe that everyone fantasizes continuously, that fantasy suffuses reality pervasively. Psychotherapy is an occasion for me and someone else to explore the imagination together. It is an opportunity for us to appreciate that fantasy is a reality just as real as any other reality, as well as an opportunity for us to appreciate the extent to which reality is also fantasy.

I do love the imagination. Interpretation is a Logos operation; imagination, an Eros operation. If I am a psychotherapist for love of the imagination, it is because, for me, images have an erotic value (which may simultaneously and perhaps paradoxically be both an attraction and a repulsion – not all images are intrinsically lovely in any simplistic sense). If I once left the imagination, or if it once left me, psychotherapy now enables me to return to it, as, in the myth, Psyche finally returns to Eros to give birth to Pleasure. (Perhaps there is not so much difference, after all, between what Freud calls the pleasure principle and what I call the fantasy principle.)

11

References

Adams, M.V. (1996a) "Flowers and Fungi: Archetypal Semiotics and Visual Metaphor," *Spring: A Journal of Archetype and Culture*, 59: 131–55.

Adams, M.V. (1996b) *The Multicultural Imagination: "Race," Color, and the Unconscious*, London: Routledge.

Adams, M.V. (1997) "Metaphors in Psychoanalytic Theory and Therapy," *Clinical Social Work Journal*, 25,1: 27–39.

Adams, M.V. (2004) *The Fantasy Principle: Psychoanalysis of the Imagination*, Hove: Brunner-Routledge.

Adams, M.V. (2008) "The Archetypal School," in P. Young-Eisendrath and T. Dawson (eds.), *The Cambridge Companion to Jung*, 2nd rev. ed., Cambridge: Cambridge University Press: 107–24.

Bachelard, G. (1969) *The Poetics of Reverie*, trans. D. Russell, New York: Orion.

Blake, W. (1976a) *Milton*, in *Blake: Complete Writings with Variant Readings*, ed. G. Keynes, London: Oxford University Press: 480–535.

Blake, W. (1976b) "A Vision of the Last Judgment," in *Blake: Complete Writings with Variant Readings*, ed. G. Keynes, London: Oxford University Press: 604–17.

Bohm, D. (1981) *Wholeness and the Implicate Order*, London: Routledge & Kegan Paul.

Brown, N.O. (1959) *Life Against Death: The Psychoanalytical Meaning of History*, Middletown, CT: Wesleyan University Press.

Cohen, D., and MacKeith, S.A. (1991) *The Development of Imagination: The Private Worlds of Childhood*, London: Routledge.

Douglas, C. (1993) *Translate This Darkness: The Life of Christiana Morgan*, New York: Simon & Schuster.

Hillman, J. (1975) *Re-Visioning Psychology*, New York: Harper & Row.

Hillman, J. (1977) "An Inquiry into Image," *Spring: An Annual of Archetypal Psychology and Jungian Thought*: 62–88.

Hillman, J. (1979) *The Dream and the Underworld*, New York: Harper & Row.

Jung, C.G. (1911–12/1952) *Symbols of Transformation: An Analysis of the Prelude to a Case of Schizophrenia*, *CW* 5.

Jung, C.G. (1921) *Psychological Types*, *CW* 6.

Jung, C.G. (1927/1931) "Mind and Earth," *CW* 10: 29–49.

Jung, C.G. (1931) "The Aims of Psychotherapy," *CW* 16: 36–52.

Jung, C.G. (1934) "The Practical Use of Dream-Analysis," *CW* 16: 139–61.

Jung, C.G. (1963) *Memories, Dreams, Reflections*, ed. A. Jaffé, trans. R. and C. Winston, New York: Pantheon Books.

Jung, C.G. (1997) *Visions: Notes of the Seminar Given in 1930–1934*, ed. C. Douglas, Princeton, NJ: Princeton University Press, 2 vols.

Kearney, R. (1988) *The Wake of Imagination: Toward a Postmodern Culture*, Minneapolis, MN: University of Minnesota Press.

Leyda, J. (1969) *The Melville Log: A Documentary Life of Herman Melville, 1819–1891*, New York, Gordian Press, 2 vols.

Leyda, J. (1973) "Herman Melville, 1972," in M.J. Bruccoli (ed.), *The Chief Glory of Every People: Essays on Classic American Writers*, Carbondale, IL: Southern Illinois University Press: 161–71.

Marcuse, H. (1955) *Eros and Civilization: A Philosophical Inquiry into Freud*, Boston: Beacon Press.

Melville, H. (1971) *Pierre; or the Ambiguities*, ed. H. Hayford, H. Parker, and G.T. Tanselle, *The Writings of Herman Melville*, Evanston, IL, and Chicago: Northwestern University Press and Newberry Library, vol. 7.

Melville, H. (1988) *Moby-Dick; or the Whale*, ed. H. Hayford, H. Parker, and G.T. Tanselle, *The Writings of Herman Melville*, Evanston, IL, and Chicago: Northwestern University Press and Newberry Library, vol. 6.

Modell, A.H. (1990) *Other Times, Other Realities: Toward a Theory of Psychoanalytic Treatment*, Cambridge, MA: Harvard University Press.

Polanyi, M. (1966) *The Tacit Dimension*, Garden City, NY: Doubleday.

Raine, K. (1968) *Blake and Tradition*, Princeton, NJ: Princeton University Press, 2 vols.

Samuels, A. (1993) *The Political Psyche*, London: Routledge.

Storr, A. (1988) *Solitude: A Return to the Self*, New York: The Free Press.

Watkins, M. (1984) *Waking Dreams*, Dallas, TX: Spring Publications.

Watkins, M. (1986) *Invisible Guests: The Development of Imaginal Dialogues*, Hillsdale, NJ: The Analytic Press.

2

IMAGINOLOGY

The Jungian Study of the Imagination

In *The Fantasy Principle: Psychoanalysis of the Imagination*, I state that "Jungian psychology is what I would call *imaginology*, and Jungian psychologists are *imaginologists*" (Adams 2004: 7). Imaginology is the study of the imagination, and imaginologists are students of the imagination. Other psychologists study drives, the ego, objects, or the self (Pine 1990). Jungian psychologists study images. The emphasis on the imagination is what is unique about Jungian psychology, which is an imaginal psychology.

"Anxiety" is one of the most important technical terms in psychoanalysis. "The ego," Freud says, "is the actual seat of anxiety" (1923, *SE* 19: 57). According to Freud, "It is always the ego's attitude of anxiety which is the primary thing and which sets repression going" (1926 [1925], *SE* 20: 109) – or, more generally, I would say, which sets defenses going. Freud says that "anxiety is a reaction of the ego to danger" (1926 [1925], *SE* 20: 129). That is, the ego reacts anxiously – and then repressively or defensively – to what it regards as dangerous. Jung says: "In this way, as Freud rightly says, we turn the ego into a 'seat of anxiety,' which it would never be if we did not defend ourselves against ourselves so neurotically" (1934b, *CW* 10: par. 360). In a very real sense, every neurosis is an anxiety neurosis.

What Jung means when he says that we defend ourselves against ourselves is that the anxious ego neurotically defends itself against the unconscious. As a practitioner of imaginal psychology, I prefer to say, instead, that the anxious ego-image neurotically defends itself against non-ego images. James Hillman says of the ego that "it too is an image." It is what he calls the "imaginal ego" (1979: 102). "Ego" means "I." The ego-image is the "I"-image. It is who or how I imagine myself to be. The psyche – or the imagination – comprises an ego-image and a variety of non-ego images.

In effect, I advocate that Jungians adopt a new terminology that I believe would be advantageous. The terms *ego-image* and *non-ego images* emphasize that, as Jung says, "the psyche consists essentially of images" (1926, *CW* 8: par. 618). As I define "unconscious," it is what the ego-image is unconscious *of. Ironically, it is not the unconscious that is unconscious. Rather, it is the ego-image that is unconscious, and what it is unconscious of are non-ego images.* To the extent that the ego-image is unconscious of non-ego images, it tends to react anxiously and defensively because it regards them as dangerous.

The function of non-ego images is transformative. Non-ego images are what I call "images of transformation." They attempt to contact and impact the ego-image in an effort to transform it. The ego-image, however, regards non-ego images as dangerous precisely because they are transformative. That is, non-ego images are only ostensibly dangerous, from the perspective of the ego-image. The ostensible danger that non-ego images pose is to the partial, prejudicial, or defective attitude of the ego-image. Non-ego images present alternative perspectives on the attitude of the ego-image. If the ego-image is not defensive but receptive, it may entertain these alternative perspectives seriously, consider them critically, and then either accept or reject them. How might the ego-image be less defensive and more receptive? It would have to be less anxious and, I would say, more curious about non-ego images.

"Curiosity," in contrast to "anxiety," is not a technical term in psychoanalysis. Freud does, however, discuss curiosity. True to form, he derives it from and reduces it to sexuality. Civilization, Freud says, progressively conceals the body and, as a result, provokes "sexual curiosity." He says: "This curiosity seeks to complete the sexual object by revealing its hidden parts" (1905, *SE* 7: 156). Sexual curiosity, Freud says, is perfectly normal, although it may also be prurient or even perverse, as in voyeurism. It is ultimately, he says, "curiosity to see other people's genitals" (1905, *SE* 7: 192). According to Freud, sexual curiosity in particular is the very origin of curiosity in general. From this perspective, curiosity is originally an urge to see the unseen – and, more specifically, what I might call the "sexual unseen," the hidden parts of the body, the genitals of other people. I would say, however, that curiosity is neither derivative from nor reducible to sexuality. Sexual curiosity in particular is merely one variety of curiosity in general. In this respect, I would say that curiosity is an urge to know the unknown, or, more specifically, what I might call the "imaginal unknown" – non-ego images of which the ego-image is unconscious. From this perspective, a defensive ego-image is an anxious ego-image, and a receptive ego-image is a curious ego-image.

It is a notorious fact that the ego-image rarely exhibits any initiative in regard to non-ego images. Seldom does the ego-image approach non-ego images. Most frequently it is non-ego images that approach the ego-image, that attempt to contact and impact the ego-image in an effort to transform it. Rather than approach non-ego images, all too often the ego-image avoids them, or, when non-ego images approach it, attacks them – demonstrates just how neurotically defensive it is and exactly how it is defensive, in an effort to protect the ego-image. The ego-image employs the familiar, famous defenses of "flight" and "fight." An anxious ego-image is a suspicious ego-image – even, at the extreme, a paranoid ego-image. In contrast, a curious ego-image would be an inquisitive ego-image. It would inquire into non-ego images.

Jung declares that it does not matter – or matters very little – what the image is. What matters to Jung is not the image but the concept – for example, the concept of the treasure or the monster. Jung says that "it does not matter" if the treasure is a ring, a crown, a pearl, or a hoard (1929, *CW* 8: par. 229). Similarly, Jung says: "It matters little if the mythological hero conquers now a dragon, now a fish or some other monster" (1928/1931, *CW* 8: par. 718).

Gregory Bateson notes that in formal logic a class is on "a *different level of abstraction*" from the members of the class (1987: 202). As a result, the class cannot be a member of the class, and a member cannot be the class. In this respect, the concept "treasure" is a class, and the images "ring, "crown," pearl," and "hoard" are members of the class; the concept "monster" is a class, and the images "dragon" and "fish" are members of the class. Logically, a treasure is on a different level of abstraction from a ring, crown, pearl, or hoard, and a monster is on a different level of abstraction from a dragon or fish. In effect, Jung privileges the class over the members of the class. What matters to Jung is the class (or concept). The members (or images), he says, do not matter or matter little. Jung commits a version of what Alfred North Whitehead calls the "fallacy of misplaced concreteness." Whitehead defines this fallacy as "mistaking the abstract for the concrete" (1967: 51). When Jung says that the concept of a treasure matters more than the image of a ring, a crown, a pearl, or a hoard and when he says that the concept of a monster matters more than the image of a dragon or a fish, he regards the abstract concept as more important – in effect, more "concrete" – than the concrete image.

On the contrary, I would argue that it matters a great deal if the treasure is a ring, a crown, a pearl, or a hoard – or if it is, in fact, a treasure at all – and if it is a dragon, a fish, or some other monster – or if it is a monster at all – and that it matters a great deal if the hero attempts to conquer the dragon, fish, or monster or engage it in some other way. Why it matters – and why it matters so much – is that, in contrast to a concept, which is an abstract form, an image is a concrete content. The concept is nondescript; it possesses no distinctive qualities. In contrast, the image possesses quite distinctive qualities that imply, with exquisite exactitude, an essence. It is in and through those distinctive qualities that it is possible to ascertain accurately what is essentially implicit in the image.

Consider a dream that Fritz Perls cites. The dream is of a lake with water that is drying up. The dreamer says:

> And I think that there's one good point about the water drying up, I think – well, at least at the bottom, when all the water dries up, there will probably be some sort of treasure there, because at the bottom of the lake there should be things that have fallen in, like coins or something, but I look carefully and all that I can find is an old license plate.
>
> (1969: 81)

The dreamer anticipates that she will find at the bottom of the lake a treasure, but all that she finds is an old license plate. In contrast to a treasure, which as an abstract concept possesses no distinctive qualities, an old license plate, as a concrete image, possesses quite distinctive qualities. The dreamer says that the license plate is "outdated." She notes that the essential function of a license plate is "to allow – give a car permission to go" (1969: 81). An out-of-date license plate is, in this respect, essentially dysfunctional. What this image essentially implies is that even if the dreamer has a car and may want or need to go somewhere in it on the archetypal journey of "individuation," she does not effectively possess the wherewithal, the means to that end – an up-to-date license plate that would allow or give that car permission to go there. This image is, truly, the license plate "hard to attain."

Jung is what I call a *conceptual essentialist*. He privileges the concept over the image. He derives the image from and reduces it to a concept. He replaces the image with a concept. For Jung, the image is incidental – relatively trivial, even utterly irrelevant. What is ultimately important to Jung is the concept, for "some other monster," as he says, would serve the same purpose just as well as a dragon or a fish. From this perspective, a dragon might as well be a fish, and a fish might as well be a dragon, for both are monsters. The dragon and the fish are merely examples of the monster. They are images that exemplify a concept. For Jung, the images of the dragon and the fish possess the same essence, and that is the concept of the monster.

I, too, am an essentialist, but I am what I call an *imaginal essentialist*. I maintain that images have essences, implicit ones, and that the Jungian methods of interpretation and active imagination can render these essences explicit. Although it is extremely difficult – I would say, impossible – to define the essence of a concept, because a concept is an abstract form, I argue that it is possible, as Hillman says, to "stick to the image" (1983: 54; 2004: 21) and accurately define the essence of an image, because an image is a concrete content with distinctive qualities. Hillman emphasizes "the actual qualities of the image" (1977: 69). It is the actual qualities of the image that enable the elaboration of a definitional consensus through the Jungian methods of interpretation and active imagination. Conceptual essentialism is futile, for it results in incessant, vain definitional conflict over concepts that are intrinsically vague. In contrast, imaginal essentialism is feasible, for it relies on the distinctive qualities implicit in images.

The images of the dragon and the fish possess very different essences that are neither derivative from nor reducible to the concept of the monster. These different essences are a function of the distinctive qualities of these images. *Functionally, an image is a qualitative distinction with an essential difference.* A dragon is a dragon is a dragon – and not a fish. A fish is a fish is a fish – and not a dragon. The one is not equivalent to the other, and neither the image of the dragon nor the image of the fish is commensurable with the concept of the monster. Different images serve different – often vastly different – purposes.

17

I do not merely prefer concrete contents to abstract forms. I do not just have a predilection for images over concepts. For me, the decisive consideration is purely pragmatic. Images simply have more practical value than concepts. What is so practically valuable about images is that they are more informative than concepts. The images of a dragon and a fish possess more information than the concept of a monster. Concepts are generalizations; images are particularizations. In this respect, it is the unique nuances, the details, of a specific image that eloquently articulate and heuristically indicate what it essentially implies and that pragmatically inform the conduct of any analysis.

Of course, from a certain perspective, "dragon" and "fish" are also concepts and not images. "Dragon" and "fish" are classes with members – for example, Richard Wagner's "Fafner" and Steven Spielberg's "Jaws." As concepts, "dragon" and "fish" are not as abstract as the concept "monster," but they are not as concrete as the images of Fafner and Jaws, which are *a* dragon and *a* fish with not only distinctive qualities but also proper names and very specific narratives.

"What others call a neurosis," Ginette Paris says, "let's call a 'monster'" (2007: 68). She says that a monster is an image, in contrast to a neurosis, which is an "abstract concept" (2007: 69). I agree with Paris that a neurosis is an abstract concept, but I disagree with her that a monster is an image. A monster is also a concept. It is no more a concrete image than a neurosis is. Catherine Atherton notes that the concept of the monster is "vague, malleable, and inconsistent" and that, as a result, "any general theory about what monsters are and what they do" must acknowledge "this uncertainty." Atherton says that "it is we who decide – in some sense of 'decide' – what counts as monstrous." She says that different definitions of the monster are a function of "different times, places, and cultures" or of different perspectives within a culture (1998: x). That is, in teratology, or the general theory of monsters, the definition of the monster, as a concept, is indefinite. I would say that it is the ego-image that decides what counts as monstrous. What the ego-image counts as monstrous are non-ego images, which it tends to regard as dangerous. A monster is just a non-ego image that an anxious and defensive – or neurotic – ego-image considers a danger.

In this respect, Jung mentions "the totally erroneous supposition that the unconscious is a monster." This notion, he says, is just "fear of nature and the realities of life" (1934a, *CW* 16: par. 328). The unconscious, Jung asserts, is not a monster but "a natural entity" that is "completely neutral." He contends that the unconscious "only becomes dangerous when our conscious attitude to it is hopelessly wrong." He says of the unconscious: "To the degree that we repress it, its danger increases" (1934a, *CW* 16: par. 329). Or, as I prefer to say, non-ego images from the unconscious become dangerous only when the anxious and defensive – or repressive – attitude of the ego-image wrongly regards them as monstrous.

"Monster" is an epithet by which the ego-image disparages a non-ego image. This is an example of the process that Bateson calls "teratogenic," which he defines as "a creating of monsters" (1991: 292). A teratogenic ego-image creates a "monster" merely by calling it so. A non-ego image is a "so-called" monster. Calling it so "monsterizes" a non-ego image and immediately restricts the options at the disposal of the ego-image. For example, calling it so may excuse killing a non-ego image.

Among the seven types of plot that Christopher Booker identifies as basic, the very first is what he calls "Overcoming the Monster." I might say that the hero does not "undergo" the monster but "overcomes" it. Booker says that the monster is what "the hero must confront in a fight to the death" (2004: 22). From this perspective, overcoming the monster entails slaying the monster. The contemporary monster, Booker says, is the "monster of global terrorism" (2004: 695). He notes that the first war in Iraq, in 1991, did not "overcome Saddam Hussein," did not "slay the monster." Thus, the second war against Iraq, which began in 2003, was an effort by America and George W. Bush to complete the plot, but, as Booker says, "the plot was not quite so simple," for, even if Saddam Hussein was to a certain extent a monster, he was not as monstrous as all that. He did not possess weapons of mass destruction, and, from another perspective, Booker says, "of course, it was not Saddam who was the monster" but "America and Bush" (2004: 696).

Monster-slaying is a recurrent but not, as Jungians tend to assume, a universal theme. Of fifty cultures that Clyde Kluckhohn surveyed, the monster-slaying theme is indigenous to only thirty-seven (1960: 51). Although by definition killing is a putting to death in any manner, while slaying is a putting to death in a deliberate, violent, even wanton manner, slaying has a more heroic connotation than killing – hence the Jungian preference for monster-slaying over monster-killing. To "slay" is more poetic – and, I might say, more euphemistic – than to "kill." Slaying justifies, dignifies, even glorifies killing.

When the ego-image regards a non-ego image as a monster, it tends to commit what I call *imagicide*. The tendency is for the ego-image to "kill" the non-ego image, the "monster." Consider, in this respect, the ego-image and non-ego image in the following dream:

> I'm walking in the dark. A very strange animal arrives. The body is of a big dog. The face is of a rabbit with two very big teeth like a snake's. The animal keeps biting me and literally taking part of my flesh. I grab the animal, twirl it in the air, and throw it away. At that moment, I'm thinking: "Yes, it's dead. I've killed it."

In dreams, Anthony Stevens says, "from the psychological perspective, the monster is the 'monster within'" (1995: 188). Edward C. Whitmont and Sylvia Brinton Perera assert that monsters "are not uncommon in dreams."

Such images, they contend, epitomize "energy that is, in actuality, or felt to be, 'monstrous.'" Frequently, they say, the image of the monster is "an unnatural combination of qualities" (1989: 109). In this dream, the ego-image does not explicitly identify the non-ego image as a monster. It describes the non-ego image as a "very strange animal." David Williams notes, however, that prominent among "monsters of earthly form" are those that are "combinations of various animal forms" (1996: 179). The animal in this dream is just such an unnatural combination of qualities. It is a combination of three animal forms – a dog's body, a rabbit's face, and a snake's teeth. After the dreamer recounted the dream to me, I asked him why he had killed the animal. "When you asked me why I killed it," he replied, "I was lost – I had no answer." Then he said: "In the dream, I felt that I had to protect myself, that I had to kill it." The non-ego image bites the ego-image and literally takes part of its flesh. The ego-image responds defensively, as ego-images tend to do, and kills the non-ego image. It does not occur to the ego-image to engage the non-ego image in any other way. The ego-image just reacts; it does not pause and reflect and consider that there might be any viable alternatives but to kill the non-ego image.

Not only is it impossible, in a strict sense, to kill the monsters that emerge from the unconscious – as Paris says, they "can never entirely be eliminated" (2007: 69) – but it is also imprudent even to attempt to kill them. In the first place, a non-ego image may not be a monster at all but only a "monster" in the paranoid projection of an anxious, excessively protective ego-image. In the second place, even if a non-ego image is, in some respect, a monster, to kill it is to obviate any necessity – and any opportunity – for the ego-image to engage it in some other way.

For example, a curious ego-image might inquire into the non-ego image in this dream – might inquire of it why it is such a very strange animal, a combination of a dog's body, a rabbit's face, and a snake's teeth, and why it bites the ego-image and literally takes part of its flesh – why the non-ego image contacts and impacts the ego-image in just this way in an effort to transform it. Engaging the non-ego image in "some other way" than, for example, killing it (or censoring it) would require an ego-image capable of seriously entertaining, with no bias, a variety of options.

Not only in dreams does the ego-image kill non-ego images. England and America also kill non-ego images – dragons and fish. England has St. George and the dragon; America has Captain Ahab and the fish. St. George lances the dragon; Captain Ahab harpoons the fish. Jung says that, topographically, the unconscious is "something below your feet, and you are St. George standing upon the dragon." This image, he says, "is the medieval ambition, to kill the dragon and stand on top of it" (1988, 1: 155).

I would say that this image is not only the medieval ambition but also the contemporary ambition, and it is not only, I would emphasize, a male ambition but also a female ambition. Consider, for example, the account that Williams provides of St. Margaret and the dragon (1996: 317–18). Margaret is a convert from paganism to Christianity. A local prefect attempts to seduce her and force her to worship pagan gods, but she refuses. From prison, she prays to God. Instantly, the enemy manifests as a dragon, which swallows her. In the belly of the dragon, she makes the sign of the cross. The dragon explodes, and Margaret emerges. Then, however, the enemy manifests again, this time as a handsome young man who attempts to seduce her. "But," Jacobus De Voragine says, "Margaret laid hold of him by the head, stretched him on the ground, and put her right foot upon him, saying: 'Proud demon, lie prostrate beneath a woman's foot!'" (1991: 353). Like Kali the Hindu goddess, Margaret the Christian saint stands on top of a prostrate man. This is feminist – or "genderist" – triumphalism with a vengeance. What an ambition! To kill the dragon, to kill the unconscious, to kill the enemy, to kill the handsome young man, to kill the demon, to kill the non-ego image, and then to stand on top of it!

In this iconography, it is not only female figures who stand on top of prostrate men but also male figures who stand on top of prostrate women – as, for example, in the statue *Civic Virtue* in New York. This statue is a marble sculpture that was originally situated near City Hall in Manhattan but was eventually relocated near Borough Hall in Queens. As Jeff Vandam describes the statue, it is "a muscular nude male youth with two vanquished women representing corruption and vice at his feet" and "with a sword over his shoulder" (2007). The statue has never been popular. Fiorello LaGuardia and Robert Moses loathed it, and feminists despise it as a politically incorrect, sexist image because it depicts civic virtue as a man and corruption and vice as women.

"The implacable mutual hostility between man and dragon, as exemplified in the myth of St. George," Carl Sagan says, "is strongest in the West." It is not, however, "a Western anomaly," he says, but "a worldwide phenomenon" (1977: 140–1). In the motif-index that Stith Thompson provides, this theme is type "B11.11. *Fight with dragon*" (1955 1: 354), but it is not, in spite of what Sagan says, universal. The Western tradition, of course, equates the dragon with the devil. Rather than analyze the dragon, the Western tradition moralizes the dragon. Moralistically equating the dragon with the devil, the very epitome of evil, conveniently excuses killing the dragon. St. George is a variation on St. Michael, who fights the dragon in the Apocalypse: "And there was war in heaven: Michael and his angels fought against the dragon; and the dragon fought and his angels, And prevailed not; neither was their place found any more in heaven. And the great dragon was cast out" (Revelation 12: 7–9). June Allen and Jeanne Griffiths say that "St. Michael threw the dragon out of heaven and left St. George to deal with him once he landed on earth" (1979: 51). As a result, it is easier, they say, to identify with the down-to-earth St. George than the up-in-heaven St. Michael.

Hillman notes that the tradition of St. George and the dragon is "the major Western paradigm" of the hero myth. "Killing the dragon in the hero myth," he declares, "is nothing less than killing the imagination" (1991: 169). Hillman recounts how in the 1950s he was present when Esther Harding delivered a presentation "in favor of killing the dragon." Harding was, he exclaims, "so moralistic!" (Marlan 2006: 192). The hero may have, as Joseph Campbell says, a thousand faces (1968), but the face of the hero in the Western tradition is that of a killer. The implications are absolutely incredible: culturally, socially, politically, militarily, religiously, sexually, ecologically – and, of course, psychoanalytically.

Jung considers *Moby-Dick* "the greatest American novel" (1930/1950, *CW* 15: par. 137). Why is the novel so great? I would say that it is great because Melville so radically deconstructs the hero myth. Captain Ahab does not kill the fish. The fish kills Captain Ahab – and all the sailors except Ishmael, who survives only by accident. In an attempt to commit imagicide, or kill the image, Captain Ahab, in effect, commits suicide and homicide. Melville explicitly diagnoses Captain Ahab as a case of monomania. Captain Ahab is not neurotically defensive; he is psychotically offensive. As Melville deconstructs the hero myth, it is insane. Of course, this deconstruction does not prevent America from chasing the "White Whale" – however elusive, even illusory, it may be – and then harpooning it. America kills the fish first and asks questions later, if ever.

When Karl Rove, Deputy Chief of Staff and Senior Advisor to the President, resigned from the administration of George W. Bush, he cynically appropriated the image of the White Whale for partisan political purposes. He quoted opponents who said, "Rove is the big fish." In this case, the harpoon was a subpoena that Democrats might issue to a Republican with a grandiose persecution complex to compel him to testify before Congress. "You know," Rove said, "I feel like I'm Moby Dick and we've got a couple of people on Capitol Hill auditioning for the role of Captain Ahab." In this paranoid projection, Rove did not know whether he was the hero or the dragon. "Let's face it," he said, "I mean, I'm a myth, and they're – you know, I'm Beowulf. You know, I'm Grendel. I don't know who I am. But they're after me" (2007).

Many villages and towns in England have traditions of dragon-killing heroes. These traditions recount local details about the hero and the dragon. For example, the version that Jacqueline Simpson provides of Jim Pulk and the Knucker of Lyminster even includes which pub the hero visits after he kills the dragon:

> Jim Pulk was a farmer's boy, who baked a huge Sussex pie and put poison inside it, and drew it on a farm cart to the Knucker Hole [at Lyminster], while he himself hid behind a hedge. The Dragon came out, ate the pie, died, and Jim Pulk then emerged and cut off his head with his scythe. He then went down to the Six Bells Inn, had a drink to celebrate his victory, and fell down dead. Presumably, he had got

some poison on his hand, which, no doubt, very properly, he drew across his mouth after downing his pint.

(1980: 45)

Apparently, the ironically hygienic moral of this tradition is that, however civil the manners of the dragon-killing hero may be, in order to survive a beer perhaps he should also be an obsessive-compulsive hand-washing hero.

In *The Mythological Unconscious*, I acknowledge that I committed an egregious error when I interpreted a dream that a young man had about a dragon. I erred when I assumed that the ego-image must kill the non-ego image – that, in order to become a hero, the young man must slay the dragon. The young man cautioned me that the dream did not stipulate that "the dragon must be slain." There was no dragon-slaying indication in the dream. The young man pondered the image of dragons and quite properly wondered: "Why does everyone want to *kill* them?" (Adams 2010: 396). At least on that occasion, he was a much more astute psychoanalyst than I was. I deserved a rebuke. Rather than "stick to the image," I had unconsciously – and uncritically – projected onto the dream the Jungian concept of the "dragon-slaying hero." I had killed the image. The dream, I had to admit, did not indicate that the young man must slay the dragon but, at most, only that he "must effectively engage the dragon *in some way*" (Adams 2010: 399).

"Those of us who are students of psychology," Mary Watkins says, "have become heirs to a potential arsenal of ways to kill the image." The effect is to lead "away from direct experience of an image," she says, "towards a concept" (1984: 135). Psychoanalysts – among them, Jungian psychoanalysts – routinely kill images. Hillman says that this killing occurs by interpreting images – that is, by deriving them from and reducing them to concepts. As Hillman defines interpretation, it is a conceptualization of the imagination. Interpreting a dream, he says, is "killing its images with interpretative concepts" (1979: 116). Replacing images with concepts – for example, interpreting a snake as "fear," "sexuality," or the "mother-complex" – is, Hillman says, "killing the snake" (1975: 39). A black snake may be an image in a dream, and in an analytic session an individual "can spend a whole hour with this black snake, talking about the devouring mother, talking about the anxiety, talking about the repressed sexuality, talking about the natural mind," Hillman says, and then the individual "leaves the hour with a concept about my repressed sexuality or my cold black passions or my mother or whatever it is, and you've lost the snake" (1983: 53–4). From this perspective, any concept is the very death of any image. Not all interpretation, however, is conceptual. There is also what I call *imaginal interpretation*. Interpretation need not kill the image with a concept. Rather than replace the image with a concept, it may respect the image and, by meticulous attention to the distinctive qualities of the image, render explicit the essence that is implicit in the image.

Of course, interpretation is not the only Jungian method. There is also "active imagination." Active imagination requires an ego-image that is curious and inquisitive. The ego-image actively engages the non-ego image in a dialogue. Active imagination is a conversation between the ego-image and the non-ego image. It is not a dictation but a negotiation. In this sense, active imagination is a variety of diplomacy. It is not only a "talking cure" but also a "listening cure." In active imagination, the ego-image talks to the non-ego image and listens to it, and the non-ego image talks to the ego-image and listens to it. Active imagination is *interactive imagination*. Both the ego-image and the non-ego image pose questions, and both provide answers. There is no imperative, I would emphasize, for the ego-image to capitulate to the non-ego image. In active imagination, the only obligation is for the ego-image to entertain seriously and consider critically what the non-ego image has to say. What the non-ego image has to say is not necessarily the "truth." It is an *opinion* that the ego-image may either accept or reject. In the process, not only may the non-ego image persuade the ego-image, but also the ego-image may convince the non-ego image. The non-ego image may transform the ego-image, and the ego-image may transform the non-ego image. In active imagination, the ego-image is just as much an "image of transformation" as the non-ego image is.

Actively imagine a dialogue between St. George and the dragon or between Captain Ahab and the fish: not St. George lancing the dragon or Captain Ahab harpooning the fish – not a concept killing the image – but St. George and the dragon and Captain Ahab and the fish conducting a reciprocal conversation and experiencing a mutual transformation. Or actively imagine a dinner and a drink, a pie and a pint, with no poison, between Jim Pulk and the Knucker of Lyminster at a pub. Or actively imagine, as Nicholas D. Kristof does, a direct negotiation between America and North Korea over the issue of nuclear proliferation. "We sometimes," Kristof says, "do better talking to monsters than trying to slay them or wish them away" (2006).

Whether in contemporary American culture the hero has to slay monsters in order to be a hero was a most important political issue in the 2008 American presidential election. In a column that Maureen Dowd wrote at the time, she said that Barack Obama "doesn't pay attention to the mythic nature of campaigns, but if he did, he would recognize the narrative of the classic hero myth." In order to attain the treasure – whether it is "a golden fleece or an Oval Office" – the hero, Dowd said, "has to kill monsters" (2008). In this case, the allusion was to Jeremiah Wright, the African-American minister whom many white Americans consider a "monster." Wright has noted that historically America has perpetrated many abominations – among them, the racist atrocities of slavery and segregation. He has described the terrorist attacks of "9/11" as retribution for terrorist acts that America has committed. He has said that America may have employed AIDS for genocidal purposes. He has said "God damn America" rather than "God bless America." Many Americans, especially white Americans, consider such comments "monstrous." They insisted that Obama not only denounce these remarks but also renounce Wright – or, in psychoanalytic terms, "dissociate" Wright – and Obama finally did so. The alternative to dissociation was persistent guilt by association. From a psychoanalytic perspective, Wright is a non-ego image that the ego-image of many Americans would prefer to repress and remain unconscious of. Obama may or may not be a "monster-slaying hero," but he is now a "minister-slaying hero." When Obama repudiated Wright, he "killed the monster" – or at least attempted to do so. (Whether the repudiation was rhetorically forceful enough to be persuasively "heroic" for white Americans was a question for which there was no immediately conclusive answer.)

I would say that what distinguished Obama as a presidential candidate in 2008 was an effort to be a new style of hero. For example, rather than "bomb, bomb, bomb" Iran (as John McCain said he would consider doing) or "obliterate" Iran (as Hillary Clinton said she would consider doing), Obama said that he would engage Iran in a direct negotiation over the issue of nuclear proliferation. In this sense, the alternatives in the 2008 American presidential election were between different styles of hero. Stylistically, Obama presented a challenge to the narrative of the classic hero myth in the Western tradition. Obama has an ego-image that does not immediately "monsterize" a non-ego image and "kill" it but attempts to engage it in some other, more effective way – dialogically and diplomatically. Whether in contemporary American culture, at this stage in the history of consciousness, this new style of hero is politically plausible was the issue.

Why does the ego-image tend to kill non-ego images rather than engage them in some other way? I would argue that it does so because it regards non-ego images as "opposite" rather than "different." The neurotic reaction of the ego-image to non-ego images is a function of what I call moralistic, scientific, and aesthetic oppositions – good versus evil, true versus false, and beautiful versus ugly. These oppositions provide the ego-image with a convenient excuse to repress – or "kill" – non-ego images that it considers evil, false, or ugly – and, as a result, dangerous. "Evil," "false," and "ugly" are, of course, concepts. When the ego-image applies these concepts to non-ego images, these oppositions eradicate the differences, the distinctive qualities, that are intrinsic to non-ego images.

If Jungian psychology were an imaginology, it would be deconstructive rather than repressive. Such an imaginology would be a combination of Jungian psychology and Derridean philosophy. It would emphasize "differences," as Jacques Derrida does (1973). The ego-image would not repress non-ego images. Non-ego images would deconstruct the ego-image. The ego-image would not be "opposite" to non-ego images. Non-ego images would be "different" from the ego-image. An ego-image that non-ego images have deconstructed would be an ego-image that does not regard non-ego images as an array of oppositions that it must repress (evil, false, or ugly non-ego images as a danger to the good, true, and beautiful ego-image) but as a profusion of differences that it may contemplate and then engage in appropriate ways. This project would entail not conceptual interpretation but imaginal differentiation. As Hillman says: "We need an imaginal ego that is at home in the imaginal realm, an ego that can undertake *the major task now confronting psychology*: the differentiation of the imaginal" (1975: 37).

References

Adams, M.V. (2004) *The Fantasy Principle: Psychoanalysis of the Imagination*, Hove: Brunner-Routledge.

Adams, M.V. (2010) *The Mythological Unconscious*, 2nd rev. ed., Putnam, CT: Spring Publications.

Allen, J., and Griffiths, J. (1979) *The Book of the Dragon*, Secaucus, NJ: Chartwell Books.

Atherton, C. (1998) "Introduction," in C. Atherton (ed.), *Monsters and Monstrosity in Greek and Roman Culture*, Bari: Levante Editori: vii–xxxiv.

Bateson, G. (1987) "Toward a Theory of Schizophrenia," in *Steps to an Ecology of Mind: Collected Essays in Anthropology, Psychiatry, Evolution, and Epistemology*, Northvale, NJ: Jason Aronson: 201–27.

Bateson, G. (1991) "The Case against the Case for Mind/Body Dualism," in *Sacred Unity: Further Steps to an Ecology of Mind*, ed. R.E. Donaldson, New York: HarperCollins: 291–3.

Booker, C. (2004) *The Seven Basic Plots: Why We Tell Stories*, London: Continuum.

Campbell, J. (1968) *The Hero with a Thousand Faces*, Princeton, NJ: Princeton University Press.

Derrida, J. (1973) "Difference," in *Speech and Phenomena: And Other Essays on Husserl's Theory of Signs*, trans. D.B. Allison and N. Garver, Evanston, IL: Northwestern University Press: 129–60.

De Voragine, J. (1991) *The Golden Legend*, trans. G. Ryan and H. Ripperger, Salem, NH: Ayer.

Dowd, M. (April 30, 2008) "Praying and Preying," *The New York Times*: A19.

Freud, S. (1905) *Three Essays on the Theory of Sexuality*, SE 7: 123–243.

Freud, S. (1923) *The Ego and the Id*, SE 19: 1–66.

Freud, S. (1926 [1925]) *Inhibitions, Symptoms and Anxiety*, SE 20: 75–172.

Hillman, J. (1975) *Re-Visioning Psychology*, New York: Harper & Row.

Hillman, J. (1977) "An Inquiry into Image," *Spring: An Annual of Archetypal Psychology and Jungian Thought*: 62–88.

Hillman, J. (1979) *The Dream and the Underworld*, New York: Harper & Row.

Hillman, J., with Pozzo, L. (1983) *Inter Views: Conversations with Laura Pozzo on Psychotherapy, Biography, Love, Soul, Dreams, Work, Imagination, and the State of the Culture*, New York: Harper & Row.

Hillman, J. (1991) "The Great Mother, Her Son, Her Hero, and the Puer," in P. Berry (ed.), *Fathers and Mothers*, Dallas: Spring Publications: 166–209.

Hillman, J. (2004) *Archetypal Psychology, Uniform Edition of the Writings of James Hillman*, vol. 1, Putnam, CT: Spring Publications.

Jung, C.G. (1926) "Spirit and Life," *CW* 8: 319–37.

Jung, C.G. (1928/1931) "Analytical Psychology and *Weltanschauung*," *CW* 8: 358–81.

Jung, C.G. (1929) "The Significance of Constitution and Heredity in Psychology," *CW* 8: 107–13.

Jung, C.G. (1930/1950) "Psychology and Literature," *CW* 15: 84–105.

Jung, C.G. (1934a) "The Practical Use of Dream-Analysis," *CW* 16: 139–61.

Jung, C.G. (1934b) "The State of Psychotherapy Today," *CW* 10: 157–73.

Jung, C.G. (1988) *Nietzsche's Zarathustra: Notes of the Seminar Given in 1934–1939*, ed. J.L. Jarrett, Princeton, NJ: Princeton University Press, 2 vols.

Kluckhohn, C. (1960) "Recurrent Themes in Myths and Mythmaking," in H.A. Murray (ed.), *Myth and Mythmaking*, New York: George Braziller: 46–60.

Kristof, N.D. (October 10, 2006) "Talking with the Monsters," *The New York Times*: A25.

Marlan, J. (2006) "Jan Marlan Interviews James Hillman," *IAAP Newsletter*, 26: 191–5.

Paris, G. (2007) *Wisdom of the Psyche: Depth Psychology after Neuroscience*, London: Routledge.

Perls, F. (1969) *Gestalt Therapy Verbatim*, ed. J.O. Stevens, Lafayette, CA: Real People Press.

Pine, F. (1990) *Drive, Ego, Object, and Self: A Synthesis for Clinical Work*, New York: Basic Books.

Rove, K. (August 19, 2007) *FOX News Sunday with Chris Wallace*.

Sagan, C. (1977) *The Dragons of Eden: Speculations on the Evolution of Human Intelligence*, New York: Random House.

Simpson, J. (1980) *British Dragons*, London: B.T. Batsford.

Stevens, A. (1995) *Private Myths: Dreams and Dreaming*, Cambridge, MA: Harvard University Press.

Thompson, S. (1955) *Motif-Index of Folk Literature*, Bloomington, IN: Indiana University Press, 6 vols.

Vandam, J. (February 11, 2007) "Hard Times Fall on an Ill-Loved Hero," *The New York Times*, City Section: 8.

Watkins, M. (1984) *Waking Dreams*, Dallas: Spring Publications.

Whitehead, A.N. (1967) *Science and the Modern World: Lowell Lectures, 1925*, New York: The Free Press.

Whitmont, E.C., and Perera, S.B. (1989) *Dreams, A Portal to the Source*, London: Routledge.

Williams, D. (1996) *Deformed Discourse: The Function of the Monster in Mediaeval Thought and Literature*, Montreal: McGill-Queen's Press.

3

IMAGINOLOGY OVERBOARD WITH A SHARK AND AN OCTOPUS

How to Do Things with Images that Do Things

Jungian Analysis and Critical Discourse

As I experience Jungians, they tend to be insufficiently critical of other Jungians (especially of Jung) and of Jungian analysis. I would prefer Jungian discourse to be much more critical than it is.

One Jungian who does criticize other Jungians is Wolfgang Giegerich. Giegerich has, for example, criticized me – or, more specifically, an article of mine: "Imaginology: The Jungian Study of the Imagination" (Adams 2008). I welcome this criticism – and the opportunity it affords me to say more about what I mean by "imaginology."

When Giegerich criticizes what I say about images, he employs an image. He says that I have "gone overboard" (2010: 475).

Literally, to "go overboard" is to go over the side of a boat into the water. Metaphorically, it is, as Christine Ammer says, to "go to extremes" (1992: 149).

Am I an extremist? Am I all wet – that is, all wrong?

Is there a Jungian boat? Are all Jungians in the same boat? Should all Jungians row, row, row that boat? Should all Jungians get on board and stay on board? Should they never go overboard? Should they never go into the water? Jung says that among images of the unconscious, water is the "commonest" (1934/1954, *CW* 9,1: par. 40). He says that "consciousness is surrounded by the sea of the unconscious" (1948, *CW* 18: par. 754). Should Jungians (or the egos of Jungians) never go into the unconscious? Should one stay dry, or should one, under certain circumstances, get wet?

If one goes overboard, how one goes overboard is important.

One may fall overboard – as did Clark Martin, a 65-year-old man, who, after he retired as a clinical psychologist, suffered from a depression, the result of kidney cancer and chemotherapy. As a participant in an experiment to evaluate the efficacy of hallucinogens in psychotherapy, Martin ingested a dose of psilocybin. Martin employs an image to describe the effect. John Tierney quotes Martin: "Imagine you fall off a boat in the open ocean, and you turn around, and the boat is gone. And then the water's gone. And then you're gone." The six-hour psychedelic experience, Martin says, was "a whole personality shift for me" (2010: A15). Boat, water, and Martin vanish – and so does the depression.

One may leap overboard – as does Pip, the cabin boy of Captain Ahab in *Moby-Dick*. In pursuit of whales, the boats abandon Pip on the sea. When Pip goes overboard, he goes crazy. As Ishmael says:

> By the merest chance the ship itself at least rescued him; but from that hour the little negro went about the deck an idiot; such, at least, they said he was. The sea had jeeringly kept his finite body up, but drowned the infinite of his soul. Not drowned entirely, though. Rather carried down alive to wondrous depths, where strange shapes of the unwarped primal world glided to and fro before his passive eyes; and the miser-merman, Wisdom, revealed his hoarded heaps; and among the joyous, heartless, ever-juvenile eternities, Pip saw the multitudinous, God-omnipresent, coral insects, that out of the firmament of waters heaved the colossal orbs. He saw God's foot upon the treadle of the loom, and spoke it; and therefore his shipmates called him mad. So man's insanity is heaven's sense; and wandering from all mortal reason, man comes at last to that celestial thought, which, to reason, is absurd and frantic; and weal or woe, feels then uncompromised, indifferent as his God.
>
> (Melville 1988: 414)

When Pip goes overboard, the soul of Pip goes underwater – down, down, down to the bottom of the sea, where he experiences images of the archetypes of the collective unconscious. The scene is so profound as to render Pip psychotic.

Ishmael also goes overboard. On the third day of the chase, he is in a boat with Captain Ahab, who harpoons the White Whale. The White Whale writhes and rolls against the boat. Ishmael is one of three men who are "flung" from the boat, which then abandons him, "afloat and swimming," on the sea (Melville 1988: 569). He neither falls from the boat nor leaps from the boat – he is *tossed* from the boat (Melville 1988: 573). Eventually, a ship rescues him. Ishmael does not die, he does not sink and drown – he lives to tell the story.

As an imaginal psychologist, I believe that one should always, as James Hillman says, "stick to the image" (1983: 54). I do not, however, believe that one should always "stick to the boat." As Ishmael says: "Now, in general, *Stick to the boat*, is your true motto in whaling; but cases will sometimes happen when *Leap from the boat*, is still better" (Melville 1988: 413). In analyzing, as in whaling, one should sometimes leap from the boat.

If I am in the same Jungian boat as Captain Wolfgang, I prefer to leap from it rather than stick to it. I prefer to go overboard.

Here I go!

Man overboard!

A New Terminology: "Ego-Image" and "Non-Ego Images"

Giegerich criticizes me for advocating that Jungians adopt a new terminology and for not explaining the advantages of that new terminology. I had imagined that I had offered an explanation. Perhaps Giegerich means that I have not offered what he would consider a satisfactory explanation. What he says, however, is that I have offered no explanation. "Why and how this new terminology would be advantageous," Giegerich says, "is not explained" (2010: 475).

What is this new terminology? Instead of (or in addition to) the terms "ego" and "unconscious," I have proposed that Jungians employ the terms "ego-image" and "non-ego images."

When I proposed this new terminology, I did not imagine that most (or even many) Jungians would immediately (or even eventually) adopt it. I merely imagined that the terms "ego-image" and "non-ego images" might appeal to some Jungians.

Jung says, emphatically, that "image *is* psyche" (1929, *CW* 13: par. 75) – or, as I prefer to say, the imagination is the psyche. To be a Jungian psychologist is to be an imaginal psychologist. It is to be an "imaginologist," a psychologist who studies the imagination – or, more specifically, a psychologist who studies the images that emerge from the psyche. (Rather than say "the imagination," it might be more accurate to say "imagining," which would emphasize that the emergence of images from the psyche is a continuous process.)

Images as Imagos

By "images," I mean "psychic images" – that is, images in the psyche. There are, of course, images in external reality, but what most interest me, as an imaginal psychologist, are images in internal reality, or "psychic reality."

Images in internal reality may refer to objects in external reality. This is what Jung means by the "objective level." Of course, images in internal reality may not refer to objects in external reality. Such images are pure figments of the imagination. Even when images in internal reality refer to objects in external reality, however, those images do not necessarily correspond accurately and exhaustively to those objects. That is, the correspondence theory of truth does not apply to images in internal reality. The notion of an identity between an image in internal reality and an object in external reality, Jung says, is a "naïve assumption" (1916/1948, *CW* 8: par. 516).

Jung says that "the psychic image of an object is never exactly like the object." For example, when an image in internal reality refers to a person in external reality, that image does not necessarily correspond accurately and exhaustively to that person. In this respect, Jung says that "we would do well to make a rigorous distinction between the image or *imago* of a man and his real existence" – by which Jung means the existence of that man as an object in external reality. He says that "the *imago* should not be assumed to be identical with the object" (1921, *CW* 6: par. 812). (Both what I call the ego-image and non-ego images are, in this sense, imagos.) That is, the image should be assumed to be different from the object, however similar the image and the object may be. Both ontologically and epistemologically, there is an ineliminable difference between image and object.

When an image in internal reality refers to a person in external reality, that image is, rhetorically, a personification, and the personification should not be assumed to be identical with the person. In addition, whether or not an image in internal reality refers to a person in external reality, Jung says that the image should be regarded as the personification of "a certain aspect" of the psyche (1917/1926/1943, *CW* 7: 90, par. 141). For example, images in dreams should not only be regarded as personifications of persons as objects but should also be regarded as personifications of certain aspects of the psyche of the dreamer as a subject. This is what Jung means by the "subjective level." *Where the object is, the image (or imago) always already was, is, and ever shall be.*

The Advantages of "Ego-Image" and "Non-Ego Images"

Why did I propose the terms "ego-image" and "non-ego images"? I have no interest in the proliferation of jargon. I merely imagined that this new terminology might be of practical value to Jungians, that these terms might serve as a constant reminder, as Jung says, that "the psyche consists essentially of images" (1926, *CW* 8: par. 618). I imagined that it might be practically valuable for Jungians to employ a terminology that would constantly remind them of this fact. Whatever practical value there may be to the terms "ego" and "unconscious," they do not emphasize that the psyche consists essentially of images. Jung says that he eschews "too abstract a terminology" (1928, *CW* 7: par. 340) – and so do I. In this respect, the terms "ego-image" and "non-ego images" are more concrete than the terms "ego" and "unconscious."

I continue to employ concepts, but, as an imaginal psychologist, I prefer images to concepts. In contrast to concepts, which are abstract generalizations, images are concrete particularizations. Images are more specific than concepts. This specificity is a function of the distinctive qualities intrinsic to images.

The terms "ego" and "unconscious" are concepts, not images, and, as such, they have no distinctive qualities. Although the terms "ego-image" and "non-ego images" are also concepts, not images, and also have no distinctive qualities, they are concepts that have an advantage over the terms "ego" and "unconscious." They are concepts that direct attention to images that do have distinctive qualities. Meticulous attention to the distinctive qualities, the nuances, of images is the *sine qua non* of any accurate interpretation of the psyche.

What is the advantage to the term "ego-image" over the term "ego"? The term "ego-image" emphasizes that the ego is also an image. As Hillman says of the ego, "it too is an image." (The "too" emphasizes that the ego is one image among the many images in the psyche.) What Hillman considers problematic about the ego is that it neither knows nor acknowledges that it is an image. That is, the ego is unconscious of the fact that it is, as Hillman says, an "imaginal ego" (1979: 102). In this respect, the ego is truly, if tautologically, egoistical or egotistical. The ego imagines that it is an exception to the rule that the psyche consists essentially of images.

What is the advantage to the term "non-ego images" over the term "unconscious"? There is a radical irony to the term "unconscious," for the unconscious is not unconscious. Rather, the unconscious is what the ego-image is unconscious of – and what the ego-image is unconscious of are the non-ego images that emerge spontaneously and autonomously from the psyche. In addition, the definite article "the" in "the unconscious" promotes the misimpression that the unconscious is a unity, when, in fact, it is a multiplicity. The unconscious is not one thing. It is many things, and those many things are the non-ego images that emerge from the psyche.

Images as Agents

Giegerich criticizes me for regarding images as agents. He means that I say that images do things. "An image is just an image," he says. "It does not do anything" (2010: 476). Although Giegerich concedes that "we are used" to saying that images do things (2010: 477), he disdains this usual usage as fallacious or at least infelicitous. He prefers a language that is not ordinary language. I do say that images do things. In contrast to Giegerich, I prefer usual usage, or ordinary language.

Images have not only distinctive qualities but also distinctive action capacities. That is, to the extent that an image is an agent, it is an image that has the capacity to act, or to do things. The action capacities of images are an example of what David Freedberg calls the "power of images" (1989). If images did not do things, there would not be such an effort to repress them – or to censor them.

Images do things in both external reality and internal reality, but the sense in which they do things is very different. For example, in external reality a pornographic image may arouse a person, or a blasphemous image may offend a person. Although, in this sense, images in external reality do things, such images are not agents. Only images in internal reality are agents. In this respect, what interest me are the things that images do in internal reality and, especially, the things that they do to other images in internal reality – for example, in dreams. The action capacities of images in internal reality include interaction capacities.

The Real I and the Imaginal "I"

When Giegerich criticizes me for regarding images as agents, he mentions what he calls the "real I" (2010: 477). By the "real I," he means an object that, as an agent, is also functionally a subject. Such an object can do things, Giegerich says, but an image cannot.

In effect, Giegerich advocates a variety of what Roy Schafer calls "action language." Schafer says that it is fallacious or infelicitous for psychoanalysts to employ the term "unconscious" as a noun, as if the unconscious were a substantive that does things. Rather than the noun "unconscious," he says that psychoanalysts should employ the adverb "unconsciously" (1976: 243–4). It is not the unconscious that does things, Schafer says, but I who do things unconsciously. Similarly, Giegerich says that it is not images that do things but the real I that does things. As an object that is functionally a subject, the real I, he says, has action capacities, but an image does not.

"When the real is no longer what it was," Jean Baudrillard says, "nostalgia assumes its full meaning" (1994: 6). In this respect, it is rather quaint for Giegerich, at this phase in the history of psychoanalysis, to invoke the real I – an I that is not now what it once was (if it ever was that) – as if it were an I that is the epitome of what Freud calls the "reality principle."

As I define the ego-image, it is not the real I but an imaginal "I." I place this "I" in quotation marks to differentiate between the real I (the I that I am in external reality) and the imaginal "I" (the "I" that I am in internal reality – for example, in dreams). In contrast to the real I that is the person that I am in external reality, the imaginal "I" is a personification, in internal reality, of who or how I imagine myself to be. The ego-image is an imago, an imaginal "I" that, although it may refer to the real I, does not necessarily correspond accurately and exhaustively to the real I.

Giegerich imagines that he refutes me by an appeal to the real I that I am. To the extent that I exist in external reality, I am a real I. Really! Jung was also a real I. In the crisis that Jung experienced after the separation from Freud, this real I was existentially important to him. "I have a medical diploma from a Swiss university," Jung says, "I must help my patients, I have a wife and five children, I live at 228 Seestrasse in Küsnacht." These reflections, he says, "proved to me again and again that I really existed" (1963: 189). Similarly, I have graduate degrees in the humanities and social sciences from an American university and an English university, a clinical degree from an American university, as well as a psychoanalytic certificate from an American institute; I must help my patients; I have a wife and two children; I live at 1 Washington Square Village in New York City. I really exist. I am a real I.

In fact, I am not just one I but many I's. (In this respect, the ego is no more a unity than the unconscious is – it, too, is a multiplicity.) When Georg Groddeck describes the I, he emphasizes "its manifold nature" (1976: 319). He says that the I is momentary:

Inside a few moments it will turn towards us the most diverse sides of its serried and scintillating surface. At one moment it is an "I" that comes out of our childhood, later it is twenty years old; now it is moral, now sexual, and again, it is the "I" of a murderer. Now it is pious, a moment later, impertinent. In the morning it is the professional "I," the officer or the civil servant, at midday perhaps the married "I," and in the evening a card player or a sadist or a thinker.

(1976: 319)

Groddeck says that "all these 'I's' – and one could quote untold numbers more – are simultaneously present in the man" (1976: 319).

Which of these I's is the real I? Are they all equally real? Is one more real than another? Or are all of these I's imaginal "I's"?

To me, the internal reality of images (for example, the imaginal "I") is just as real as the external reality of objects (for example, the real I), although the realities of images and objects are different. In contrast to the imaginal "I," the real I is relatively irrelevant, especially in psychoanalysis. In psychoanalysis, images are more important than objects, for the internal reality of images is primary and constitutive while the external reality of objects is secondary and derivative. That is, images in internal reality are not only psychologically but also logically prior to objects in external reality (Adams 2004: 6).

In this respect, the imaginal "I" is both psychologically and logically prior to the real I. The things that I (as a real I) do are the result of who or how I (as an imaginal "I") imagine myself to be. *Imagination precedes action.*

Images as Subjects

Giegerich also criticizes me for regarding images as subjects. As I do, he appreciates what Hillman says of the ego – that "it too is an image." Giegerich says that this proposition has a grammatical advantage over the term "ego-image." He notes that, in the proposition "the ego too is an image," the image is grammatically "in the position of the predicate" (2010: 477). In contrast, in the term "ego-image," he says, the image is no longer in the position of the predicate but is now in the position of the "subject," while the prefix "ego-" is what he calls "a specifying attribute" (2010: 478).

In the new terminology that I propose, the image, Giegerich says, is neither the predicate of the ego as the subject nor "an adjective" (2010: 479) – as, for example, in the phrase "imaginal ego," where the adjective "imaginal" modifies the noun "ego." What exasperates Giegerich is that in the term "ego-image," the ego is not the subject – the image is the subject. To Giegerich, it is preposterous to attribute subjectivity to an image. Subjectivity, he fastidiously insists, is exclusive to the ego.

To criticize the term "ego-image" on this basis is, if I may say so, to quibble – to cavil about words. Rather than the term "ego-image," I could have employed the term "image-ego." In the term "image-ego," the ego would be in the position of the subject, and the prefix "image-" would be a specifying attribute. The term "image-ego" would be functionally equivalent to the phrase "imaginal ego." Presumably, Giegerich would endorse such a reversal, for the term "image-ego" is consistent with the notion that only the ego, not the image, has subjectivity.

I have no objection to the term "image-ego" (although it might promote the misimpression that there is some other ego that is not an image – and there is no ego that is not an image). I prefer, however, to retain the term "ego-image." Grammatically, the term "ego-image" is a compound noun. The hyphenation specifies an attribute of the image. This image is not just any image – it is specifically an ego-image. I regard the term "ego-image" as a succinct paraphrase, a convenient abbreviation, of the proposition that "the ego too is an image." To me, "ego-image" is a term that concisely expresses that fact. What Hillman says is radically important. *There is no ego that is not always already an image.*

What is at issue is whether images – not only the ego-image but also non-ego images – have subjectivity. Are images ever subjects? I would say that in internal reality images do have subjectivity, at least functionally. Personifications in internal reality – for example, the ego-image and non-ego images in dreams – function just as much as subjects as any person in external reality functions as a subject.

One World or Many Worlds

Is there one reality – or are there many realities? William James says that there are "many worlds" (1983: 920). As examples of these many worlds, he mentions the "world of sense, or of physical 'things,'" the "world of science," the "world of ideal relations, or abstract truths," the "world of 'idols of the tribe,' illusions or prejudices," the "various supernatural worlds" of religion and mythology, the "various worlds of individual opinion," and the "worlds of sheer madness and vagary" (1983: 921–2). Among the many worlds, James also mentions the "world of dreams" (1983: 923n.). In a discussion of "multiple realities," Alfred Schutz, who cites James with approval, says of these many worlds that "there are several, probably an infinite number of various orders of realities, each with its own special and separate style of existence" (1962: 207).

In psychoanalysis, there is not one reality but two realities – external reality and internal reality, or psychic reality. What Freud and Jung call psychic reality I prefer to call "imaginal reality." From this perspective, external reality consists essentially of objects, and internal reality consists essentially of images. (Although object relations psychoanalysts say that there are objects in internal reality – objects that have been internalized from external reality – I regard this nomenclature as a misnomer. What object relations psychoanalysts call internal objects are not objects but images of external objects.) In psychoanalysis, there is not one world but two worlds – the external world and the internal world. In contrast to the external world, the internal world is an imaginal world, what Eva T.H. Brann calls the "world of the imagination" (1991).

Images as Entities

Giegerich criticizes me for regarding images as entities (2010: 479). An entity is a thing or being with a separate and distinct existence. I do regard images as entities. Just as there are entities in the external world, there are entities in the internal world. The entities in the external world are objects (physical things – among them, persons), and the entities in the internal world are images (psychic things – among them, personifications).

The entities in the internal world are what John R. Searle calls fictional entities. Searle mentions "fictional (and also legendary, mythological, etc.) entities." He says that such entities are *fictional characters* that *exist in fiction* (1969: 78). Such entities are characters in the same sense as characters in novels. These fictional entities do not exist as objects in the external world – they exist as images in the internal world. They have an imaginal existence.

Fictional Worlds

The mythological world, the religious world, and the dream world are examples of what Thomas G. Pavel calls "fictional worlds" (1986). By "fictional worlds," I do not mean only literary worlds that are fictions – for example, a novelistic world. To me, the internal world, the psychic world, or the imaginal world is a fictional world. The entities in fictional worlds are fictional things that are, as Pavel says, "fictional beings" (1986: 27).

The fictional entities in the mythological world, the religious world, and the dream world have an existential status identical with that of fictional characters in other fictional worlds – for example, the novelistic world. In novels, images do various things. In dreams, images also do various things – they think, feel, speak, and do many other things. To me, it is neither fallacious nor infelicitous to say that images in internal reality are agents or subjects – that is, entities that do things. *Images do, indeed, do deeds – they are fictional entities that do fictional things in fictional worlds.*

Images and Concepts

Giegerich criticizes me for saying that images are more specific than concepts – that in contrast to images, which have distinctive qualities, concepts have no distinctive qualities and are nondescript. In this respect, he quotes a sentence from a dream that Jung recounts. "Suddenly," Jung says, "I had the feeling that something was coming up behind me" (1963: 88). What interests Giegerich is the "something" in this dream. "This 'something,'" he remarks, "has hardly any distinctive qualities." It is, he says, "nondescript." Among nouns as names of persons, places, or things, a thing is the most indefinite. A thing could be anything. (The only thing it could not be is nothing, for that would be a contradiction in terms.) By definition, a "something" is a thing so unspecific as to be indeterminate. In this sense, a "something" would be a concept – that is, a thing with no distinctive qualities. As Giegerich defines the "something" in this dream, however, it is not a concept but an image, for it is, he says, a "this" (2010: 495). By this definition, any "this" is an image, however nondescript it may be.

In fact, however, the "something" in this dream does have distinctive qualities. The very next sentence (which Giegerich does not quote, perhaps from a concern that it would compromise the purity of the position that he espouses) is quite specific. "I looked back," Jung says, "and saw a gigantic black figure following me." This image is not at all nondescript. It is specifically a figure with the distinctive qualities of "gigantic" and "black." The image also has distinctive action capacities. This "something" is a non-ego image that does something. The non-ego image is "coming up behind" and "following" the ego-image. It is precisely these qualities and action capacities that prompt the ego-image to do something. Jung says that "I was conscious, in spite of my terror, that I must keep my little light going through night and wind, regardless of all dangers." In the dream, the ego-image reacts to the non-ego image – the gigantic black figure – with fright but also with determination. "I knew, too," Jung says, "that this little light was my consciousness, the only light I have." In the dream, the ego-image resolves to protect the light of consciousness against the "powers of darkness" – the night, the wind, and the gigantic black figure – that threaten at any moment to extinguish it (1963: 88).

Rather than the distinctive qualities of images, Giegerich emphasizes what he calls the "thisness" of images. What, however, is the "ness" of an image as a "this" but a function of the distinctive qualities, as well as the distinctive action capacities, of the image? When Giegerich criticizes me, he says that I count, "as it were, *the number* of qualities in order to distinguish image from concept" and that this is a "quantitative" method (2010: 496). Giegerich imagines that I regard interpretation as a problem in mathematics with addition as the solution. Although I do say that the more distinctive qualities an image has, the more specificity the image has (and the more possibility there is of an accurate interpretation of the image), I never say that the specificity of an image is the sum of the distinctive qualities of the image. The method by which I interpret images is not a quantitative method – it is a qualitative method. That is why I employ the expression "distinctive qualities." What I emphasize is qualitative distinctions. In spite of what Giegerich says, I do not just enumerate the distinctive qualities of an image. To me, what an image means is a function of the distinctive qualities and

37

distinctive action capacities intrinsic to the image. It is those qualities and action capacities that endow a specific image with "thisness."

Jung says that the psyche consists essentially of images – he does not say that the psyche consists exclusively of images. Dreams may include concepts as well as images. What most interests me is not whether a "this" in a dream is an image or a concept. For me, the issue is not concepts in dreams but concepts in the interpretation of images. The objection that I have is to interpretation as a reductive conceptualization of the imagination – that is, the tendency of psychoanalysts complacently to replace an image with a concept, as if the substitution of an abstract generalization for a concrete particularization were a satisfactory interpretation. Such a conceptualization does violence to the imagination, for it reduces what is more specific (an image) to what is less specific (a concept). The reduction obliterates the details (the distinctive qualities and distinctive action capacities) that are the very basis of an accurate interpretation of any "this."

Possible and Impossible Worlds

Recently, there has been much discussion, in modal logic, of "possible worlds" and, in contrast, "impossible worlds." Lubomír Doležel differentiates between three alethetic modalities: "possibility, impossibility, and necessity" (1998: 115). In modal logic, there is the "actual world," and there are various fictional worlds. The actual world is the natural world. In contrast to a fictional world, the actual world is a factual world, or a nonfictional world. In the actual world, objects obey the laws of nature. Among fictional worlds, some are possible worlds in which images obey the laws of nature, while others are impossible worlds in which images violate the laws of nature.

Natural Fictional Worlds

Some fictional worlds are natural fictional worlds. "If the modalities of the actual world determine what is possible, impossible, and necessary in the fictional world," Doležel says, the result is "a natural fictional world." As Doležel defines a natural fictional world, it is a possible world in which "nothing exists and nothing happens that would violate the laws of the actual world." Among the entities in a natural fictional world are characters that can only do things that persons in the actual world can do. For example, Doležel says that "walking is possible" for such a character, "while becoming invisible is not" (1998: 115).

Such fictional worlds are mimetic worlds. Images (psychic things) in these internal worlds both refer to and correspond to objects (physical things) in the external world. Such images in the internal world obey the laws that govern objects in the external world. The things that these images do in the internal world are only what it is possible for objects to do in the external world.

Supernatural Fictional Worlds

Other fictional worlds are supernatural fictional worlds. "Fictional worlds that violate the laws of the actual world," Doležel says, "are physically impossible, supernatural worlds" (1998: 115). Examples of supernatural worlds are what James calls the worlds of mythology and religion. What is impossible in the natural world is possible in a supernatural world. Among the things in a supernatural world are physically impossible beings. "Physically impossible beings – gods, spirits, monsters, and so on – inhabit the supernatural world," Doležel says. These physically impossible beings in a supernatural world can do things that physically possible beings – for example, human beings – in the natural world cannot do. Doležel says that gods, spirits, monsters, and so on in a supernatural world are agents that have "action capacities" that exceed those of persons in the natural world. In this respect, any entity with a capacity to act, or to do things, is, by definition, an agent. Doležel also says that certain extraordinary persons in a supernatural world are agents that selectively have "action capacities that are not available to ordinary persons" in a supernatural world. Among the things that these extraordinary persons can do, Doležel says, are "becoming invisible, flying on a carpet, and so on." Examples of such extraordinary persons, he says, are "heroes of myth, fairy tales, and legends." In addition, not only animate objects such as extraordinary persons but also inanimate objects in a supernatural world may be personifications. For example, Doležel says that in a supernatural world "a statue becomes an agent," or in the supernatural world of fairy tales "a mirror talks" (1998: 116). Animate objects such as animals in the supernatural world of fables are agents, he says, that also have action capacities such as "speech." Doležel also says that there are various "intermediate worlds" between the natural world and supernatural worlds. "Dreams, hallucination, madness," he says, are "physically possible" experiences in the natural world, but "physically impossible persons, objects, and events," he notes, also appear in such intermediate worlds (1998: 117).

Some fictional worlds – for example, the mythological, religious, and dream worlds – are, either in whole or in part, impossible worlds. A fictional world may not be a mimetic world. Images in the internal world may not be images of objects in the external world. That is, images in the internal world may not correspond to objects in the external world – they may not even refer to them. The things that images do in the internal world – for example, in the mythological, religious, and dream worlds – may be things that are impossible for objects to do in the external world.

Miraculous and Transnatural Worlds

Images in the internal world may violate the laws that govern objects in the external world. That is, among the things that images in some fictional worlds may do is to do miracles. "A miracle," as Hume defines it, "is a violation of the laws of nature" (1992: 93). Some fictional worlds are miraculous worlds. In such fictional worlds – for example, in the supernatural worlds of mythology and religion – there may be a suspension or an interruption of the laws of nature.

The world of dreams may also be a world of miracles. The dream world is not, however, a supernatural world. It is a fictional world that, as Michael Polanyi says, is "*trans*natural" – that is, a world that goes "beyond the 'natural'" (Polanyi and Prosch 1975: 125). The dream world is a world that transcends the natural world. Images in the transnatural world of dreams can do things that objects in the natural world cannot do. For example, the oneiric world is not an entropic world. The second law of thermodynamics does not apply to the internal world as that law of nature obtains in the external world. In contrast to objects in the external world, images in the internal world can do anything and everything. What is utterly impossible in the external world is quite possible in the internal world.

The Dream World and the Naturalistic Fallacy

Some psychoanalysts, Hillman says, assume that the world of dreams "should accord with" the world of nature (1979: 95). To do so is to commit the naturalistic fallacy. As Hillman defines the naturalistic fallacy, it is the assumption that "the way it *is* in nature is the norm for how it *should* be in dreams". This normative assumption is not only fallacious but also facile. "The naturalistic fallacy is common," Hillman says, "because it requires least effort on the part of an interpreter" (1975: 84). It is hardly hard – it is, in fact, all too easy – for an interpreter to assume that images in the dream world not only refer to but also should correspond to objects in the natural world, and that is why psychoanalysts, both Freudians and Jungians, commonly commit the naturalistic fallacy.

For such psychoanalysts, the natural is the normal. They regard images that are deviations from the naturalistic norm as pathological. The dream world is not, however, reducible to the natural world. "A multicolored child, a woman with an erected penis, an oak tree bearing cherries, a snake becoming a cat who talks," Hillman says, "are neither wrong, false, nor abnormal because they are unnatural" (1975: 85) – or, as I would say, transnatural.

Objects and Images: The Shark and the Octopus

Yoram Kaufmann is one Jungian who emphasizes the importance of images and who proposes a method for the accurate interpretation of images. Images, he says, are what inform any interpretation. That is, for Kaufmann, images are the only reliable source of information for an accurate interpretation. It is images, he says, that establish the parameters of any interpretation – that delimit and discipline an interpretation. Kaufmann argues, as I do, that scrupulous, systematic scrutiny of specific images is the basis of any interpretation that aspires or purports to be accurate. I respect the effort to articulate precise principles for the interpretation of images, and I admire Kaufmann for it. I share the interest that he has in images and interpretation. I also appreciate that he values critical discourse.

Kaufmann, however, is a Jungian who commits the naturalistic fallacy. He assumes that images in the dream world accord – or should accord – with objects in the natural world. As examples of images, he mentions the shark and the octopus. He notes that, as an object in the external world, the shark is "quite different" from the octopus by "nature." The shark, Kaufmann says, is "very dangerous," in contrast to the octopus, which is "very gentle" (2009: 11). Arthur O. Lovejoy and George Boas list 66 different meanings of the word "nature" in the history of ideas (1935). By "nature," Kaufmann means the instincts of an organism – in this instance, those of the shark and the octopus.

What do experts say about the shark and the octopus as objects in the external world? They say, as Kaufmann does, that the shark is dangerous – but what of the octopus? Jacques-Yves Cousteau and Philippe Diolé say that the octopus is quite timid. "The octopus," they say, "far from being the aggressive monster so dear to fiction writers and filmmakers, is a shy, retiring creature" (1973: 12). What is at issue is the reputation of the octopus. The putative monstrosity is a myth, in the sense of a false notion. Cousteau and Diolé propose "to put an end to the calumnies of which the unfortunate octopus has been the target" and "to demythologize the fabulous monsters." Octopuses are not monsters, they say, but "marvelous animals" (1973: 36). The octopus is a monster only to the ignorant. Cousteau and Diolé investigate a report that describes "a long and bloody battle" with a 200-pound octopus, as well as a report that describes the bite of a giant octopus as "sufficiently poisonous to kill a man," but they conclude that no octopus, not even a giant one, is dangerous (1973: 41).

What, however, of the shark and the octopus as images in the internal world? To Kaufmann, there is no shark that is not dangerous, and there is no octopus that is not gentle – whether the shark and the octopus are objects in the external world or images in the internal world. In accordance with the nature of the object – or what Kaufmann calls "the nature of the beast" – he says that when a person dreams of a shark, the image is "a real dangerous content of the unconscious." The image of the shark, he says, is evidence of "an unconscious complex" that is "a real threat" (2009: 11). (By "real," Kaufmann means that the threat is serious.) In contrast, if a person dreams of an octopus, even if the image has "a menacing feel" to it, Kaufmann says that the image is not a real dangerous content of the unconscious, not a real threat. The image of the octopus is, he says, "quite benign" (2009: 12).

For Kaufmann, images in the internal world are in strict conformity with objects in the external world, and any response to the image should be in strict compliance with the nature of the object. Kaufmann conflates objects and images. In effect, he reduces images to objects. He perpetrates a reductive objectification of the imagination. To Kaufmann, images in the internal world refer to objects in the external world, and those images do – or should – correspond to those objects. If those images do not correspond to those objects – for example, if a shark in a dream is very gentle and an octopus in a dream is very dangerous, or if a person regards the shark as gentle and the octopus as dangerous – this is evidence, he says, of a complex (2009: 12).

In spite of what Kaufmann says, the natural world is not the norm for the dream world, and images of a gentle shark and a dangerous octopus are not deviations. Such images are not abnormal – they are transnatural. The dream world is a transnatural world where all things, even things that are impossible in the natural world, are possible. That is, the dream world is a miraculous world where, in violation of the laws of nature, a shark can be gentle and an octopus can be dangerous. The notion that images in the dream world accord with objects in the natural world is a *non sequitur*. Even if all sharks as objects in the natural world are dangerous, it does not follow that all sharks as images in the dream world are dangerous, for the dream world is a transnatural world.

The Dream World and the Literalistic Fallacy

Hillman mentions "the literalistic and naturalistic fallacies" (1975: 198). Kaufmann commits both fallacies – he literalizes as well as naturalizes the images in dreams. When Kaufmann interprets dreams, he takes the images literally rather than metaphorically. He does not appreciate that the images in dreams are metaphors.

Kaufmann cites a dream that an analyst presented as evidence of the success of an analysis. The dream does not include the shark or the octopus as images, but it does include the sea as an image. "In the dream," Kaufmann says, "the patient and the analyst are scuba-diving in the ocean to a depth of three thousand feet." He says that the analyst presented the dream as an example of a profound analysis – one that attains "great depths." Both the patient and the analyst, he says, "were impressed by the depth of the dive." Kaufmann says that they regarded the image as "a very positive statement from the unconscious" (2009: 14).

To Kaufmann, however, the image is a very negative statement from the unconscious – for it is, he notes, "literally impossible to dive down three thousand feet." He takes the image of the depth of the dive literally. "The pressure of the water increases drastically as one goes deeper," he says, "and after a while, long before three thousand feet, one would explode as a result of this pressure" (2009: 14). (Actually, one would implode.)

As Kaufmann interprets this dream, it is a negative statement from the unconscious about the conduct of the analysis of the patient. What the dream indicates, he says, is that the analyst "is taking him to depths" that will be "disastrous." Kaufmann says that the patient "is being taken to depths that will tear him apart" (2009: 15).

It is important, however, to note what the images in a dream do and do not do. By the literalistic criteria that Kaufmann applies to this dream, the ego-image of the patient should implode – but it does not. An implosion is a violent compression. If there were an implosion in this dream, it might indicate that the analysis is a disaster, but there is no implosion. Why does the ego-image not implode?

Hillman says of images in dreams: "Nothing is literal; all is metaphor" (1975: 175). The dream world is a metaphorical world. In such a world, where images are metaphors, what is literally possible or impossible is irrelevant. In the dream world, it is metaphorically possible for the ego-image to dive to a depth of three thousand feet, even to dive all the way down to the very bottom of the sea – and not implode.

In this dream, the most important metaphor is water pressure. Psycho-analytically, water is a metaphor for the unconscious – and, by extension, water pressure is a metaphor for unconscious pressure. In any analysis that is not superficial – that is, in any analysis that does not simply remain on the surface – the unconscious ultimately exerts enormous pressure on the patient. There are, of course, analysts who conduct analyses that are too deep and who subject patients to too much pressure from the unconscious – and there are patients who cannot withstand any pressure at all from the unconscious. What this dream indicates, however, is that this patient, with this analyst, is able to withstand the pressure of an in-depth analysis, for the ego-image in the dream is able to withstand the pressure of the unconscious.

In spite of what Kaufmann says, this dream is a positive statement about the conduct of the analysis – as well as a positive statement about the action capacities of the ego-image. If this analysis were a disaster, the dream would employ images that demonstrate unequivocally that it is. This dream indicates that the ego-image has the action capacity to dive down very, very deep into the unconscious, where it might eventually encounter various non-ego images – among them, perhaps, images of the shark or the octopus.

A Shark Dream

"Let us assume," Kaufmann says, "that a person has a dream in which a shark appears" (2009: 11). Although Kaufmann discusses the image of the shark as if it appears in a dream, he never presents an example of a dream – much less a sample of dreams – in which the image of a shark does appear. Only when an analyst presents the entirety of a dream verbatim, not just a summary or a paraphrase, do other analysts have an opportunity to assess whether an interpretation of the images in the dream is accurate or not. In this respect, Kaufmann is more declarative than demonstrative. Any image of a shark that appears in any dream, he just assumes – and asserts – is a threat.

One thing that an image of a shark may do in a dream is appear, but images of sharks in dreams do many more things than appear. As a non-ego image, a shark may, for example, threaten the ego-image. Consider a dream in which a shark does threaten the ego-image. Dean Crawford quotes a recurrent nightmare that Peter Gimbel recounts:

> This nightmare, which also popped up occasionally as an inner vision by day, always followed the same pattern. I was swimming among the great blues in the middle ground. Abruptly, they disappeared beyond my perimeter of vision leaving only the gray-blue blankness of the open ocean. I spun round and round, trying to look in all directions at once, sensing that something enormous was just out of sight. A form appeared, huge beyond imagining. It came rapidly toward me and materialized as the great white shark, the man-eater. It bore straight in with overwhelming speed, and as the jaws opened to swallow me I would awaken and begin thinking of what desperate measures to take if the nightmare – or daymare – came true.
>
> (2008: 9)

The dream ends abruptly. Gimbel sleeps, dreams, and then wakes when the non-ego image of the shark threatens to devour the ego-image. In the dream, the ego-image does not respond to the threat.

Gimbel is not just a person who dreams of sharks. He is a former banker who has organized an expedition to research sharks and has produced a film to document that experience. It is hardly a surprise that a person who has swum with sharks, as Gimbel has, might also dream of sharks – and might reflect on what to do in the event of an attack by a shark as an object in external reality. Should Gimbel react to the shark defensively with "flight" or "fight"? How should he deal with the shark? The dream does not say – it poses a question but provides no answer.

Another Shark Dream

An appearance of an image of a shark in a dream is not, as such, a threat. If the only thing that an image of a shark does in a dream is to appear, what the image means in that dream is indeterminate. Consider a dream in which a shark does appear. A patient of Walter Bonime recounts the dream: "I was in a large tank like a swimming pool. There was also a shark in the water. I was swimming frantically to get away from him" (1962: 126).

In the interpretation that Bonime proposes, the shark is an image of the psychoanalyst, and the dream is a wish-fulfillment. Bonime says that the patient "frantically wished to elude the analyst" (1962: 126). In this dream, the patient reacts with fright and then defensively with "flight." Presumably, Kaufmann would consider this evasive reaction prudently appropriate, for the patient considers the shark as an image just as dangerous as a shark as an object. What an image means, however, is a function not only of what it is but of where it is and what it does.

Where is the shark in this dream? The dream says that the shark is in a swimming pool with the patient. A swimming pool, of course, is not the sea. The sea is the natural habitat, or environment, of a shark. A swimming pool and the sea are both bodies of water, but, as Hillman emphasizes, it is important to differentiate "the *kind* of water in a dream" (1979: 152). In this respect, the sea is a large, very deep body of water, and a swimming pool is a small, relatively shallow body of water. In this dream, the patient and the shark are together, within the confines of a swimming pool. The shark is in the immediate vicinity of the patient. The patient is in proximity to the shark. In such a situation, it might be appropriate for a patient to err on the side of caution – not only to swim away from the shark but also to get out of the swimming pool.

In this dream, what does the shark do – and not do? The dream says that the shark is in the water. Presumably, the shark is just swimming. The dream does not say that the shark is threatening the patient. The dream does not say that the shark is attacking or even approaching the patient. There is no indication in the dream that the shark is even aware that the patient is in the water with it. Sharks as objects in external reality are predators that attack other fish. Although sharks may attack humans, they do so only occasionally. The voracity of sharks is notorious, but sharks do not have an instinctive appetite for humans. Humans are not the prey of sharks. Sharks may bite or even eat humans, but sharks, even hungry sharks, do not hunt humans. Although there is no indication in this dream that the shark has any intention or motivation to attack or even approach the patient, the patient frantically swims away from the shark.

"Stick to the Image"

To have any opportunity to interpret an image accurately, it is necessary, as Hillman says, to "stick to the image." In this dream, the patient does not pause and reflect on the image. What the patient does is react to the image – defensively. The patient does not stick to the image of the shark long enough to ascertain whether the shark is even aware of him, whether the shark has any interest in him, and, if so, what the intention or motivation of the shark might be.

As I do, Hillman says that images do things. In a discussion of images of animals in dreams, he says that it is important to observe patiently – to wait and see – what things these images as animals do. "To find out who they are and what they are doing there in the dream," Hillman says, "we must first of all watch the image and pay less attention to our own reactions to it." Only then might it be possible, he says, to interpret the image accurately, to discern

45

"what it means with us in the dream." In this respect, to stick to the image is to attend to the image – to pause and reflect on the image and not just react to the image. Hillman says that "no animal ever means one thing only, and no animal simply means death" (1979: 148). In spite of what Kaufmann says, no image of a shark simply means only one thing – for example, danger. What an image of a shark means is a function not only of where the image is but also of what the image does or does not do. A shark that placidly swims in a dream has a very different meaning from a shark that viciously attacks in a dream.

The Literal and the Metaphorical

In the interpretation that Bonime proposes of the dream, the shark is an image of the analyst. That is, he says that the patient experiences the analyst as a shark. Literally, a shark is a fish. Taxonomically, a shark is an elasmobranch fish of medium to large size with a fusiform body, lateral branchial clefts and a tough, usually dull gray skin. Metaphorically, a shark is a rapacious person who preys on other people through usury, extortion, or trickery – for example, a "loan shark." In this respect, a shark is an image of the archetype of the "trickster." Whether sharks as objects in the external world are, in fact, tricky, or whether this notion is an anthropocentric conceit is, at least in psychoanalysis, irrelevant, for sharks as images in the internal world – for example, in the dream world – may be tricky.

No analyst, of course, is literally a shark. Any patient who regarded an analyst as a literal shark would be not neurotic but psychotic. Such a notion would be a delusion or even a hallucination. Are there, however, analysts who are metaphorical sharks? Are there rapacious analysts who prey on patients? Are there analysts who are tricksters? I imagine so.

Is the analyst in the dream that Bonime presents a metaphorical shark? All that is certain is that – at least as Bonime interprets the dream – the patient experiences the analyst as a shark. Does the analyst, in fact, have qualities and action capacities the same as or similar to those of a shark, or does the patient merely impute those qualities and action capacities to the analyst? An analyst may not be frightening, but, even so, in spite of that fact, a patient may be frightened. Bonime does not say whether he regards the image as a perception or a projection.

In the new terminology that I advocate, whether or not the shark is an image of the analyst, and whether or not that image is a perception or a projection, the shark is a non-ego image. Although in the dream the non-ego image never threatens the ego-image of the patient, the ego-image reacts to it with fright and then defensively with "flight." In this dream, the ego-image just assumes that the shark as a non-ego image is dangerous – as Kaufmann just assumes that all sharks in dreams are dangerous.

Jung says that the unconscious is "dangerous only because we are not at one with it and therefore in opposition to it" (1917/1926/1943, *CW* 7: par.

195). That is, the unconscious is not intrinsically dangerous. "It only becomes dangerous when our conscious attitude to it is hopelessly wrong," Jung says. "To the degree that we repress it, its danger increases" (1934, *CW* 16: par. 329). Or, as I prefer to say, a non-ego image that emerges from the unconscious is not dangerous as such but only becomes dangerous when the attitude of the ego-image is partial, prejudicial, or defective. To the extent that the ego-image is repressive in particular – or defensive in general – the danger of a non-ego image increases. For Kaufmann, a shark is absolutely dangerous. For Jung, a non-ego image, even a shark, is only relatively dangerous. Whether a non-ego image is dangerous and, if so, how dangerous it may be – or become – is relative to how repressive or how defensive the attitude of the ego-image is.

When an apparently dangerous non-ego image from the unconscious pursues the ego-image in a dream, Jung says that it means "this wants to come to me." The ego-image, however, tends to react defensively, with the result, he says, that the non-ego image "just becomes all the more dangerous." Rather than repress the non-ego image, Jung recommends that the ego-image respond receptively: "The best stance would be: 'Please, come and devour me!'" (2008: 19).

Another Shark Dream

Consider another dream that a patient, a 48-year-old man, recounted to me:

> Somebody asks me about how my thinking has changed about the ocean. I say: "I initially studied a part of the ocean close to the coast. ('Close to the coast' means that I'm safe.) Then the conditions of the ocean changed so much that there's a difference between what's going on close to the coast and what's going on deeper in the ocean where everything is more dangerous and there are sharks".

This patient has experienced a change in how he thinks about the unconscious. In this dream, what does the ego-image do and not do? The ego-image does not enter the ocean – the image of the unconscious. Rather, the ego-image studies the ocean. Initially, the ego-image studies only a part of the ocean – the part close to the coast, where the ego-image is safe. Eventually, however, as the ego-image continues to study the ocean – and not just a part of it but the whole of it – the conditions change, not just a little but a lot. The conditions of the ocean change so much that there is a difference between what is happening near to the coast, where the water is shallow and safe, and what is happening far from the coast, where the water is deeper and more dangerous – and where there are sharks, which (although the dream does not say so), presumably, the ego-image also considers dangerous. As the ego-image studies the scene, it thinks about what it might experience – and what it might encounter – were it to enter the unconscious.

That the ego-image in this dream was so studious – that it would study the unconscious rather than immediately enter it – was no surprise, for this patient was a professor at a university. I do not mean that, for him, analysis was, in the pejorative sense of the word, "academic." Study of the unconscious is, however, no substitute for experience of the unconscious. Unless and until a patient enters deeply into an analysis and the ego-image enters deeply into the unconscious, any expectation of danger – or anticipation of sharks – is merely a surmise.

Another Shark Dream

In a *Red Book Dialogue* that I conducted with the comedian Sarah Silverman at the Rubin Museum of Art in New York (Adams 2009), I mentioned a dream that Silverman recounts in the film *Jesus Is Magic* (2006). In the dream, Silverman dives into a swimming pool. "As I'm diving in," she says, "there's a shark coming up from the water – with braces."

It is not impossible for a shark, as an object in the external world, to have braces. However improbable that may be, it is possible. Although sharks do not have dentists, much less orthodontists, it is possible that an ichthyologist might wire braces onto the teeth of a shark for some experimental purpose. That a shark, as an image in the internal world, has braces is not miraculous. It is not, however, in the nature of sharks to have braces. That is not the nature of the beast.

Silverman does not say that the shark in the dream frightened her. Presumably, the image of the shark with braces amused her, for she recounts the dream as a joke. By the naturalistic criteria that Kaufmann employs, the image of the shark would be a dangerous content of the unconscious, and Silverman should have regarded it as a threat. The shark should have frightened her. In a discussion of jokes and the unconscious, Freud presents examples of dreams that demonstrate that the unconscious has a sense of humor (1905, *SE* 8). For Kaufmann, however, a shark in a dream is no laughing matter. Even a shark with braces is no joke.

In the dream, Silverman is the ego-image, and the shark is a non-ego image. Both the ego-image and the non-ego image do things. The thing that the non-ego image does is to come up from the water, and the thing that the ego-image does is to look at the non-ego image. If, as Jung says, water is the commonest image of the unconscious, the shark in the dream is a content of the unconscious. Whether the non-ego image is a dangerous content that is a threat to the ego-image is, however, problematic.

However much a shark with braces may amuse Silverman as an adult, she says that sharks did frighten her as a child. "I was afraid of sharks – even in pools," she says in the *Red Book Dialogue*. "I'm from the *Jaws* era!" (Adams 2009).

The shark in *Jaws* frightened an entire generation. A woman who watched the film on a date with a man in a theater recounted to me an anecdote about just how much the shark frightened the audience. When the shark came up from the water, a man in the seat next to her date clapped his hands over his eyes, buried his head in her date's lap, knocked her date's popcorn all over the place, and grabbed her date around his waist so hard that he scratched her date through his shirt. "Sorry, man!" he exclaimed. "Sorry!"

The very week when I was revising the final version of this essay, I had an experience that was, if not "synchronistic," at least ironic. I went for a dental appointment to have my teeth cleaned. The hygienist, it so happened, was a film enthusiast. As I lay there, jaws wide open, while she probed, scraped, and polished my teeth, she named all of her favorite films. Suddenly, she mentioned *Jaws*. (I had not said to her that I was writing an essay that included images of sharks – among them, Jaws.) She said that the film had so "freaked out" everyone that, for weeks afterward, everyone had expected to see sharks on the sidewalks of New York. She then mentioned a comedy sketch from an episode of *Saturday Night Live*. In the skit as she recounted it, there was a knock at the front door of a house. A voice said, "Mailman!" A woman opened the door, and there – surprise, surprise – was Jaws. "Land shark!" the woman exclaimed.

"Sharks inspire terror out of all proportion to their actual threat," Crawford says. How to account for this disparity between the threat and the terror of sharks? "We may wonder what they did to earn such special attention," Crawford says. "Did they chomp down on our prehistoric ancestors often enough to create an evolutionary memory, a kind of monster profile in the lower cortices of our brains?" This speculation about evolution is, of course, more Lamarckian than Darwinian. It is also rather Jungian, although Crawford emphasizes the brain and Jung emphasizes the psyche. Is there a "monster archetype" in the collective unconscious? Crawford says that "some sharks are genuine monsters." Sharks can – and occasionally do – attack humans, although Crawford notes that "sharks on average kill fewer than twenty" in the entire world in a single year (2008: 7).

In the origin of species, humans date to 200 thousand years ago. One fossil of a shark dates to more than 400 million years ago. There are more than 450 species of sharks. "Some of these species are indeed the monsters of our nightmares – if not in behaviour then surely in appearance," Crawford says. "But, in fact, sharks outstrip our imaginations not only in the terror that they induce, or in their improbable shapes and designs, but also in their connection to an evolutionary past so distant as to defy human comprehension" (2008: 46).

The shark in *Jaws* is not just any shark – it is a rogue shark. "According to mythology, the rogue shark prowls the beaches, haunts the harbours and even swims upstream in his monstrous quest for innocent people to maim and kill," Crawford says. "*Jaws* uses this myth as its central sensation and conceit" (2008: 65). Even as the film frightens, it also entertains. "Fright entertainment, the creating and inflaming of phobias," Crawford says, "is a Western cultural norm." He offers an explanation that is both religious and psychoanalytic.

Crawford says that "we're haunted by visions of hell and – at least since Freud – fascinated by our own inner recesses and dark depths" (2008: 69). Or, as I would say, *Jaws* appeals to the cultural unconscious of the West.

The Archetype of the "Sea Monster"

As an object in the external world, the shark is a sea creature. In the internal world, however, the shark is an image of the archetype of the "sea monster." In the index that Stith Thompson compiles of motifs in folk literature, this is type "G308. *Sea monster*" (1955, 3: 347).

R.E.L. Masters and Jean Houston quote the transcript of a psychedelic experience of a 40-year-old man who ingested 100 micrograms of LSD. In the session, the man appears as a little boy who encounters a sea monster that threatens to devour him and a fisherman:

> a huge sea monster … opens its jaws and snaps them shut on half of the fisherman's boat. With the next bite it will swallow both of us. A thunderbolt comes out of the sky and smashes the boat in two, leaving half of it stuck in the monster's gullet. The fisherman takes me in his arms and swims with me towards shore …. The sea monster pursues us … Just as we reach the shore it snaps off the fisherman's leg. The fisherman continues to hold me and crawls with me in his arms to a nearby hut. His wife is there. She nurses her husband and puts me into a cradle. I am raised by this couple as their own son. They are very kind to me … tell me I must be very special seeing as how I was drawn from the water … They call me Aquarion. The years pass. I am now four years old but already am tremendously strong and powerful … They tell me I must avenge myself on the sea monster who tried to destroy me and bit off my fisher-father's leg. I dive into the water to go and find the sea monster … For many hours I swim around and finally find it. It is swimming towards me at tremendous speed. It has grown gargantuan and horrible ugly … opens its jaws to consume me but I evade them and get a strangle hold on its throat. For many days we battle together … The sea is crimson with our blood … Great waves are created by our combat … I am the conqueror … tear open its belly … In its stomach I find the leg of my fisher-father. I take the leg back to land and fit it onto his stump. It instantly joins and he is whole again.
>
> (1966: 227)

This sea monster is rather generic, not very specific. It devours a part (a leg) of the fisherman. The little boy is an image of the archetype of the "monster-slaying hero." He tears open the belly of the sea monster, retrieves the leg and reattaches it, so that the fisherman is again whole. "Aquarion" is, of course, an appropriate name for a hero from the 1960s, the "Age of Aquarius."

In *Moby-Dick*, the sea monster is specifically a whale monster. Captain Ahab and Captain Boomer compare a leg and an arm. The White Whale has devoured the leg of Captain Ahab and the arm of Captain Boomer. Captain Boomer says that the White Whale "doesn't bite so much as he swallows." Bunger, the surgeon on the ship, says that, if so, Captain Boomer should "give him your left arm for bait to get the right." He says that "the digestive organs of the whale are so inscrutably constructed by Divine Providence, that it is quite impossible for him to completely digest even a man's arm." The arm of Captain Boomer, Bunger says, is intact in the belly of the White Whale. He says that if Captain Boomer were agile enough, he could retrieve the arm (which the White Whale has devoured but not digested) – not in order to reattach it but to bury it. "Yes, Captain Boomer," Bunger facetiously says, "if you are quick enough about it, and have a mind to pawn one arm for the sake of the privilege of giving decent burial to the other, why in that case the arm is yours; only let the whale have another chance at you shortly, that's all." Captain Boomer politely declines. He says that the White Whale is "welcome to the arm he has, since I can't help it, and didn't know him then; but not to another one" (Melville 1988: 441).

Sea monsters may be whale monsters as in *Moby-Dick*, crocodile monsters as in *Peter Pan*, or shark monsters as in *Jaws*. In the new terminology that I advocate, sea monsters are non-ego images that the ego-image regards as dangerous. A sea monster may threaten to devour the ego-image (for example, Captain Ahab in *Moby-Dick*, Captain Hook in *Peter Pan*, or Captain Quint in *Jaws*) either in whole or in part (for example, either a leg or an arm). An example from the world of art is *Watson and the Shark* by John Singleton Copley (Crawford 2008: 71). Copley paints a shark monster that devoured a part (a foot) of Brook Watson, a 14-year-old boy in Havana in 1774. In the Bible, of course, a whale monster devours the whole of Jonah. Jung calls the archetype of the sea monster the "'Jonah-and-the-Whale' complex, which has any number of variants" (1911–12/1952, *CW* 5: par. 654).

Crawford offers a psychoanalytic interpretation of sea monsters – among them, shark monsters. "Sharks and sea monsters, rising as they do from the deep, enjoy special symbolism in relation to the unconscious," he says. "If the abyss of the ocean symbolizes our own inner depths, then it would follow that the monster represents our repressed fears and desires" (2008: 110).

Images of Octopus Monsters

Sea monsters may also be octopus monsters, as in the Polynesian myth of Rata and Nganaoa, who is an image of the archetype of the "monster-slaying hero." Rata is in a boat on the sea. He encounters three different sea monsters – a clam monster, an octopus monster, and a whale monster. Nganaoa slays them all, one after the other. Jung quotes the myth as Leo Frobenius recounts it:

Yet soon the voice of the ever watchful Nganaoa was heard again: "O Rata! Another fearful enemy is rising up from the sea!" This time it was a mighty octopus, whose giant tentacles were already wrapped round the boat to destroy it. At this critical moment Nganaoa seized his spear and plunged it into the head of the octopus. The tentacles sank down limply, and the dead monster floated away on the surface of the ocean.

(1911–12/1952, CW 5: par. 538n.)

There is also an octopus monster in *The Toilers of the Sea* by Victor Hugo. In that novel, Gilliatt is another image of the archetype of the "monster-slaying hero." In a cave, he encounters an octopus monster. One after another, the tentacles of the octopus monster wrap Gilliatt around the arm, wrist, elbow, shoulder, waist, and chest. As the constriction and the suction of the tentacles increase and as the octopus monster is about to bite him, Gilliatt stabs the octopus monster to death. He plunges a knife into the head of the octopus monster (1892). In spite of what Kaufmann says, the octopus monsters in the myth and the novel are hardly gentle. They are just as dangerous as any shark monster.

Consider a dream that a two-year-old girl recounts in a video on YouTube (*Octopus Monster – Bad Dream – Funny 2 Year Old Girl*, March 27, 2008). The girl tells her father that, in the dream, she saw an octopus monster at Home Depot. She tells him that the octopus monster had sharp, big teeth. Although she says that the octopus monster does not eat two-year-old girls or fathers but eats only octopus food, she says that they have to kill the octopus monster with a knife – "a tiny knife," she says. In this dream, she reacts with fright and then defensively with "fight." In effect, the girl and her father are images of the archetype of the "monster-slaying hero."

Consider also a dream that a schizoid patient recounted to Harry Guntrip. The patient had many dreams but could never remember any of them. Guntrip says that the patient "decided to take pencil and paper to bed and write down his dreams during the night," but he "just stopped dreaming" (1969: 298). Eventually, however, the patient did have a dream – a dream of an octopus monster. "It will come as no surprise that this patient finally dreamed of going down into his cellar to free a young man who was in the grip of an octopus," Guntrip says. "He opened the door, and then shut and locked it again and came upstairs, and promptly decided to end his analysis" (1969: 298–9). In this dream, the patient reacts with fright and then defensively with "flight."

To be in the grip of an octopus monster is to be in the grasp of tentacles – elongate, tactile, prehensile appendages. In this respect, Medard Boss mentions a woman who had dreams of a variety of sea monsters. "In this nocturnal venture she flung herself courageously into the depths of the sea," Boss says. "There, innumerable slimy slithering tentacles of octopi and other monsters came clutching at her from all sides" (1963: 150).

52

Similarly, a man recounted to me a nightmare that he had as a six-year-old boy. It was, he said, the earliest dream that he could remember:

In the dream, I am with my father. We are physically quite close. More particularly, I am close to his head. Perhaps my father is holding me. Writhing tentacles begin to grow out of his head – first one, then another, then another, and so on until there are quite a few of them. Each one has a suction cup on the end. These tentacles are reaching out to me to attach themselves to me. The colors of my father's head and the tentacles are dark and – well, octopus-like: blacks and blues and greens. My father smiles at me in a menacing way. All of this is frightening.

The boy reacted to the dream with fright and then defensively with "flight" – but, ironically, where he fled was to the bed of his father and mother. This dream of an octopus monster was, the man said, "frightening enough that I went and got into bed with my parents." His father kindly reassured him: "If you came and got into bed with me, the dream couldn't have been that bad."

An example from the world of art is *St. George Fighting the Octopus* by Salvador Dalí (Thorn 1990: 92). In this watercolor, the octopus monster is very aggressive and very sexual. Dalí paints a knight who fights an octopus monster that rapes a damsel in distress. In addition to tentacles, this octopus monster has four dangling penises with red tips, one of them dripping with semen.

Bernard Heuvelmans mentions another example from the world of art – a votive picture that Pierre Denys de Monfort cites as evidence of an octopus monster that attacked and almost sank a ship off the coast of Angola. In the account that Heuvelmans provides, the sailors prayed to St. Thomas to save them. They then cut off the tentacles of the octopus monster with cutlasses and axes. When they returned home, they immediately went to the chapel of St. Thomas, where they gave thanks for deliverance. The votive picture, Heuvelmans says, is a sensational, hyperbolic dramatization of the incident "by an artist who was not present." The tentacles "of so monstrous a beast would have been more than 10 feet thick," he remarks, and "no sailor could have cut through them," even with the help of St. Thomas (1968: 56).

A shark monster and an octopus monster may even fight each other, as in the film *Mega Shark versus Giant Octopus* (2009). Mega Shark bites an airplane, a ship, a submarine, and the Golden Gate Bridge with its teeth. Giant Octopus crushes an offshore oil rig and swats an airplane with its tentacles. Ultimately, these enormous sea monsters engage each other in teeth-to-tentacles combat to the death. Mega Shark and Giant Octopus are images of the archetype of the "monster-slaying monster."

As a monster, the octopus is what Federico de Luca Comandini calls an "imaginal animal." In this respect, he notes that Christian theology, in disregard of biology, associated the octopus with "temptation," "flattery," and "lust" (1988: 96) – even with "Judas" and the betrayal of Jesus (1988: 97).

The unconscious, Hanscarl Leuner says, is "just as unfathomable as the sea in its expanse and its depths" (1984: 64). To a patient, Leuner says, the sea as an image of the unconscious "can also hide monsters and monstrous animals, such as huge octopuses or large hostile fish, such as the whale or the shark, which could devour him" (1984: 64–5).

A Shark Anecdote

Where images do things may be more important than the things that images do. Consider an anecdote that a patient, a 42-year-old man, recounted to me:

> I've been reading *Finding Nemo* as a bedtime story to my two-year-old daughter. One part of the book has a shark trying to eat the protagonist, who's a fish. The other night, my daughter said: "Well, I don't have to be scared of the shark because the shark is *there* in the book, and I'm *here* in the bedroom." She wasn't really saying, "The shark can't eat me because it's unreal." What she said wasn't a statement about ontology. She was saying, "The shark's in a different location than I am. It's in the book, while I'm on the bed in this room – so I don't have to worry about the shark eating me." It wasn't that the shark was less real. It was just located somewhere where it couldn't get to her. The shark was located "over there on that page."

In this anecdote, a shark in a book is just as real as a shark in a bedroom, but what these sharks can – and cannot do – is a function of where they are. The little girl intuitively realizes that if a shark were in the bedroom with her, it could eat her but that the shark that is in the book cannot, for she is not in the book with that shark. That shark and the little girl are in different locations – that is, in different worlds, the world of the book and the world of the bedroom. The shark that is in the book can eat only what is in the book with it – for example, the fish. As a result, the little girl does not react to the shark with fright or defensively with "flight" or "fight."

Precocious as she is, the little girl does not yet have the sophistication to differentiate between objects in the external world and images in the internal world – or a fictional world – but she does differentiate between the world of the bedroom and the world of the book – or, as she says, between "here" and "there." For the little girl, the decisive issue is "where" the shark is. In contrast to Kaufmann, she appreciates that the habitat of the shark – which world the shark inhabits – is important to what a shark can or cannot do and whether the shark is a threat or not. The little girl has impressive ecological acumen. To her, the action capacity of a shark is a function of the environment in which the shark exists. Even if all sharks were dangerous, they would be so only in the respective, restrictive worlds that they inhabit.

Another Shark Anecdote

Consider another anecdote that a patient, a 53-year-old man, recounted to me:

> When I was a little boy, my two older brothers and I played a game at the local swimming pool. In turn, each of us kids would push off from the side of the pool and then swim very fast toward one of the others and grab his crotch. It was a very sexual game. I can remember getting excited – probably hard – when I was only five, six, or seven years old. We called the game "Shark." I had – I still have – a very strong fear of sharks in the water, so much so that I've been unable to relax in bathtubs, or I've had to get out of bathtubs.

This is a game of make-believe. Alternately, each brother pretends to be a shark that attacks one of the other brothers. The game is an example of what Heinz Werner and Bernard Kaplan call *child-play*, or, more specifically, a game that is "patently make-believe" (1963: 94).

A Freudian interpretation of this anecdote would regard the game as an expression of sexual and aggressive instincts. Each brother grabs the crotch of the other brothers – attempts, as it were, to castrate them. The masculine, homoerotic play so excites the little boy that he gets an erection (or probably does so, at least as the patient remembers the game). The game arouses the little boy and, presumably, simultaneously frightens him.

Instinctively, all children play sexual games, some of which are also aggressive games. The only peculiar aspect of this anecdote is that the patient, as an adult, has what is, in effect, an obsessive-compulsive "shark complex." Although he does not say that the phobia is a traumatic result of the game that he played as a child, he intimates that it is.

The patient appreciates how absurd it is for him to imagine that a shark might be in a bathtub with him – and to be unable to relax in the bathtub or have to get out of the bathtub. There is no shark as an object in the bathtub with this patient – there is only a shark as an image in the psyche of this patient. In the bathtub, however, he reacts to the image of the shark with fright and then defensively with "flight." In contrast to the little girl who differentiates between the shark in the book and the shark in the bedroom, when this patient is under the influence of the "shark complex," he does not differentiate between the shark as an image in the psyche and the shark as an object in the bathtub. For him, "there" is "here."

It is as if this patient constructs a syllogism that contravenes the principles of elementary logic:

Sharks are in water.
Bathtubs contain water.
A shark is in the bathtub.

Such a syllogism, E. von Domarus says, is "paralogical," for it affirms a consequent on the basis of "identical predicates" (1944: 111). In this instance, the syllogism predicates an element – water – common to both sharks and bathtubs, and, as a consequence, the patient imagines that a shark is in the bathtub.

Compensation and Transformation

What most interest me, as an imaginal psychologist, are not the things that objects in the external world do but the things that images in the internal world do to other images in the internal world – for example, what non-ego images do to the ego-image and what the ego-image does to non-ego images in the dream world. Jung says that in dreams the basic function of the unconscious is "compensatory." What the unconscious does in dreams is to attempt to compensate the attitude of the ego. The attitude of the ego, Jung says, is partial, prejudicial, and – at the extreme – defective.

The unconscious compensation, Jung emphasizes, "always" addresses the ego attitudes that are "the most strongly defended." The attitudes about which the ego is most defensive, he says, are those that are "the most questionable." The ego tends to experience the unconscious compensation as a threat and to engage it defensively rather than receptively. To the ego, the unconscious compensation has an "apparently hostile aspect," but this impression "merely reflects" what Jung calls "the surly face" of the ego. "In reality," he says, "the unconscious compensation is not intended as a hostile act but as a necessary and helpful attempt" to redress the most problematic attitudes of the ego (1955–56, CW 14: par. 314).

In the new terminology that I advocate, non-ego images that emerge spontaneously and autonomously in dreams do so in an effort to compensate the attitude of the ego-image. These non-ego images are purposive. They are what I call "images of transformation." Such images attempt to contact and impact the ego-image – that is, to compensate and, in the process, to transform the partial, prejudicial, or defective attitude of the ego-image. Cumulatively, this effort may culminate in what Jung calls "individuation." The effort may, however, either succeed or fail. Non-ego images present for consideration alternative perspectives on the attitude of the ego-image. Whether the effort at compensation and transformation by non-ego images is a success or a failure is a function of whether the ego-image is reactive or reflective.

An ego-image that is anxious and defensive reacts to non-ego images and rejects the alternative perspectives that they present. Such an ego-image summarily and peremptorily dismisses these alternative perspectives. In contrast, an ego-image that is curious and receptive pauses and reflects on non-ego images. Such an ego-image wonders and ponders what non-ego images may mean – and then either accepts the alternative perspectives that non-ego images present or at least entertains these alternative perspectives seriously, assesses them critically, and attempts to engage them effectively. There is no imperative for the ego-image to capitulate to non-ego images. The only obligation is for the ego-image to inquire into non-ego images and mull over the alternative perspectives that they present.

Imaginal Essentialism versus Conceptual Essentialism

Douglas Medin and Andrew Ortony differentiate between "metaphysical essentialism" and "psychological essentialism." Metaphysical essentialism assumes that things have essences – that is, that essences are intrinsic to things. In contrast, psychological essentialism does not assume that things have essences but emphasizes that people may believe that things have essences. Medin and Ortony regard "such a belief" as psychologically relevant "however erroneous it may be." They say that "if people believe that things have essences, we had better not ignore this fact" (1989: 183).

Kaufmann says that Jung is an essentialist and that he is, too. That is, Kaufmann believes that images have essences. When he interprets images, he employs the method that I call *conceptual essentialism*. Kaufmann not only reduces sharks as images in the internal world to sharks as objects in the external world but also reduces all sharks, whether they are images in the internal world or objects in the external world, to the shark as a concept, or abstract generalization, which he defines by the adjective "dangerous" and the noun "threat," which, I would emphasize, are also concepts.

This is interpretation as (1) a reductive objectification of the imagination and (2) a reductive conceptualization of the imagination. It is what I might call an "I-O-C" reduction:

I = Images = Sharks as Images

O = Objects = Sharks as Objects

C = Concept = Shark as Concept (Dangerous, Threat)

Such a reduction disregards all of the distinctive qualities and distinctive action capacities that are indispensable to an accurate interpretation of the image – that is, a specific interpretation of a specific image.

When Kaufmann reduces the shark as an image to the shark as a concept, he commits the "fallacy of misplaced concreteness," which Alfred North Whitehead defines as "mistaking the abstract for the concrete" (1967: 51). In effect, Kaufmann regards the shark as an abstract concept as more "concrete" than the shark as a concrete image. The result is an interpretation that is an abstraction – any and every image of a shark is dangerous and a threat. In contrast, any accurate interpretation of an image is a concretion. It is an interpretation that is just as specific as a specific image in a specific dream.

Images are vivid, in contrast to concepts, which are vague. In this respect, when Kaufmann reduces the image to a concept, he defines what is more definite by what is less definite. The shark that Kaufmann interprets is an abstract, collective shark, not a concrete, individual shark. It is a universal, conceptual shark, not a unique, imaginal shark.

Jungians (among them, Jung) also employ the method of conceptual essentialism when they reduce images to archetypes, for archetypes are concepts, abstract generalizations rather than concrete particularizations. Such an interpretation is a reductive typification of the imagination. It is, as Jung says, "a reduction to general types" (1914, *CW* 3: par. 413). To interpret a particular image (for example, a shark) as a general type (for example, a sea monster) is to reduce what is complex (an image) to what is simple (a concept). It is to reduce the higher order of complexity of the image to the lower order of simplicity of the concept. At the extreme, it is to reduce the unique to the universal.

It is not that the "archetypes" of Jung (or the "types" of Thompson) are of no practical value, but to reduce a particular image to a general type is not to interpret that image on the basis of the specificity of the image. Simply to say that a shark is a sea monster is not to say very much. Such a reduction disregards what is special about the image. The more specific an interpretation, the more accurate the interpretation.

I, too, believe that images have essences. These essences are implicit in images. Imaginal reality is an example of what David Bohm calls an "implicate order" (1981). The essences implicit in images are a function of the distinctive qualities and action capacities intrinsic to images. The method that I employ to interpret images is what I call *imaginal essentialism*. What is at issue is the integrity of the image. Rather than reduce the image to a concept, I engage the image as an image, or concrete particularization, and render the essence of the image explicit by recourse to the distinctive qualities and distinctive action capacities specific to the image. Any accurate interpretation of an image entails the specification of those qualities and action capacities.

Mandates versus Options

Kaufmann says that the alternative perspectives that non-ego images present to the ego-image are *mandates* (2009: 4). A mandate is, by definition, an authoritative command. For Kaufmann, it is mandatory for the ego-image to acquiesce in the alternative perspectives that non-ego images present, for these alternative perspectives are authoritative commands. Kaufmann advocates submission to the mandates of images. "Not to submit to these mandates," he says, "is a violation of the spirit of the image" (2009: 19). To Kaufmann, the ego-image should, in all instances, be unconditionally submissive.

The alternative perspectives that non-ego images present to the ego-image are not, however, mandates but options for the ego-image to consider. These alternative perspectives are opinions of non-ego images about the attitude of the ego-image. They are not authoritative commands, and the ego-image is under no obligation to accept them. It is at the discretion of the ego-image either to accept or to reject them – the ego-image may be compliant, or it may be defiant. Were the alternative perspectives that non-ego images present to the ego-image mandates, it would be incumbent on the ego-image just to follow the orders of non-ego images. Jungian analysis would be a very simple affair.

What Kaufmann calls a mandate is, in effect, a dictate – that is, non-ego images mandate, or dictate, how the ego-image should respond. Kaufmann says that what is mandated by an image is "dictated" (2009: 23). Non-ego images are not, however, dictatorial. The alternative perspectives that non-ego images present to the ego-image are not edicts – and they are certainly not infallible edicts. In this respect, Jung says that "one would do well" not to assume that a dream "infallibly guides life in the right direction" (1916/1948, *CW* 8: par. 494).

Jungian analysis is not a monological dictation but a dialogical negotiation. It is a conversation between the ego-image and non-ego images. Non-ego images do not dictate to the ego-image, nor should the ego-image submit to non-ego images. Rather, the ego-image should converse with and negotiate with non-ego images in what Mary Watkins calls "imaginal dialogues" (1986).

The alternative perspectives that non-ego images present to the ego-image have a variety of what J.L. Austin calls "illocutionary forces" (1962: 99). In dreams, there are instances when a non-ego image presents to the ego-image an alternative perspective that has the illocutionary force of a command. A non-ego image may command the ego-image to do this or that thing. For example, a non-ego image may say to the ego-image: "Slay the sea monster!" A command is an order. Commanding, or ordering, is an example of what Austin calls "exercitives" (1962: 150) – or what Searle calls "directives" (1979: 21–2). Even in such instances, however, it is the prerogative of the ego-image to regard the command as just the opinion of a non-ego image. The ego-image retains the option either to accept or to reject the alternative perspective. *An ego-image that engages a non-ego image should not be unconditionally submissive but should be critically decisive.*

Knowledge: Unconscious, Instinctive, and Scientific

In this respect, Jung says that a little knowledge about dreams is a dangerous thing. "Many people who know something, but not enough, about dreams," he says, assume that "the unconscious always knows best" – or, as I would say, that the non-ego images that emerge from the psyche always know best what things the ego-image should do. Such people, Jung says, leave "the dreams to take the necessary decisions" (1945/1948, *CW* 8: par. 568). These people abdicate the responsibility – and the opportunity – to decide whether to accept or reject what the unconscious says.

Although Kaufmann knows a lot about dreams, not just a little, he is one of those people who assume that the unconscious always knows best – that is, that the unconscious knows what the ego does not know, which is what is best for the ego. He calls this a "strong assumption." Even if the ego knows none of the "biological facts" about a shark and an octopus, Kaufmann says that the psyche – by which he means the unconscious or, more specifically, the collective unconscious – knows all of these facts. He says that "the *ego* may not know, but the *psyche* knows" (2009: 13). This notion is, as Kaufmann says, a strong assumption, but it is also, if I may say so, a wrong assumption. It is an audacious assumption but an implausible assumption.

There is unconscious knowledge – or, as Freud says, "*instinctive* knowledge" (1918 [1914], *SE* 17: 120). Instinctive knowledge is, however, hardly scientific knowledge. Biological facts are not innate in the psyche. They are not inherited – rather, they are acquired through an arduous process of research. Progress in scientific knowledge is notoriously incremental, tentative, and provisional. Even if in theory all of the biological facts about a shark and an octopus were always already present in the psyche – and, to me, this is a radically problematic assumption – in practice these facts are not immediately available to the ego. Kaufmann never says why this should be so, other than that a complex may prevent access to these facts. The history of science amply demonstrates just how difficult it is to discover biological and other facts – among them, I might add, psychological facts. If all of these facts were innate in the psyche, it would be ironic – even perverse – for it to be so difficult to discover them, and, if I may say so, the difficulty of discovery is surely not just a function of the complexes of scientists.

Two Shark Dreams

Consider these two dreams that a patient, a 60-year-old woman, recounted to me in two successive analytic sessions. This is the first dream:

> I'm in a boat with a man. He's pulling something out of the water. The thing being pulled out is something that's been in the deep water a long time. What's visible looks slanted, shaped like a large fin. I say to the man: "You know what it is. You can tell me. You know what's under the water."

After the patient recounted the dream, she remarked to me: "It seems that something that's long been unconscious is being brought to the surface." This is the second dream:

> I'm in a boat, and I'm being thrown overboard, headfirst. My hands are behind my back, and my wrists and ankles are bound in heavy chains. I feel as if I'm sinking. A shark appears. My initial feeling is: "It's all over." Rather than attacking me, however, the shark goes right for the chains and begins to gnaw them.

The patient interprets the thing in the water in the first dream as a content of the unconscious. What is visible is not the whole of the thing but only a part of the thing. Although the first dream is not explicitly a shark dream, the large fin implies that the thing in the water is a shark – and the shark in the second dream confirms that this is so. Both dreams are shark dreams. It is as if the second dream is an elaboration on the first dream.

In the second dream, the ego-image, which is bound in chains, is thrown overboard. Woman overboard! In this dream, when the ego-image goes overboard, it feels that it is sinking – and, presumably, drowning. When the shark suddenly appears, the ego-image anticipates that the shark will attack it. The shark, however, does no such thing. Rather, the shark gnaws the chains that bind the ego-image.

As I interpret the second dream, the heavy chains are an image of the partial, prejudicial, or defective attitude to which the ego-image is in bondage. As a result of the heavy chains, the ego-image cannot swim – it sinks. It is then that the shark suddenly appears. The ego-image reacts to the non-ego image of the shark not so much with fright as with resignation. Apparently, the ego-image expects the shark to attack it – to swallow and devour it. To the surprise of the ego-image, however, the shark gnaws the chains that bind the ego-image.

The Archetypes of the "Helpful Animal" and the "Rescuer"

In the second dream, the shark is an image of the archetype of the "helpful animal." The shark is an example of the motif that Thompson calls type "B300. *Helpful animal*" (1955, 1: 422). Thompson also mentions type "B470. *Helpful fish*" (1955, 1: 438), as well as types "B471. *Helpful shark*" (1955, 1: 438) and "B477. *Helpful octopus*" (1955, 1: 439).

In contrast to what Kaufmann says, Jung says that whether an animal is frightening or not is a function of the attitude of the ego toward the unconscious – or, as I prefer to say, the attitude of the ego-image toward the non-ego image. In this respect, Jung says of this attitude: "if it is negative towards the unconscious, the animals will be frightening; if positive, they appear as the 'helpful animals' of fairytale and legend" (1911–12/1952, *CW* 5: par. 264). In spite of what Jung says, the attitude of the ego-image is not absolutely but only relatively decisive. Helpful animals do not appear only when the ego-image has a positive attitude toward the unconscious – they may also appear when the ego-image has a negative attitude toward the unconscious. For example, in the second dream, the attitude of the ego-image toward the shark is initially apprehensive – and, at least to that extent, negative. In spite of this attitude, the shark is a helpful animal.

To Kaufmann, a shark in the internal world is just as dangerous and should be just as frightening as a shark in the external world. He admits no exception to this rule. In the internal world, however, animals that are dangerous and frightening in the external world may not be harmful but, as Jung says, helpful. The naturalistic criteria that Kaufmann applies to the image cannot account for a helpful shark. To Kaufmann, a helpful shark is an oxymoron.

What an image is – for example, a shark – is important. What an image does and does not do is also important, perhaps even more important than what an image is. That is, the distinctive action capacities of an image are just as important as or perhaps even more important than the distinctive qualities of an image.

In the second dream, the shark does not attack the ego-image but gnaws the chains that bind the ego-image. Although it is not utterly impossible for a shark in the external world to gnaw chains, it is quite improbable. In the internal world, however, it is possible for a shark not only to gnaw chains but also to gnaw through chains. A shark in the dream world, which is not a natural world but a transnatural world, may do miracles. For example, a shark may gnaw through chains in an effort to rescue the ego-image from the attitude that binds it and that would drown it. Such a shark is an image of the archetype of the "rescuer" – an example of the motif that Thompson calls type "R150. *Rescuers*" (1955, 5: 282) or, more specifically, type "B540. *Animal rescuers or retrievers*" (1955, 1: 449).

What this dream indicates is that there is, in the psyche of this patient, a certain aspect that, although it appears as the image of a shark, demonstrates an intention or motivation to rescue the ego-image from what is a sink-or-swim, life-or-death situation. As an image of the archetype of the "helpful animal," the shark in this dream is an example of the motif that Thompson calls type "B520. *Animals save person's life*" (1955, 1: 443).

Perhaps the most famous example of this motif is the myth of Arion and the dolphin. Arion sails to Sicily, where he wins a musical competition. On the voyage back to Corinth, the crew of the ship plot to kill him and steal the prizes. Arion asks permission to sing a last song. When he plays the kithara, the melody attracts dolphins. At the end of the song, Arion leaps from the ship. He goes overboard – goes over the side of the ship into the water. One of the dolphins rescues him and carries him to safety. The myth is an example of the motifs that Thompson calls type "B473. *Helpful dolphin*" (1955, 1: 438) and type "B551.1. *Fish carries man across water*" (1955, 1: 452).

This archetype recurs in the experience of Élian González, a little boy who with his mother was one of the boat people who sailed from Cuba for America in the year 2000. His mother died on the voyage, but Élian lived to tell the story. Roberto Cespedes (2000) provides this account of the miraculous rescue of Élian:

> His rescue, after seeing his mother and nine others drown when their boat capsized trying to get to Florida, was itself a miracle. He survived 48 hours on an inner tube. The fishermen who rescued him spoke of swordfish leaping around the boy; but Elian repeated over and over that they were dolphins. The legend began to circulate that dolphins, mythical animals since the time of the ancient Greeks, had saved the little boy from the jaws of sharks.

Although it is not impossible, it is improbable that this six-year-old boy was familiar with the myth of Arion and the dolphin. This variation on the theme of the animal that saves a person's life demonstrates the persistence of the archetype of the "rescuer" in the contemporary cultural unconscious.

Interpretative Contextualism

When Kaufmann interprets images, he emphasizes the context (2009: 8). To interpret the meaning of an image with any accuracy, it is necessary to interpret the image in context. There are, however, many contexts, not just one context. In this respect, Freud says that the same image may have "a different meaning" in "various contexts" (1900, *SE* 4: 105). That is, the meaning of an image is not constant – it is variable. The meaning of a specific image is a function of a specific context.

There are internal contexts and external contexts. For example, a dream is a text, but the text of the dream is also an internal context – it is a context for the images internal to the dream. Although Kaufmann discusses the shark as if it were an image in a dream, he never presents any dreams in which there are images of sharks. That is, he never interprets the image of a shark in the internal context of a specific dream. In this respect, Kaufmann interprets the image of the shark out of context – or, more specifically, out of any internal context. Although Kaufmann does not interpret the image of the shark in an internal context, he does interpret it in context – or, more specifically, in an external context. This is the external context of the shark as an object in the natural world.

The interpretation of the image of the shark out of any internal context and in one and only one external context, the natural world, is what enables Kaufmann to say, arbitrarily, that all images of sharks have the same meaning – that they are all, without exception, dangerous. Had Kaufmann interpreted the image of the shark in the internal context of dreams and not only in the external context of the natural world but also in the external context of a supernatural or transnatural world, he would have had to concede that images of sharks have different meanings in various contexts. The evidence that images of sharks are not invariably dangerous would have been too obvious for him to ignore or deny.

Classes and Members

In formal logic, there are classes with members. A class may be a concept, and the members of that class may also be concepts. For example, the class "fish" is a concept, and the concept "shark" is a member of that class. An image may also be a member of a class that is a concept. For example, the class "shark" is a concept, and the image "Jaws" is a member of that class.

In this respect, there is what I might call a declension of classes with members from the abstract to the concrete, from the general to the particular. For example, "animal" is a concept more general than "sea creature," and "sea creature" is a concept more general than "fish," and "fish" is a concept more general than "shark," and "shark" is a concept more general than "Jaws," which is not a concept but an image much more particular than any of these concepts.

"Jaws" is, in fact, a unique image. Not all images of sharks are unique, as "Jaws" is, but any concrete image of a shark – for example, in a dream – is more particular than any abstract concept of a shark. *Unique images have not only (1) distinctive qualities and (2) distinctive action capacities but also (3) distinctive locations in distinctive worlds, (4) distinctive identities, even proper names, (5) distinctive intentions or motivations, and (6) distinctive narratives.*

Another Shark Dream and Shark Anecdote

Consider another dream that a patient, a 35-year-old man, recounted to me:

> I'm at the beach. I go into the sea and start swimming, with my head in the water, heading offshore. I swim for a while, when suddenly I bump into a big steel gate. The gate is located in an underground tunnel. I wonder how I ended up in a dry underground tunnel while swimming in the wet water of the sea. On the gate is a warning: "Danger of Death." I notice that there are two other gates before that gate and two other gates after it. Although there is no water in the underground tunnel, the warning makes me think of sharks, and that thought suffices to convince me not to go further. Behind me is a tall blond man. He is dressed in a suit and tie. He seems to be the guardian in charge of the gates. Very gently, he persuades me that it would be dangerous for me to go further and that I should go back the way I have come.

This dream is an example of the archetype of the "rite of passage." In the dream, the ego-image passes through two gates, bumps into another gate that it does not pass through, and then looks at two other gates that it does not pass through. The dream is also an example of the archetype of the "descent to the underworld." In the *Divine Comedy*, Dante approaches the entrance to the underworld where he sees the warning "Abandon all hope ye who enter here." In this dream, the ego-image descends to an underground tunnel where it sees the warning "Danger of Death." It is then that the thought of sharks convinces the ego-image not to go further. In contrast to Dante, who passes through hell and purgatory to paradise, this ego-image passes through two gates but does not pass through three other gates. In addition, in contrast to Dante, who has Virgil as a guide, the ego-image has a tall blond man as a guardian – a non-ego image that persuades the ego-image that it would be dangerous to go further and to go back the way it has come.

Three years later, this patient recounted an anecdote to me. "I've always been afraid of sharks," he said, "ever since my uncle took me as a child to see *Jaws*." He had seen the film in French. The title, he said, was *Les Dents de la Mer* – "The Teeth of the Sea." Recently, the patient had been living in Paris, and he had mentioned the film to a friend who has an interest in the psychoanalysis of Jacques Lacan. The friend had started singing – and punning in Lacanian style: "Les dents du père, les dents de la mère" (in English, "The teeth of the father, the teeth of the mother"). The effect of the word-play, the patient said, had been "mind-blowing." He said that he had immediately visualized "the shark as the image of the mother." The patient said: "I have many reasons to be afraid of my mother as a shark. When I was a child, she was eating me up – eating up my spirit." In effect, he interpreted the shark as an image of the archetype of the "terrible mother." To the patient, the shark was an example of what Jung calls "the Terrible Mother in the form of a voracious fish, a personification of death" (1911–12/1952, *CW* 5: par. 369).

Although there were no sharks in the dream that the patient recounted to me, when he had seen the warning "Danger of Death" on the gate in the dream, he had thought of sharks. In contrast to Dante, the patient had abandoned all hope – had abandoned the descent to the underworld. "I refrained from going deeper," he said, "because I thought of the presence of sharks." In the dream, the ego-image had reacted to the non-ego image of sharks with fright and then defensively with "flight." Presumably, Kaufmann would regard this defensive reaction as appropriate. Is the patient not warned of the "Danger of Death"? Does he not think of sharks? Is he not persuaded by the tall blond man that it would be dangerous to go further and to go back the way he has come? Are not all these images a cogent indication that the ego-image in this dream reacted appropriately?

When the patient had an opportunity to pause and reflect on the images in this dream, rather than react to them, he was, however, less defensive and more receptive. Three years later, he interpreted the image of the shark as an image of the mother. As he interpreted the dream, the image of the shark was a certain aspect of the psyche – a "shark complex" that was a "mother complex." That is, he interpreted the image of the shark not only on the objective level but also on the subjective level. The image was not only an outer shark, his mother who had eaten up his spirit as a child. "The shark is me also, so I need to accept it," the patient said. "I hope that I'm no longer so afraid of my inner shark."

Psychoanalysis is not a surface psychology, or ego psychology. It is, as Freud says, "a depth-psychology or psychology of the unconscious" (1933 [1932], *SE* 22: 158). Topographically, the unconscious is a subconscious. "If 'the unconscious', as an element in the subject's waking thoughts, has to be represented in a dream," Freud says, "it may be replaced very appropriately by subterranean regions" (1900, *SE* 5: 410). That is, the unconscious is an underworld. "To know the psyche at its basic depths, for a true depth psychology," Hillman says, "one must go to the underworld" (1979: 46). Although, in this dream, the ego-image goes to the underworld, it does not, as Dante does, go through the underworld.

The dream is an example of the archetype of the "journey." This ego-image does not, however, complete the journey – it abandons the journey. The ego-image goes only a part, not the whole, of the way. In the underground tunnel, at the third of five gates, the middle of the way, the ego-image goes back the way it has come. Rather than go all the way down, the ego-image goes back up. Thinking makes it so. When the ego-image thinks of sharks, it goes no further, goes no deeper. At the first thought of sharks, it ascends from the underworld, ascends from the depths to the surface. Three years later, however, the patient has second thoughts. He hopes that he is no longer so afraid of the shark, which he interprets as an image in the internal world, or the underworld of the psyche. That is, he was not then ready but may now be ready, in spite of the sharks, to complete the journey through all five gates.

Imagicide and the Archetype of the "Monster-Slaying Hero"

Even if a non-ego image – for example, a shark – is dangerous, even deadly so, Jung never says that the ego-image should react with "flight." In fact, Jung says that the ego-image should react with "fight." In this respect, he describes the encounter between the ego-image and the non-ego image of the sea monster as a battle. Jung says: "It is easy to see what the battle with the sea monster means: it is the attempt to free the ego-consciousness from the deadly grip of the unconscious" (1911–12/1952, *CW* 5: par. 539). In effect, he says that the ego-image should be a "monster-slaying hero." Jung says that heroes "purposely expose themselves to the danger of being devoured by the monster of the maternal abyss." He says that "if a man is a hero," it is "because, in the final reckoning, he did not let the monster devour him, but subdued it, not once but many times" (1928, *CW* 7: par. 261).

To slay an image is not, however, the only way to engage an image effectively. To do so is to commit what I call *imagicide*. Rather than react to a non-ego image defensively with "fight," the ego-image might stick to the non-ego image, might pause and reflect on it, might inquire into it and mull over other ways to deal with it. There are many more ways than one for the ego-image to deal effectively with a non-ego image. There are many more ways than one for the ego-image to be a hero.

Rather than subdue a non-ego image, the ego-image might, for example, circumvent the non-ego image. Or, as in the method of active imagination, the ego-image might address the non-ego image. The ego-image might question the non-ego image, and the non-ego image might answer the ego-image. That is, the ego-image might engage the non-ego image in dialogue and negotiation. In this process, the ego-image might ascertain what the intention or motivation of the non-ego image is and might then decide, among various options, what the most effective response would be. (There might, of course, be more than one viable option.)

I do not say that the ego-image should never slay a non-ego image. Under certain circumstances – for example, a "slay-or-be-slain" situation – it may be vitally important for the ego-image to slay a non-ego image. Imagicide is, however, only one among many options, and, in a specific instance, it may not be an appropriate (much less the most effective) option.

In psychoanalysis, whether Freudian or Jungian, the conventional paradigm is one of conflict between the ego-image and non-ego images. This adversarial assumption is a bias that privileges violent confrontation between the ego-image and non-ego images – rather than, for example, nonviolent communication between them. In contrast, as Tzvetan Todorov says, "Nonviolent communication exists, and we can defend it as a value" (1984: 182). The "image-slaying ego" (or "monster-slaying hero") is a prevalent, even pervasive assumption. The objection that I have is to any *a priori* notion, any axiomatic or dogmatic position, about the relation between the ego-image and non-ego images. What I advocate is a position that is heuristic and pragmatic.

In many if not most dreams, the ego-image is instantly, indiscriminately, and excessively defensive. The ego-image tends to react to non-ego images with fright and then defensively with either "flight" or "fight." Statistically, this is just a fact, but why should it be so? Simply to describe defenses as instincts with survival value, the result of evolution through natural selection, is not to provide an adequate account of why the ego-image in dreams is so consistently defensive – and so disproportionately defensive.

To the extent that the ego-image is neurotic, it is anxious rather than curious about non-ego images. To the extent that the ego-image is psychotic, it is paranoid about non-ego images. For example, to schizophrenics, the unconscious is extremely "fishy." To them, the unconscious is a "sea" replete with "monsters." In contrast, Jung says that it is "totally erroneous" to suppose that "the unconscious is a monster" (1934, *CW* 16: par. 328). He says that the unconscious is not monstrous but is "completely neutral" (1934, *CW* 16: par. 329). The ego-image tends, however, to "monsterize" non-ego images, and this teratogenic tendency provides the ego-image with an all too convenient excuse to "slay" non-ego images.

What is unique about psychoanalysis is that it is an occasion to do things with images that do things – or, more specifically, non-ego images that emerge spontaneously and autonomously from the unconscious in an effort to compensate and transform the partial, prejudicial, or defective attitude of the ego-image. How, however, to do things with images that do things? The thing that the ego-image tends to do to non-ego images is to react to them defensively with either "flight" or "fight," on the assumption that non-ego images are intrinsically dangerous or monstrous.

Psychoanalysis is an opportunity for the ego-image to pause and reflect on non-ego images, to "stick to the image" long enough to determine what things these images are doing – and why they are doing these things – and then to decide what things (which might be anything or nothing) to do with these images. Ultimately, what things I may do with these images that do things is a function of who or how I imagine myself to be – what I am as an imaginal "I" – and how defensive or receptive the ego-image is to non-ego images.

References

Adams, M.V. (2004) *The Fantasy Principle: Psychoanalysis of the Imagination*, Hove: Brunner-Routledge.

Adams, M.V. (2008) "Imaginology: The Jungian Study of the Imagination," in S. Marlan (ed.), *Archetypal Psychologies: Reflections in Honor of James Hillman*, New Orleans: Spring Journal Books: 225–42.

Adams, M.V. (October 30, 2009) *Red Book Dialogue with Sarah Silverman*, New York: Rubin Museum of Art: DVD.

Ammer, C. (1992) *Have a Nice Day – No Problem! A Dictionary of Clichés*, New York: Dutton.

Austin, J.L. (1962) *How To Do Things with Words: The William James Lectures Delivered at Harvard University in 1955*, New York: Oxford University Press.

Baudrillard, J. (1994) *Simulacra and Simulation*, trans. S.F. Glaser, Ann Arbor, MI: University of Michigan Press.

Bohm, D. (1981) *Wholeness and the Implicate Order*, London: Routledge & Kegan Paul.

Bonime, W. (1962) *The Clinical Use of Dreams*, New York: Basic Books.

Boss, M. (1963) *Psychoanalysis and Daseinsanalysis*, trans. L.B. Lefebre, New York and London: Basic Books.

Brann, E.T.H. (1991) *The World of the Imagination: Sum and Substance*, Lanham, MD: Rowman and Littlefield.

Cespedes, R. (April 4, 2000) "The Mystical Power of Elian," *The New York Times*: A23.

Comandini, F. de L. (1988) "The Octopus: Metamorphoses of an Imaginal Animal," trans. R.M. Mercurio, *Spring: A Journal of Archetype and Culture*: 91–107.

Cousteau, J.-Y., and Diolé, P. (1973) *Octopus and Squid: The Soft Intelligence*, trans. J.F. Bernard, Garden City, NY: Doubleday.

Crawford, D. (2008) *Shark*, London: Reaktion Books.

Doležel, L. (1998) *Heterocosmica: Fiction and Possible Worlds*, Baltimore: Johns Hopkins University Press.

Freedberg, D. (1989) *The Power of Images: Studies in the History and Theory of Response*, Chicago: University of Chicago Press.

Freud, S. (1900) *The Interpretation of Dreams*, SE 4 and SE 5.

Freud, S. (1905) *Jokes and Their Relation to the Unconscious*, SE 8.

Freud, S. (1918 [1914]) "From the History of an Infantile Neurosis," *SE* 17: 1–122.

Freud, S. (1933 [1932]) *New Introductory Lectures on Psycho-Analysis*, SE 22: 1–182.

Giegerich, W. (2010) "Imaginal Psychology Gone Overboard: Michael Vannoy Adams' 'Imaginology': A Defense of the Image against the Detraction by Its Devotees," in *The Soul Always Thinks: Collected English Papers*, vol. 4, New Orleans: Spring Journal Books: 475–500.

Groddeck, G. (1976) *The Book of the It*, trans. V.M.E. Collins, New York: International Universities Press.

Guntrip, H. (1969) *Schizoid Phenomena, Object-Relations, and the Self*, New York: International Universities Press.

Heuvelmans, B. (1968) *In the Wake of the Sea-Serpents*, trans. R. Garnett, New York: Hill and Wang.

Hillman, J. (1975) *Re-Visioning Psychology*, New York: Harper & Row.

Hillman, J. (1979) *The Dream and the Underworld*, New York: Harper & Row.

Hillman, J., with Pozzo, L. (1983) *Inter Views: Conversations with Laura Pozzo on Psychotherapy, Biography, Love, Soul, Dreams, Work, Imagination, and the State of the Culture*, New York: Harper & Row.

Hugo, V. (1892) *The Toilers of the Sea*, trans. M.W. Artois, Philadelphia: George Barrie & Son, vol. 4.

Hume, D. (1992) "Of Miracles," in *Essays: Moral, Political, and Literary*, in *The Philosophical Works*, ed. T.H. Green and T.H. Grose, Darmstadt: Scientia Verlag Aalen, 4: 88–108.

James, W. (1983) *The Principles of Psychology*, Cambridge, MA: Harvard University Press.

Jesus Is Magic (2006) Visual Entertainment: DVD.

Jung, C.G. (1911–12/1952) *Symbols of Transformation: An Analysis of the Prelude to a Case of Schizophrenia*, CW 5.

Jung, C.G. (1914) "On Psychological Understanding," *CW* 3: 179–93.

Jung, C.G. (1916/1948) "General Aspects of Dream Psychology," *CW* 8: 237–80.

Jung, C.G. (1917/1926/1943) *On the Psychology of the Unconscious*, CW 7: 1–119.

Jung, C.G. (1921) *Psychological Types*, CW 6.

Jung, C.G. (1926) "Spirit and Life," *CW* 8: 319–37.

Jung, C.G. (1928) *The Relations between the Ego and the Unconscious*, CW 7: 121–241.

Jung, C.G. (1929) "Commentary on 'The Secret of the Golden Flower,'" *CW* 13: 1–55.

Jung, C.G. (1934) "The Practical Use of Dream-Analysis," *CW* 16: 139–61.

Jung, C.G. (1934/1954) "Archetypes of the Collective Unconscious," *CW* 9,1: 3–41.

Jung, C.G. (1945/1948) "On the Nature of Dreams," *CW* 8: 281–97.

Jung, C.G. (1948) "Psychology and Spiritualism," *CW* 18: 312–16.

Jung, C.G. (1955–56) *Mysterium Coniunctionis: An Inquiry into the Separation and Synthesis of Psychic Opposites in Alchemy*, *CW* 14.

Jung, C.G. (1963) *Memories, Dreams, Reflections*, ed. A. Jaffé, trans. R. and C. Winston, New York: Pantheon Books.

Jung, C.G. (2008) *Children's Dreams: Notes from the Seminar Given in 1936–1940*, ed. L. Jung and M. Meyer-Grass, trans. E. Falzeder with T. Woolfson, Princeton, NJ: Princeton University Press.

Kaufmann, Y. (2009) *The Way of the Image: The Orientational Approach to the Psyche*, New York: Yahav Books.

Leuner, H. (1984) *Guided Affective Imagery: Mental Imagery in Short-Term Psychotherapy*, ed. W.A. Richards, trans. E. Lachman, New York: Thieme-Stratton.

Lovejoy, A.O., and Boas, G. (1935) "Some Meanings of 'Nature,'" in *Primitivism and Related Ideas in Antiquity*, Baltimore: Johns Hopkins University Press: 447–56.

Masters, R.E.L., and Houston, J. (1966) *The Varieties of Psychedelic Experience*, New York: Holt, Rinehart and Winston.

Medin, D., and Ortony, A. (1989) "Psychological Essentialism," in S. Vosniadou and A. Ortony (eds.), *Similarity and Analogical Reasoning*, Cambridge: Cambridge University Press: 179–95.

Mega Shark versus Giant Octopus (2009) Asylum Home Entertainment: DVD.

Melville, H. (1988) *Moby-Dick; or, The Whale*, ed. H. Hayford, H. Parker, and G.T. Tanselle, *The Writings of Herman Melville*, Evanston, IL, and Chicago: Northwestern University Press and Newberry Library, vol. 6.

Octopus Monster – Bad Dream – Funny 2 Year Old Girl (March 27, 2008) YouTube: video.

Pavel, T.G. (1986) *Fictional Worlds*, Cambridge, MA: Harvard University Press.

Polanyi, M., and Prosch, H. (1975) *Meaning*, Chicago: University of Chicago Press.

Schafer, R. (1976) *A New Language for Psychoanalysis*, New Haven, CT: Yale University Press.

Schutz, A. (1962) "On Multiple Realities," in *Collected Papers I: The Problem of Social Reality*, ed. M. Natanson, The Hague: Martinus Nijoff: 207–59.

Searle, J.R. (1969) *Speech Acts: An Essay in the Philosophy of Language*, Cambridge: Cambridge University Press.

Searle, J.R. (1979) *Expression and Meaning: Studies in the Theory of Speech Acts*, Cambridge: Cambridge University Press.

Thompson, S. (1955) *Motif-Index of Folk Literature*, Bloomington, IN: Indiana University Press, 6 vols.

Thorn, M. (1990) *Taboo No More: The Phallus in Fact, Fiction and Fantasy*, New York: Shapolsky Publishers.

Tierney, J. (April 12, 2010) "Hallucinogens Have Scientists Tuning in Again," *The New York Times*: A1 and A15.

Todorov, T. (1984) *The Conquest of America: The Question of the Other*, trans. R. Howard, New York: Harper & Row.

Von Domarus, E. (1944) "The Specific Laws of Logic in Schizophrenia," in J.S. Kasanin (ed.), *Language and Thought in Schizophrenia: Collected Papers*, Berkeley: University of California Press: 104–14.

Watkins, M. (1986) *Invisible Guests: The Development of Imaginal Dialogues*, Hillsdale, NJ: The Analytic Press.

Werner, H., and Kaplan, B. (1963) *Symbol Formation: An Organismic–Developmental Approach to Language and the Expression of Thought*, New York: Wiley.

Whitehead, A.N. (1967) *Science and the Modern World: Lowell Lectures, 1925*, New York: The Free Press.

4

GOLDEN CALF PSYCHOLOGY

James Hillman Alone in Pursuit of the Imagination

For Jung, psyche and imagination are not two different things – they are one and the same thing. When Jungians analyze the psyche, they analyze the imagination. What most interest Jungians are images. "Every psychic process," Jung says, "is an image and an 'imagining'" (1939, *CW* 11: par. 889). As a process, imagining is a continuous, spontaneous, autonomous, purposive emerging of images. Jung says that "the psyche consists essentially of images" (1926, *CW* 8: par. 618). The very essence of psyche is imagination. Jung says, emphatically, that "image *is* psyche" (1929, *CW* 13: par. 75). From this perspective, the theme of the First Conference of the International Association for Jungian Studies in 2006 should have been not "Psyche and Imagination" but "Psyche as Imagination."

In celebration of the 80th birthday of James Hillman, the program of the conference included a session with the title "Why Hillman Matters." It was especially appropriate to ask that question, for, more than any other Jungian after Jung, Hillman emphasizes the imagination.

When, in preparation for the conference, I began to imagine what I might say in regard to the question why Hillman matters, a passage from *Memories, Dreams, Reflections* occurred to me. It is the passage in which Jung says: "In retrospect I can say that I alone logically pursued the two problems which most interested Freud: the problem of 'archaic vestiges,' and that of sexuality" (1963: 168). I would say that James Hillman has alone logically pursued the problem that most interested Jung: the problem of the imagination.

Imagine my surprise when a few days later, as I was rereading Wolfgang Giegerich's criticism of Hillman's imaginal psychology in *The Soul's Logical Life*, I read this passage:

> HILLMAN is probably the only one who was responsive to what was germinally inherent in the Jungian project. JUNG had said that he had been the only one who logically pursued the two problems that most interested FREUD. In the same way we can say that HILLMAN logically further developed what JUNG had been most interested in.
>
> (1999: 104)

When I had first read *The Soul's Logical Life*, I had marked this passage in pencil in the margin. There was, therefore, no doubt that the passage had previously impressed me. Before it had occurred to me that, among all Jungians, Hillman is the one Jungian who has logically pursued what most interested Jung, it had also occurred to Giegerich. I had not consciously remembered what Giegerich had said about Hillman and Jung. Had I conveniently forgotten it, even repressed it? Was this an instance of cryptomnesia, tantamount to unconscious plagiarism? Or was it merely that Giegerich and I had independently imagined Hillman in the same way. Does it matter? Does Hillman matter? If he does matter, then why does he matter?

Giegerich does not say that what most interested Jung was the imagination and that it is Hillman alone who has logically pursued that interest. Perhaps because what most interests Giegerich and what he so logically pursues is the soul, he says that what Hillman pursues is also the soul. In *Re-Visioning Psychology*, Hillman does say that what interests him is "a psychology of soul," but he immediately also says that what he bases that project on is "a psychology of image" (1975: xi). The very basis of Hillmanian psychology is the imagination.

Hillman might agree with me that the imagination was the problem that most interested Jung, but he would not, I imagine, agree with me that, after Jung, he alone has pursued that problem. He would probably say that the imagination has been a pursuit of many others. Whether or not Hillman alone has pursued the imagination, I would argue that had he not pursued it as he has, contemporary Jungian Studies would be even more only "Jung Studies" than it still is.

What would Jungian Studies be without Hillman? What if Hillman had never existed? Would Jungians have had to invent him? Would Jungians have had to imagine him? Jung may have said: "Thank God I am Jung and not a Jungian." I might reverse that and say: "Thank God I am a Jungian and not Jung." Or, I might say: "Thank God I am a Hillmanian." Or, I might ask: "Is it imaginable that there might eventually be an International Association for Hillmanian Studies?"

Hillman denies that he has founded a "school" of psychology. He insists that he has merely emphasized a certain "direction" in Jungian psychology (Adams 2008: 109). What direction is that? Post-Jungian psychology has been "taken seriously over the last thirty years," especially in Britain, Christopher Hauke says, "largely due to the work of the American Jungian analyst James Hillman" (2000: 8). Hillman may or may not be "post-Jungian" (I am personally dubious that there are, in the strict sense, any "post-Jungians" except, perhaps, Giegerich), but Hillman is most definitely "post-Jung." He is one – and by far the most original – of the first generation of Jungians after Jung. Hillman was at the C.G. Jung Institute of Zurich while Jung was still alive, but he was not there with Jung in any intimate way. "In fact, it's funny to say, but I didn't even try to see Jung, even when I could have," Hillman says. "I saw him at lectures or parties in the fifties, and sometimes met with him about Institute matters, but there were four years when I had the opportunity to go there and I never did" (1983b: 102–3). If Hillman did not go there, where did he go? He went in the direction of the imagination.

I first heard the name "James Hillman" from the poet and Blake scholar Kathleen Raine in London 40 years ago. Raine said to me that when I returned to America, I should meet Hillman. William Blake says: "The Imagination is not a State: it is the Human Existence itself" (1976: 522). Raine advised me to meet Hillman because he, too, regards the imagination not as a mere state but as the very existential basis of humanity.

In "The Importance of Being Blasphemous," the last chapter of *The Fantasy Principle: Psychoanalysis of the Imagination* (Adams 2004), I declare that I am a Jungian atheist. As I say, I prefer reprofanation over resacralization. One evening, however, my daughter, at the age of 16, said to me: "Dad, I know who your god is." I asked, quizzically: "Who is that?" She replied: "James Hillman."

A month before, Hillman had spoken at a colloquium of the Jungian Psychoanalytic Association in New York, and I had taken several photographs of him on that occasion. Hillman hates photographs, especially of him. He said to me: "You take too many photographs." I said: "It's funny that someone who loves images so much hates photographs so much." He said: "Photographs aren't images." I printed and framed two of the photographs (Figures 4.1 and 4.2). It was those photographs that prompted my daughter to say that Hillman is my god.

I feel about Hillman in a way that I do not feel about Jung or any other Jungian. I do not worship Hillman, but I do really like him. Why do I like Hillman so much? I like him because I feel that he is like me. I feel akin to Hillman. He feels to me like kinfolk. I feel what Jung calls "kinship libido" (1946, *CW* 16: par. 445) between Hillman and me. In *Inter Views*, Hillman says that he feels "a kinship with people" who "are trying to re-vision things" (1983b: 28). That is exactly how I feel about Hillman. Over the years, Hillman has been to me not a god but a kindred spirit – and, like a spirit, he has inspired me. Like no other Jungian, he has been an inspiration to me. I imagine myself in the spirit of Hillman. Spirit means breath, and Hillman has been for me a breath of fresh air.

At the "Festival of Archetypal Psychology in Honor of James Hillman" at Notre Dame University in 1992, I delivered a presentation entitled "My Imaginal Hillman" (Adams 1992). Hillman has been an image for me. What image is that? It is the image of the very possibility of my being a Jungian and, at the same time, not being one – that is, the very possibility of my being myself. Paul Kugler once asked me, "Michael, when are you going to stop saying '*the* Jungians' and start saying '*we* Jungians'?" Similarly, Hillman admits that "'the Jungians' are one monstrous complex for me." He says: "I am one of them and so I can't bear them – except for some good personal

Figure 4.1 James Hillman, Colloquium of the Jungian Psychoanalytic Association, February 5, 2006, photograph by Michael Vannoy Adams.

Figure 4.2 James Hillman, Colloquium of the Jungian Psychoanalytic Association, February 5, 2006, photograph by Michael Vannoy Adams.

friends" (1983b: 36). What is so unbearable to Hillman about "the Jungians" is that they repeat Jung, over and over again, in a rote, uncritical, uncreative way. If there is a "Jung cult," it is not only a cult of personality but also a cult of theory and practice. The result is not imagination – or individuation – but merely monotonous imitation of Jung by mediocrities, so that, for them, Jungian Studies is only "Jung Studies."

David Tacey has published a critical appreciation of Hillman – or perhaps it would be more accurate to say that he has published an appreciative criticism of Hillman, for even as he appreciates Hillman, he criticizes him. In "Twisting and Turning with James Hillman," Tacey identifies me as one of "various academics" who have "rallied to Hillman's support" (1998: 220). I am an academic – I have been a faculty member at various universities and colleges for 35 years. I would not say, however, that I have supported Hillman. Rather, I would say that Hillman's imagination has supported my imagination. Happily for me, Hillman's interest in the imagination just happened to coincide with my interest in it: a happy happenstance.

In answer to the question why Hillman matters, I propose to engage just one of the issues that Tacey addresses. Hillman hardly ever mentions what Jung calls the "Self." When Andrew Samuels discusses Hillman in *Jung and the Post-Jungians*, he notes how "little he says about the self" (1985: 107). For example, in *Re-Visioning Psychology*, there is no entry in the index for "Self." When Hillman dispensed with the Self, Tacey says that "he may not have known what he was doing" (1998: 230). I would argue that Hillman knew exactly what he was doing. What he knew was that, in order to re-vision conservative, conventional Jungian psychology, he had to rebut what he calls "the dogma of self domination" (1981: 136). The Self has dogmatically dominated Jungian psychology, and Hillman knew very well that he had to repudiate it.

One reason why Hillman considers the Self dispensable is that he advocates an imaginal psychology rather than a conceptual psychology. The Self is a concept, not an image. Jung acknowledges that "the self is no more than a psychological concept" (1928, *CW* 7: par. 399). Similarly, when Hillman discusses the ego and the Self, he says that they are both "abstract concepts" and "not images" (1983b: 83). For Hillman, concepts are abstract generalizations, in contrast to images, which are concrete particularizations. Images, he notes, are much more specific than concepts. Hillman espouses a psychology of the imagination that is a psychology of specificity.

Another reason why Hillman considers the Self dispensable is that it is not just any concept. In Jungian psychology, the Self is the "concept of concepts." The Self is *the* Concept with a capital "C." It is God with a capital "G." It is Yahweh with a capital "Y." Jung says that "in the place of a jealous God" Freud substituted sexuality, which then assumed "the role of a *deus absconditus*, a hidden or concealed god." According to Jung, however, "the psychological qualities of the two rationally incommensurable opposites – Yahweh and sexuality – remained the same" – only the name was different (1963: 151). Similarly, in the place of God Jung substitutes the Self, which is just as jealous as Yahweh. Just as for Freud sexuality is God, for Jung the Self is God by another name.

When Freud discusses God, he remarks that "no image must be made of him" (1939 [1934–38], *SE* 23: 18). Freud emphasizes "the sublime abstraction" of this stricture. The second of the Ten Commandments, Freud notes, is a prohibition "against making an image of any living or imagined creature" (1939 [1934–38], *SE* 23: 19). The second commandment states: "Thou shalt not make unto thee any graven image, or any likeness of any thing that is in heaven above, or that is in the earth beneath, or that is in the water under the earth" (Exodus 20: 4). This comprehensive prohibition, which represses concrete images, is so important, Freud says, because it sublimates God as "an abstract idea" (1939 [1934–38], *SE* 23: 113) – that is, an abstract concept. Jungian psychology commits a similar sublimation and repression. The Self is sublime, and it is repressive. Prominent among the psychological qualities that the Self, as a concept, shares with Yahweh is what I would call jealousy of images. From this perspective, images are idolatrous, and the Self, as a concept, is iconoclastic.

Yet another reason why Hillman considers the Self dispensable is that it reduces multiplicity to unity. Hillman repudiates the notion of the psyche "as ultimately a unity of self" (1975: 41). In the controversy over the One and the Many, Jungian psychology is a theology. It is, as Hillman says, a "monotheism" (1981). It is a monistic theology rather than the pluralistic psychology that first Hillman and then, later, Samuels (1989) advocate.

"Monism, as a general psychological tendency," Jung says, endeavors to establish "one function or the other as the supreme psychological principle." Jung criticizes "psychological monism, or rather monotheism," as simple but defective, for it entails "exclusion of the diversity and rich reality of life and the world" and admits "no real possibility of human development" (1916, *CW* 7: par. 482). As a result, Jung says, pluralism must ultimately supersede monism. He says that eventually psychology will "have to recognize a plurality of principles and accommodate itself to them" (1916, *CW* 7: par. 483). In theory and practice, however, Jung establishes one function, the Self, as the supreme psychological principle, and he explicitly correlates it "with monotheism" (1951, *CW* 9, 2: par. 427).

In contrast, when Hillman re-visions Jungian psychology, he recognizes a plurality of principles. He espouses a psychology that values what he calls "the plurality of individual differences." He says that "precisely these differences are what we wish to keep in mind." What Hillman proposes is a psychology of "differentiation" (1981: 124). It is a psychology that multiplies rather than unifies, but Hillman does not just privilege the many over the one. He privileges, as he says, "the many and the different" over "the one and the same" (1981: 114). As I have previously noted, Gregory Bateson and Jacques Derrida emphasize "the decisive importance of 'difference'" (Adams 1991: 255) – and so does Hillman. Hillman adopts what I call a differential position in regard to images. Different images and the differences among them are what interest him. Rather than reduce the many and different images to one and the same concept, the Self – a conceptual unity – Hillman radically affirms imaginal multiplicity.

Tacey says that Hillman offers "the clinical analyst little or nothing to work with" (1998: 218). Similarly, in a recent reclassification of schools of post-Jungian psychology, Samuels says that Hillmanian psychology has been more or less "eliminated as a clinical perspective" (2008: 11). Contrary to what Samuels says, Hillmanian psychology remains a vitally active, uniquely valuable clinical perspective, and, contrary to what Tacey says, Hillman offers the analyst everything to work with clinically – and that is the spontaneous, autonomous multiplication of emergent images. What Hillman offers the analyst is what the psyche as imagination offers – images, images, and more images.

To the extent that modern Western culture derives from ancient Middle Eastern culture, it is iconoclastic. The Jewish–Christian–Islamic tradition is fundamentally image-smashing. Iconoclasm, Hillman says, is historically recurrent. As examples, he mentions "the Bible, Mohammed, Cromwell" (1983a: 70). Contemporary psychologists, both Freudians and Jungians, also smash images, Hillman says, "through conceptual interpretation" (1983a: 71). That is, when they interpret concrete images, they reduce them to abstract concepts.

In contrast to this conceptual psychology, what Hillman proposes is an imaginal psychology – what I might call "golden calf psychology," a psychology that is intrinsically idolatrous. As Moshe Halbertal and Avishai Margalit note, the golden calf is "the epitome of idolatry in the Bible" (1992: 3). While Moses receives the Ten Commandments from Yahweh on Mount Sinai, Aaron melts the golden earrings of the wives, sons, and daughters of the Israelites and, "with a graving tool," makes a graven image, "a molten calf" (Exodus 32: 4). The Israelites then play and dance. When Moses returns, he angrily breaks the two tablets on which the finger of Yahweh has written the Ten Commandments. Then he burns the golden calf in fire, grinds it to powder, strews it on water, and makes the Israelites drink it. When Yahweh offers the covenant of the Promised Land to the Chosen People, he says that he will displace the Amorites, the Canaanites, the Hittites, the Perizzites, the Hivites, and the Jebusites but that the Israelites must "break their images" (Exodus 34: 13), for Yahweh is a jealous God. In fact, the very name of Yahweh is "Jealous," with a capital "J" (Exodus 34: 14).

Jungian psychology, in which the Self is just Yahweh by another name, an iconoclastic concept, also jealously breaks images, which it regards as idolatrous. From the perspective of conservative, conventional Jungian psychology, Hillman is an idolator, not a Moses of the Self but an Aaron of images. The Hillmanian perspective is not "a theology of the Self" (1981: 122) but a psychology of images. Hillman does not revere, or "worship," images – he respects them. He plays with and dances around the golden calves that the psyche continuously graves. Ultimately, Hillman matters because images matter – images that are concrete, particular, multiple, and different.

References

Adams, M.V. (1991) "My Siegfried Problem – and Ours: Jungians, Freudians, Anti-Semitism, and the Psychology of Knowledge," in A. Maidenbaum and S.A. Martin (eds.), *Lingering Shadows: Jungians, Freudians, and Anti-Semitism*, Boston and London: Shambhala: 241–59.

Adams, M.V. (1992) "My Imaginal Hillman; or, 'James, I'll See You in My Dreams,'" Boulder, CO: Sounds True Recordings: audiotape.

Adams, M.V. (2004) *The Fantasy Principle: Psychoanalysis of the Imagination*, Hove: Brunner-Routledge.

Adams, M.V. (2008) "The Archetypal School," in P. Young-Eisendrath and T. Dawson (eds.), *The Cambridge Companion to Jung*, 2nd rev. ed., Cambridge: Cambridge University Press: 107–24.

Blake, W. (1976) *Milton*, in *Blake: Complete Writings with Variant Readings*, ed. G. Keynes, London: Oxford University Press: 480–535.

Freud, S. (1939 [1934–38]) *Moses and Monotheism: Three Essays*, SE 23: 1–137.

Giegerich, W. (1999) *The Soul's Logical Life: Towards a Rigorous Notion of Psychology*, 2nd rev. ed., Frankfurt am Main: Peter Lang.

Halbertal, M., and Margalit, A. (1992) *Idolatry*, Cambridge, MA: Harvard University Press.

Hauke, C. (2000) *Jung and the Postmodern: The Interpretation of Realities*, London: Routledge.

Hillman, J. (1975) *Re-Visioning Psychology*, New York: Harper & Row.

Hillman, J. (1981) "Psychology: Monotheistic or Polytheistic," in D.L. Miller, *The New Polytheism: Rebirth of the Gods and Goddesses*, Dallas: Spring Publications: 109–42.

Hillman, J. (1983a) *Healing Fiction*, Barrytown, NY: Station Hill Press.

Hillman, J., with Pozzo, L. (1983b) *Inter Views: Conversations with Laura Pozzo on Psychotherapy, Biography, Love, Soul, Dreams, Work, Imagination, and the State of the Culture*, New York: Harper & Row.

Jung, C.G. (1916) "The Structure of the Unconscious," *CW* 7: 269–304.

Jung, C.G. (1926) "Spirit and Life," *CW* 8: 319–37.

Jung, C.G. (1928) *The Relations between the Ego and the Unconscious*, *CW* 7: 121–241.

Jung, C.G. (1929) "Commentary on 'The Secret of the Golden Flower,'" *CW* 13: 1–55.

Jung, C.G. (1939) "Foreword to Suzuki's 'Introduction to Zen Buddhism,'" *CW* 11: 538–57.

Jung, C.G. (1946) *The Psychology of the Transference*, *CW* 16: 163–323.

Jung, C.G. (1951) *Aion: Researches into the Phenomenology of the Self*, *CW* 9, 2.

Jung, C.G. (1963) *Memories, Dreams, Reflections*, ed. A. Jaffé, trans. R. and C. Winston, New York: Pantheon Books.

Samuels, A. (1985) *Jung and the Post-Jungians*, London: Routledge & Kegan Paul.

Samuels, A. (1989) *The Plural Psyche: Personality, Morality and the Father*, London: Routledge.

Samuels, A. (2008) "New Developments in the Post-Jungian Field," in P. Young-Eisendrath and T. Dawson (eds.), *The Cambridge Companion to Jung*, 2nd rev. ed., Cambridge: Cambridge University Press: 1–15.

Tacey, D. (1998) "Twisting and Turning with James Hillman: From Anima to World Soul, from Academia to Pop," in A. Casement (ed.), *Post-Jungians Today: Key Papers in Contemporary Analytical Psychology*, London: Routledge: 215–34.

Part II

JUNGIAN INTERDISCIPLINARY APPLICATIONS

Cultural Applications

5

THE ISLAMIC CULTURAL
UNCONSCIOUS IN THE DREAMS OF A
CONTEMPORARY MUSLIM MAN

One of the most vitally important topics in "Jungian Studies" is the psychological analysis of different cultures – and of cultural differences. I have previously argued that psychoanalysts need to become "culturally knowledgeable." I have emphasized that "the acquisition of sufficient cultural knowledge demands the most serious and meticulous study of specific cultures" (Adams 2010: 143). I have also noted that one of the most dynamic contemporary academic disciplines is "Cultural Studies" but that psychoanalysts, including Jungian psychoanalysts, have remained "more or less inattentive" to culture (Adams 2004: 134).

I have a special interest in the "cultural unconscious." Joseph L. Henderson introduced that term into Jungian discourse (1990). Henderson defined the cultural unconscious as a dimension between the collective unconscious and the personal unconscious. That definition dissatisfied me, for what is cultural is obviously collective. Subsequently, I redefined the cultural unconscious as a dimension of the collective unconscious (Adams 1996: 46–7; Adams 2004: 155–6; Adams 2010: 114–15). By that redefinition, the collective unconscious includes two dimensions. In addition to a dimension that comprises archetypes and archetypal images, the collective unconscious includes a dimension that comprises stereotypes and stereotypical images – and this is what I mean by the cultural unconscious.

Among the stereotypes and stereotypical images in the cultural unconscious are what Samuel L. Kimbles and Thomas Singer call "cultural complexes" (Kimbles 2000; Singer and Kimbles 2004). As I define a cultural complex, it is a set of values about which a culture is especially emotionally sensitive. (I should perhaps emphasize that, as I employ the term "complex," it has a strictly neutral, not a pejorative – and certainly not necessarily a psycho-pathological – connotation.)

One of the dominant cultural complexes is what I call the "Middle Eastern cultural complex." This cultural complex is a function of the Jewish, Christian, and Islamic traditions. Although there are important differences between these traditions, there are also important similarities. Among these similarities is a set of values about which these traditions are especially emotionally sensitive. What constitutes this set of values is a belief in one God to whom believers are obedient (in the Jewish and Christian traditions) or submissive (in the Islamic tradition). Obedience or submission to one God is the basis of the Middle Eastern cultural complex.

I also have a special interest in what I call the "Islamic cultural unconscious." I have delivered presentations on that topic in New York, London, Atlanta, Pittsburgh, Buffalo, and Fort Lauderdale. At the New School in New York, I teach a course with the title "Psychoanalyzing Jewish, Christian, and Islamic Mythology." Students in that course analyze psychologically the Tanakh, the New Testament, and the Qur'an. While I was a psychoanalyst in training in New York, there were courses in the Jewish, Christian, Greek, Hindu, Buddhist, and other traditions but no course in the Islamic tradition. The omission of Islam seemed to me symptomatic. In relation to Islam, Jungians were not culturally knowledgeable but culturally ignorant or culturally negligent.

Islam purports to subsume and supersede all previous revelations – among them, the Jewish and Christian revelations. From this perspective, the Qur'an is the final revelation, the last word on the subject, and Muhammad is the final prophet of that revelation. "Islam" means "submission." To be a Muslim is, by definition, to be submissive to God. In this sense, there is in the Islamic cultural unconscious a "submission complex" (just as there is in the Jewish cultural unconscious and the Christian cultural unconscious an "obedience complex"). I do not mean to suggest that Muslims are necessarily more submissive than other persons. I do, however, maintain that a set of values about which a culture is especially sensitive may – and often does – exert an unconscious influence on persons. A cultural prohibition may function, for example, as a personal inhibition.

In this sense, the submission complex in the Islamic cultural unconscious has important consequences for Muslims. It problematizes individuation. For Muslims, the concern is that individuation may be an inflation of the ego, which may be an association or equation with God. For the ego to be inflated and associated or equated with God (and not submitted to God) is the sin of *shirk*, which, Rafiq Zakaria notes, is "as grave a sin as *kufr*, or the denial of the existence of God" (1991: 7). The dreams of a contemporary Muslim man demonstrate just how problematic the Islamic submission complex may be for individuation.

In 2003, a young Muslim man, 32 years old, came to me for Jungian psychoanalysis. I shall call him by the name "Nizar," a pseudonym that he chose. In Arabic, the name "Nizar" means "glance" (and the name "Nizzar" means "keen-eyed"). The young Muslim man translated "Nizar" as "vision."

As Nizar experienced his identity, there was "a war between two parts of what I am." One part was the "Arab–Islamic part." He had once rejected that part but now accepted it. The other part was the "Western part." He was "good at amalgamating identities" – for example, he spoke North African

Arabic, Eastern Arabic, Turkish, Hebrew, French, and English – but he felt "a lot of division in my being."

Nizar was in no sense provincial. He had a cosmopolitan perspective. He now lived in America – but he had previously lived in Africa, Europe, Asia, and the Middle East. Erik H. Erikson says that all individuals, as members of a nation, class, caste, sex, or race, have identities that "at the very minimum comprise *what one is never not*". This "never not" identity is the basis for the possibility of a transcendent, human identity. "What one is never not," Erikson says, "establishes the life space within which one may hope to become uniquely and affirmatively what one is – and then to transcend that uniqueness by way of a more inclusive humanity" (1969: 266). In just this way, Nizar was never not a Muslim. Islam was an essential aspect of his identity. Nizar also, however, aspired to a more inclusive humanity – and a more inclusive spirituality. He had a special interest in comparative religion. Nizar had seriously studied both Christianity and Judaism. At one time, he had even considered conversion to Judaism. He had also seriously studied Sufism. Nizar quoted Ibn 'Arabī with approval: "My heart has become a monastery for Christian monks, a tabernacle for the Torah, a Ka'ba for the pilgrims, an idol for the polytheists. My only religion is love."

Nizar had been living in Jerusalem and working for an international organization in the relief efforts for Palestinians in Gaza. He had moved to New York because he had wanted "to be where who you are or where you come from doesn't matter" and because he had wanted "to forget the Arab–Israeli conflict and the conflict between the West and Islam." Nizar had wanted "to extract myself from that state of conflict," but, he said, "ironically, synchronistically, I ended up in the very heart of it." He had arrived in New York the day before September 11, 2001 – "9/11."

While living in Jerusalem, Nizar had been in therapy for two years with a Jewish Israeli therapist. "I had two extremely impressive dreams," he said, "but my therapist couldn't find an interpretation." The reason, Nizar said, was that "the importance of spirituality for me was not understood by that therapist as a real part of my being." Nizar had come to me because he knew that, by reputation, Jungian psychoanalysis respects the importance of spirituality. I asked him if he had also come to me because he knew that I have a special interest in the psychological analysis of Islam. No, Nizar said, he had no idea. While living in Jerusalem, he had begun to read Jung. *Memories, Dreams, Reflections* had impressed him – especially the affirmation that "inner life was almost more important than outer life."

What I propose to do is to interpret three of Nizar's dreams in the context of the Islamic cultural unconscious. All three dreams are spiritual dreams. Most of the dreams that Nizar recounted to me were not spiritual dreams, but a considerable number were – more than the three that I shall interpret – and they were disproportionately frequent in comparison with the number of spiritual dreams that other persons in analysis with me have recounted. The first two dreams that I shall interpret are those for which Nizar's Jewish Israeli therapist had been unable to find an interpretation because the therapist had been unable to understand the importance of spirituality as a real part of his being. Nizar told me the two dreams in the first session of analysis with me.

Dream 1

I'm in an ancient city in south Lebanon – Tyre. There are ancient ruins. There's a swimming pool, very long, just next to the ocean on my left. The swimming pool is dry; there's no water in it. I'm walking in the swimming pool. It's marble or stone. On each side of the swimming pool are statues of gods. The statues are looking behind me at the sun. I'm walking forward, the sun behind me, very shining. The sky is blue. Although my back is to the sun, I can still see it. I'm impressed, surprised that I can see the sun while it's behind me. I'm impressed that all the idols are looking at the sun.

The ancient city of Tyre in Phoenicia (now a city by the Arabic name of Sur in south Lebanon) was a seaport famous for commerce. Tyre was also a city that Isaiah, Amos, and Joel prophesied God would destroy (Graves and Patai 1989: 52). The ancient ruins in Nizar's dream may, in this sense, be an allusion to this prophetic destruction. In the Tanakh, God strikes down and destroys the king of Tyre. God says to the king of Tyre:

By your far-flung commerce
You were filled with lawlessness
And you sinned.
So I have struck you down ...
And I have destroyed you.
(Ezekiel 28: 16)

The sin of the king (and the city) of Tyre was an emphasis on commercial values – that is, material values – rather than spiritual values.

In Nizar's dream, there is a swimming pool next to the ocean. James Hillman notes that many psychotherapists interpret "bodies of water in dreams" as the unconscious. Among these bodies of water, he specifically mentions both "swimming pools" and "oceans" (1979: 18). In Nizar's dream, there is no water in the swimming pool. Nizar is not swimming in a pool full of water but walking in a pool empty of water – that is, he is walking in what was once wet, or unconscious, but is now dry, or conscious.

On each side of the swimming pool are statues of gods. In Islam, statues of gods are idols, and idolatry is a sin. So also in Islam is polytheism a sin, and in this dream there are statues of many gods, not just one God. Although

Nizar calls the statues idols, he does not respond to them as if he considers them examples of the sins of idolatry and polytheism. Nizar simply observes that the statues are looking behind him at the sun. The sun, Jung says, is an image of "the daylight of the psyche, consciousness" (1955–56, *CW* 14: par. 501). Although the sun is behind Nizar, he can still see it. Jung says: "We have no eyes behind us; consequently 'behind' is the region of the unseen, the unconscious" (1944, *CW* 12: par. 55). It is as if Nizar has "eyes in the back of his head." He sees the sun not with the body's eye but with the mind's eye – or the imagination's eye. The dream emphasizes the difference between perception and vision. It indicates that Nizar has a special capacity to see the region of the unseen, the unconscious, and, with "the benefit of hindsight" to see the sun, the daylight psyche, consciousness – that is, that he has an exceptional aptitude for consciousness. In this sense, hindsight is insight.

Jung says that the basic function of most dreams is compensatory. What dreams compensate are the partial, prejudicial, and – at the extreme – defective attitudes of the ego. In Islam, the "spiritually correct" attitude of the ego is humble. Muhammad is the epitome of this attitude. "Before God," Zakaria says, "Muhammad always humbled himself" (1991: 7). The difficulty for Nizar was how to remain humble before God and simultaneously to acknowledge just how exceptional an aptitude he had for consciousness. From a Jungian perspective, Nizar's dream indicated that the attitude of his ego was excessively humble. Nizar knew that he had a special capacity for consciousness, but he could not or would not acknowledge that capacity because to do so would be, from the perspective of the Islamic cultural unconscious, to commit the sin of *shirk*. Nizar's concern was that he would commit a sin that would be to develop an attitude that would be an inflation of his ego. In this respect, Nizar's dream effectively compensated his "humility complex," and enabled him eventually to acknowledge just how exceptional an aptitude he had for consciousness.

At the end of the sixth session, Nizar remarked that it was necessary "to keep humble before the grace and the gift that we embody." I then asked, provocatively: "Where did you get that bright idea?" In the seventh session, Nizar said that he had been "appalled" that I could even suggest that humility might not, in all circumstances, be a virtue – that it might even be, in some circumstances, a vice. He then acknowledged that he had difficulty "listening to that voice that tells you, 'You have something special.'" He said: "It's a voice that I refused to listen to till now." The story of Nizar's whole life had been, he said, "a struggle to be ordinary." Now, however, he was realizing that "it's no shame to be extraordinary." He said: "I like the phrase to be 'out of the ordinary.'" A friend had told him that she considered him exceptional. "For the first time," he said, "I didn't blush." He was now "switching from the struggle to be ordinary to an effort to accept my sensitive, serious insight into many things."

Dream 2

My father is next to me. There are four birds that are killed and cut into pieces. Suddenly, they're resurrected. A pigeon comes to my hand. Then it's as if the sun is just in front of my face. Such a light! It's very realistic. I wake up shocked by the beauty of the light.

In this dream, Nizar's father is next to him (that is, his father complex is next to his ego). His father had been a devout Muslim. One of Nizar's happiest memories was of returning home from school as a child and spending time with his father, who would tell him stories from the Qur'an. Those stories, he said, "give you faith that in spite of all the betrayals, pain, suffering, and helplessness that you inevitably experience in life, you can emerge out of it with strength and dignity – that somehow your humanity has been resurrected." When his father died, a Sufi grand master led the procession to the cemetery, "with easily 1,000 people following." Nizar had spent the last two nights of his father's life praying with him the 99 names, or attributes, of God. He described his father as a man who was "so humble." His father, he said, "had avoided everything that could inflate his ego." That is, Nizar's "humility complex" was a function of his father complex.

One of the basic principles of Islamic dream interpretation is to identify any correspondences between a dream and a specific passage from the Qur'an. As Marcia Hermansen says, references to the Qur'an in dreams "legitimate the interpretations." Hermansen also notes that "the actual content of the dreams could contain recitations from the Qur'an" (2001: 78). Nizar's dream includes a direct reference to the Qur'an. The dream paraphrases a specific passage in which God demonstrates the miracle of resurrection:

Behold! Abraham said:
"My Lord! Show me how
Thou givest life to the dead."
He [Allah] said: "Dost thou not
Then believe?" He [Abraham] said:
"Yea! but to satisfy
My own heart."
He [Allah] said: "Take four birds;
Tie them (cut them into pieces),
Then put a portion of them
On every hill, and call to them:
They will come to thee
(Flying) with speed. Then know that Allah
Is Exalted in Power, Wise."

(Sura 2: 260)

In Nizar's dream, as in the Qur'an, four birds are cut into pieces and then resurrected. The passage from the Qur'an demonstrates the power of God to perform the impossible, which is to give life to the dead. In this context, Nizar's dream is about possibility. It indicates that even the impossible is possible.

In Nizar's dream, a pigeon comes to his hand. An Islamic dream dictionary says: "If a bird flies into one's hand in a dream, it means glad tidings" (Al-Akili 1992: 39). Similarly, the dream dictionary says: "Seeing a pigeon in a dream means glad tidings" (Al-Akili 1992: 328–9). Presumably, the pigeon that comes to Nizar's hand is one of the four birds that the Qur'an says were cut into pieces and then resurrected. After the pigeon comes to his hand, it is as if the sun is just in front of his face. When the sun confronts Nizar, he exclaims: "Such a light!" Jung says: "Light always refers to consciousness" (1936, *CW* 12: par. 259). In this sense, light is an image of the possibility of "enlightenment." The sun, which in the first dream was behind Nizar, is in the second dream in front of him. He now faces the sun, and the beauty of the light shocks him awake – that is, into consciousness. In his dream, Nizar becomes "enlightened." Nizar said that the meaning of his dream was "quite clear" to him. His dream, he said, "was forecasting the process of individuation."

Dream 3
I'm making the ritual circumambulation around the Ka'ba. I'm alone, the only one. At one point, I wonder whether my circumambulations are done in the right direction, counterclockwise. Yes, they are. At another point, at the southeast corner of the Ka'ba, I stop, totally overwhelmed by emotion. I'm crying, weeping – *deeply* – the kind you rarely have because the emotions are so strong, so powerful. I'm reciting the ritual words for the circumambulation: "Oh, God, to you. Oh, God, to you. Indeed, the grace and the praise are to you along with the kingdom."

The Ka'ba in Mecca is the holiest place in Islam. In Islamic tradition, Abraham and Ishmael built the Ka'ba. Later, the Ka'ba became a place of polytheism. It was surrounded by 360 idols. When Muhammad established Islam, he destroyed the idols and restored monotheism. At the southeast corner of the Ka'ba is the black stone. At least once in a life, all Muslims are supposed to perform the *hajj*, a pilgrimage to Mecca, where they circumambulate the Ka'ba and kiss the black stone. Nizar described the Ka'ba and the black stone as follows:

The Ka'ba is called the house of God. The southeast corner of the Ka'ba is where the black stone is located. My father used to tell me: "God sent that black stone from heaven to Abraham and Ishmael. It was a magic stone on which Abraham and Ishmael would stand, and it would lift them up (and down), so that they could build a very high Ka'ba." God sent the stone from heaven totally white. Human sins made it totally black. The black stone is where you have direct access to and contact with God. Imagine two million people going around that black stone, wanting to approach it to kiss it!

To at least some Muslims, the Ka'ba is not only an outer reality, a place in Mecca, but also an inner reality. "In Sufism, the Ka'ba is nothing else than the image of the Self," Nizar said. "I asked a Sufi master what the meaning was, and he told me that the Ka'ba is an image of the perfect man, the archetype." Similarly, Nizar said, the black stone has not only a physical reality but also a psychic reality. "The black stone is the *lapis*, or philosopher's stone," he said. "It has an alchemical capacity for transformation." For Nizar, the Ka'ba and the black stone have not only an exoteric but also an esoteric meaning. In a discussion of the visionary dream in Islamic spirituality, Henry Corbin says: "What is called 'esoteric' (*bāṭin*, interior realities), as opposed to 'exoteric' (*ẓāhir*, exterior things), has given rise to forms of consciousness, to positions taken, which are only conceivable within the framework of a prophetic religion, that is, a religion essentially based on revelation – the Book – received from a prophet" (1966: 382).

Nizar's grandfather had performed the pilgrimage to Mecca "by boat and camel." To perform the *hajj*, Nizar said, is to accomplish "a mystical journey." Nizar had asked a Sufi if he had ever performed the pilgrimage to Mecca. The Sufi had answered: "Do you think that Sufis go to Mecca without being invited by God? You must be invited by a vision or a dream." Nizar has not yet performed the outer *hajj*, the pilgrimage to the actual place in Mecca. In the dream, however, he performs an "inner *hajj*." He circumambulates the Ka'ba, and at the southeast corner, where the black stone is located, he has a profound experience. He cries, weeps – deeply. From a Jungian perspective, Nizar (the ego) has direct access to and contact with God (the unconscious). If the Ka'ba is, as Nizar says, the image of the Self, the archetype of the perfect man, and if the black stone is the *lapis*, the philosopher's stone, which has an alchemical capacity for transformation, then the strong, powerful emotions that he experiences in the dream indicate that the ego not only experiences direct access to and contact with the unconscious but also experiences the impact of the unconscious.

After his dream of the Ka'ba, Nizar decided to practice "active imagination." He knew that active imagination was a Jungian method, but he also knew that it was an Islamic method. "I don't know whether you know the works of Henry Corbin," he said to me. "Corbin resurrected the classics of Iranian philosophy, and I'm reading his books." In *Creative Imagination in the Sufism of Ibn 'Arabī*, Corbin defines active imagination as "an effort to utilize the image and the Imagination for spiritual experience" (1969: 6). To practice active imagination in this sense, he says, is to access the images in the "'ālam al-mithāl," an *imaginal* (not "imaginary" in the sense of "unreal") dimension, and to engage those "events, figures, presences directly" (1969: 43). This dimension is what Corbin calls "the *mundus imaginalis*, the place of prophetic visions" (1987: 231).

For Nizar, the Ka'ba in his dream was just such an image. Once a day, he would reimagine his dream of the Ka'ba. He would circumambulate the Ka'ba seven times and recite the ritual words. Then he would kiss the black stone. He would focus on the Ka'ba as if he was above it. From above, he would see the circumambulation and see the Ka'ba as the center of the circle. He practiced active imagination, he said, "with all my being." He would cry. He would pray. He would "talk to the Self" – not just submit to it but even (he laughed) "negotiate with it." He said: "What I'm practicing is something that I knew, but only now do I experience the deep meaning of it." Nizar said that active imagination, "dialogue with – let me call it 'God,' or the 'universal unconscious,' I don't know what to say – is amazingly great." He had "never experienced anything like it." It was, he said, "emotionally like what I experienced with my dream of the Ka'ba." The experience was "really, really intense." Nizar said, laughing: "I don't know how I made it till now without it."

From a Jungian perspective, an effective relation between the ego and the unconscious is not submission but dialogue and negotiation. Jung acknowledges one exception to this rule. He says that "in situations where there are insoluble conflicts of duty" the ego "must submit to a decision and surrender unconditionally" to the unconscious (1951, *CW* 9, 2: par. 79). Only in such extreme situations is it imperative for the ego to submit to the unconscious.

In *Memories, Dreams, Reflections*, Jung recounts a dream that exhibits a cultural style that is Islamic. This is what I call the "Millimeter to Spare Dream." In the dream, Jung and his father enter a house that has a room that is a replica of the council hall of Sultan Akbar, the Muslim emperor of Mughal India. In that room, Jung's father prays in the Islamic style. "Then he knelt down and touched his forehead to the floor," Jung says. "I imitated him, likewise kneeling, with great emotion. For some reason I could not bring my forehead quite down to the floor – there was perhaps a millimeter to spare" (1963: 219). Jung interprets the dream to mean that there were "things that awaited me, hidden in the unconscious." He says: "I had to submit to this fate, and ought really to have touched my forehead to the floor, so that my submission would be complete. But something prevented me from doing so entirely, and kept me just a millimeter away. Something in me was saying, 'All very well, but not entirely.'" What was this something that prevented Jung from complete submission? "Man always," he says, "has some mental reservation, even in the face of divine decrees. Otherwise, where would be his freedom?" (1963: 220).

To submit to God without any mental reservation is for the ego not to engage in free, critical conversation with the unconscious. In this respect, to practice prayer – or active imagination – is for the ego to exercise the freedom not to accept the opinions of the unconscious as dictates but to assess those opinions and either accept or reject them. The purpose of Jungian psychoanalysis is not for the ego to capitulate, or surrender unconditionally, to the opinions of the unconscious but to relate to them effectively – that is, freely, critically – through dialogue and negotiation. Prostration of the ego before the unconscious may be the Islamic style, but it is not the Jungian style. Dialogue or negotiation with God (or the unconscious) is very different from uncritical submission (or unconditional surrender) to God.

Initially, it was difficult for Nizar to engage the unconscious in dialogue and negotiation, because to be a Muslim is, by definition, to be submissive. Eventually, however, like Jung, he was able mentally to reserve "a millimeter to spare," the *sine qua non*, the necessary and sufficient condition, for a free, critical dialogue and negotiation between the ego and the unconscious in active imagination.

There is an important precedent in Islam for dialogue and negotiation with God. This is the relevant passage from the Qur'an, which describes the "night journey" of Muhammad:

> "Glory to (Allah)
> Who did take His Servant
> For a journey by night
> From the Sacred Mosque
> To the Farthest Mosque
> Whose precincts We did
> Bless, – in order that We
> Might show him some
> Of Our Signs"
> (Sura 17: 1)

When Muhammad journeys in one night (*isrā*) from the Ka'ba in Mecca to the site of the Temple of Solomon in Jerusalem (the location of the Al-Aqsa Mosque) and then ascends (*mi'rāj*) from the Dome of the Rock to paradise and the presence of Allah, Allah lays the duty of a certain number of prayers a day on Muhammad and all Muslims. As Muhammad descends from paradise, he encounters Moses. Moses asks Muhammad how many prayers Allah has laid on him and all Muslims. Muhammad says fifty. Moses then says: "Prayer is a weighty matter and your people are weak, so go back to the Lord and ask him to reduce the number for you and your community" (Ibn Isḥāq 1978: 186). Muhammad returns to Allah, who subtracts ten prayers. Again and again, Moses tells Muhammad to ask Allah to reduce the number. When Muhammad tells Moses that there remain "only five prayers for the whole day and night," Moses once again tells him to ask Allah to subtract more prayers, but Muhammad refuses. Muhammad says: "I replied that I had been back to my

Lord and asked him to reduce the number until I was ashamed, and I would not do it again" (Ibn Isḥāq 1978: 187). This example demonstrates that in Islam dialogue and negotiation with God is not only possible but also permissible by a precedent that Muhammad establishes. In this instance, Allah does not insist on immediate and utter submission but, with mercy on all Muslims, acquiesces to the appeals of Muhammad. Moses tells Muhammad that Muslims are too weak to pray fifty, forty, thirty, twenty, ten, or even five times a day. Again and again, until Allah finally reduces the number of prayers to only five, Muhammad engages Allah in dialogue and negotiation. In short, Allah is not unamenable to suasion.

Like Joseph's two dreams of the sheaves and the sun, moon, and stars bowing down to him (Genesis 37: 5–10; Sura 12: 4), Nizar's first two dreams indicate just how special he is, just how exceptional an aptitude he has for consciousness. Joseph eventually became the pharaoh's dream interpreter, or "psychoanalyst." What will Nizar become? As a contemporary Muslim man, he aspires to participate in and contribute to an effort to re-vision how both Muslims and non-Muslims imagine Islam. The image that many Muslims and non-Muslims have of Islam is a vulgar caricature. Nizar is acutely conscious of the fundamentalist Islam that, by a strict constructionist appeal to precedents that are conservative or even reactionary, frustrates sincere, serious efforts to affirm imaginatively a modernist Islam that would effectively address important issues. He is also conscious of the pervasive ignorance about Islam and bias against it in Western culture.

Currently, Nizar continues to work for an international organization, not in the Middle East but in Africa, where he witnesses genocidal atrocities so tragically, so traumatically inhumane as to defy description. His active imagination with his "inner Ka'ba" sustains him. Nizar is considering resigning from the international organization and moving to Europe to write a book. True to the pseudonym that he chose, he now has a "vision" that he wishes to share with others.

References

Adams, M.V. (1996) *The Multicultural Imagination: "Race," Color, and the Unconscious*, London: Routledge.

Adams, M.V. (2004) *The Fantasy Principle: Psychoanalysis of the Imagination*, Hove: Brunner-Routledge.

Adams, M.V. (2010) *The Mythological Unconscious*, 2nd rev. ed., Putnam, CT: Spring Publications.

Al-Akili, M.M. (1992) *Ibn Seerïn's Dictionary of Dreams: According to Islāmic Inner Traditions*, Philadelphia: Pearl Publishing House.

Corbin, H. (1966) "The Visionary Dream in Islamic Spirituality," in G.E. von Grunebaum and R. Callois (eds.), *The Dream and Human Societies*, Berkeley: University of California Press: 381–408.

Corbin, H. (1969) *Creative Imagination in the Sufism of Ibn 'Arabī*, trans. R. Manheim, Princeton, NJ: Princeton University Press.

Corbin, H. (1987) "The Theory of Visionary Knowledge in Islamic Philosophy," *Temenos*, 8: 224–37.

Erikson, E.H. (1969) *Gandhi's Truth: On the Origins of Militant Nonviolence*, New York: W.W. Norton.

Graves, R., and Patai, R. (1989) *Hebrew Myths*, New York: Anchor Books.

Henderson, J.L. (1990) "The Cultural Unconscious," in *Shadow and Self: Selected Papers in Analytical Psychology*, Wilmette, IL: Chiron Publications: 103–13.

Hermansen, M. (2001) "Dreams and Dreaming in Islam," in K. Bulkeley (ed.), *Dreams: A Reader on the Religious, Cultural, and Psychological Dimensions of Dreaming*, New York: Palgrave: 73–91.

Hillman, J. (1979) *The Dream and the Underworld*, New York: Harper & Row.

Holy Qur'an (1410 H.), trans. A.Y. Ali, Madhinah: King Fahd Holy Qur'an Printing Complex.

Ibn Isḥāq (1978) *The Life of Muhammad: A Translation of Isḥāq's Sīrat Rasūl Allāh*, trans. A. Guillaume, Karachi: Oxford University Press.

Jung, C.G. (1936) "Individual Dream Symbolism in Relation to Alchemy," *CW* 12: 39–223.

Jung, C.G. (1944) "Introduction to the Religious and Psychological Problems of Alchemy," *CW* 12: 1–37.

Jung, C.G. (1951) *Aion: Researches into the Phenomenology of the Self*, *CW* 9, 2.

Jung, C.G. (1955–56) *Mysterium Coniunctionis: An Inquiry into the Separation and Synthesis of Psychic Opposites in Alchemy*, *CW* 14.

Jung, C.G. (1963) *Memories, Dreams, Reflections*, ed. A. Jaffé, trans. R. and C. Winston, New York: Pantheon Books.

Kimbles, S.L. (2000) "The Cultural Complex and the Myth of Invisibility," in T. Singer (ed.), *The Vision Thing: Myth, Politics and Psyche in the World*, London: Routledge: 157–69.

Singer, T., and Kimbles, S.L. (eds.) (2004) *The Cultural Complex: Contemporary Jungian Perspectives on Psyche and Society*, Hove: Brunner-Routledge.

Tanakh: The Holy Scriptures (1985), Philadelphia: Jewish Publication Society.

Zakaria, R. (1991) *Muhammad and the Quran*, Harmondsworth: Penguin Books.

6

THE SABLE VENUS ON THE
MIDDLE PASSAGE
Images of the Transatlantic Slave Trade

Among all archetypes, the journey is perhaps the most universal. Of course, there are always variations on themes. There is the external journey, and there is the internal journey. There are personal journeys, and there are collective journeys. There is the journey as quest, but there is also the journey as conquest. There are journeys of heroes, journeys of villains, journeys of victims, and journeys of survivors. There are journeys of exploration and journeys of exploitation. Not every journey is a journey of individuation.

There is the journey to Africa – for example, the journeys of Jung to North Africa in 1920 and to East Africa in 1925–26, as well as the journey of Jungians to South Africa in 2007 for the Seventeenth Congress of the International Association for Analytical Psychology. There is also the journey from Africa. Of journeys from Africa, the most universal is the journey of all humanity from Africa, as the evidence of mitochondrial DNA has conclusively proved, but there is also another journey from Africa, not of all humanity, but the journey of Africans in the transatlantic slave trade – the "night sea journey" of the Middle Passage to the Americas.

The passengers on the ships of the Middle Passage were not immigrants but "imports." They were slaves. As James A. Rawley says, a slave was a "commodity," and the slave trade was a "business" (1981: 7). Rawley estimates the imports of slaves into the Americas, 1451–1870, at 11,345,000 (1981: 428).

The most notorious image of those ships is the diagram of the *Brookes* (Figure 6.1). Abolitionists published the diagram in 1788, when a law that would restrict that ship to 454 slaves was under consideration in the British Parliament.

One witness testified that in 1783 the ship had carried approximately 600 slaves, of whom 70, or 11.6 per cent, had died on the journey. "It was calculated," Rawley says, "that if every man slave was allowed six feet by one foot, four inches, platform space, every woman five feet ten by one foot four, every boy five feet by one foot two, and every girl four feet six by one foot, the *Brookes* could hold 451 slaves" (1981: 283).

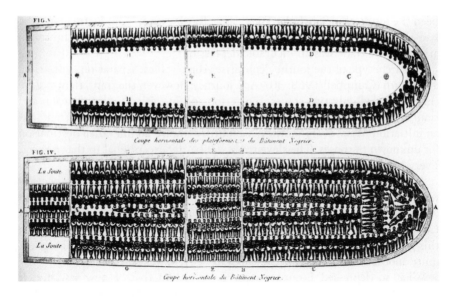

Figure 6.1 The *Brookes* diagram, 1788.

These are, of course, merely the physical dimensions of the journey – not the psychic dimensions, which Rawley aptly calls the "trauma of the Middle Passage." It was not just that Africans were traumatized when they were enslaved. They were also traumatized when they were, as Rawley says, "confined on a ship that would sail into the alien sea for an unknown destination and unknown purposes" (1981: 290).

Hardly any personal accounts of the journey exist, but one by Olaudah Equiano describes an initial experience of one such ship. "I was now," he says, "persuaded that I had gotten into a world of bad spirits, and that they were going to kill me." On the ship he saw "a large furnace or copper," and he had a fantasy that the white men on the ship were going to boil him. He fainted. When he recovered, he asked other slaves on the ship "if we were not to be eaten by those white men with horrible looks, red faces, and long hair" (1987: 33). There is, of course, a certain irony to all this, for one of the fantasies of Europeans was that Africans were cannibals who would boil them and eat them. Equiano was reassured that he was not going to be boiled and eaten, that he was not going to be killed, but he was still convinced that the world of white men that he had gotten into on the ship was a world of "bad spirits" – and that was, in fact, an accurate description of the psychic reality of the situation. The white men *were* bad spirits.

"The psychological impact," Rawley says, "of the Middle Passage upon the involuntary passengers was noted by contemporaries." For example, a doctor reported that one ship had carried 602 slaves, of whom 155, or 25.7 per cent, had died on the journey. He estimated that two-thirds of those deaths had been the result of melancholy. The doctor, Rawley says, "could cure none who had the melancholy" (1981: 291). Diagnostically, the trauma of the transatlantic slave trade was an incurable depression.

The archetype of the journey comprises three stages: separation, initiation, and return (Campbell 1968: 30). As a journey, however, the transatlantic slave trade included only two stages: separation and initiation – or separation and trauma. In a sense, of course, every initiation is a trauma, and every trauma is an initiation. Also, every journey is a journey toward an unknown destination for unknown purposes. The slave trade was hardly exceptional in that respect. Every journey is a journey of the ego into the unconscious.

As an initiatory experience, however, the slave trade was an especially traumatic experience. It was a journey with no return. On a beach in Benin (then Dahomey), there is the "Gate of No Return." It symbolizes, Henry Louis Gates, Jr., says, that "the spirits of slaves, the dead, are welcome home through this gate" (1999: 226). Of course, it is one thing to return dead and in spirit, quite another thing to return alive and in body.

What so depressed Equiano was the realization that "I now saw myself deprived of all chance of returning to my native country" (1987: 33). The result was often, if not insanity, suicide. The captain of one ship reported that slaves committed suicide because "'tis their belief that when they die they return home to their own country and friends again" (Mannix 1962: 117–18). A doctor on another ship also reported that slaves "wished to die on an idea that they should then get back to their own country." The captain of that ship devised an ingenious solution to the problem – to behead the dead in order to prevent any idea of suicide. "The captain in order to obviate this idea," the doctor said, "thought of an expedient viz. to cut off the heads of those who died intimating to them" – that is, to the slaves – "that if determined to go, they must return without heads" (Mannix 1962: 118). From a psychoanalytic perspective, decapitation is dissociation. To return without a head would be to return without spirit – or without psyche. To sever the head from the body was to sever the slave from Africa spiritually or psychically.

Of course, some contemporary descendants of slaves do return to Africa – for example, to Gorée Island off the coast of Senegal. This is not just the slave trade, in an ironic reversal, as a tourist trade, a mere exercise in nostalgia or sentimentality. It is a return to the scene of the trauma, as if such a journey might be a curative experience.

Perhaps the most egregiously perverse image of the transatlantic slave trade is the Sable Venus. "Venus" is, of course, the proper name of a goddess, but it is also a generic name, or epithet, for a woman. The most famous "Venus" from Africa is not the Sable Venus but the Hottentot Venus.

The Hottentot Venus was a real woman, Saartjie Baartman (Figure 6.2). In 1810, she was transported from South Africa to Europe, where she was exhibited as a curiosity in England and France. Europeans were fascinated by her body, which was caricatured with a Cupid on her buttocks (Figure 6.3).

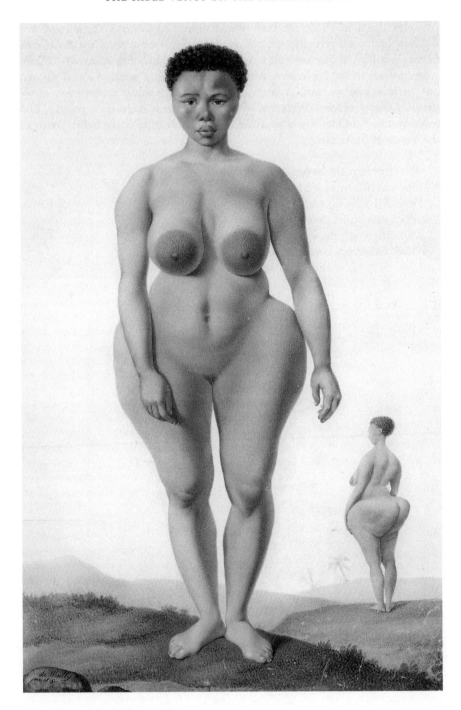

Figure 6.2 Saartjie Baartman, 1810.

After her death in 1815, her body was dissected by Georges Cuvier, and her skeleton, brain, and genitals were preserved and displayed at the *Musée de l'Homme* in Paris until 1974. Her remains were finally interred in South Africa in 2002.

In contrast to the Hottentot Venus, the Sable Venus was not a real woman but an imaginal woman. A book, *The History, Civil and Commercial, of the British Colonies in the West Indies*, by Bryan Edwards includes a poem, "The Sable Venus: An Ode," by Isaac Teale. The poem compares the Sable Venus to the Venus of Botticelli:

> The loveliest limbs her form compose,
> Such as her sister VENUS chose,
> In FLORENCE, where she's seen;
> Both just alike, except the white,
> No difference, no – none at night,
> The beauteous dames between.
> (Edwards 1801: 34–5)

Figure 6.3 The Hottentot Venus, caricature, early nineteenth century.

The second volume of the third edition of the book in 1801 includes both the poem and an image. The image is *The Voyage of the Sable Venus, from Angola to the West Indies* by Thomas Stothard, Esquire, of the Royal Academy (Figure 6.4). If any image is obscene, this is it. It is iconography as pornography. "No more preposterous misinterpretation was ever perpetrated of the 'Middle Passage,'" Hugh Honour says, than the Sable Venus. Honour remarks that neither the poem nor the image "so much as alludes to slavery: the theme of both is the physical charm of the black woman" (1989: 33).

Figure 6.4 The Voyage of the Sable Venus, from Angola to the West Indies, engraving by William Grainger after painting by Thomas Stothard for Bryan Edwards, *The History, Civil and Commercial, of the British Colonies in the West Indies*, 1801.

Daniel P. Mannix notes that "a wealth of classical details" embellishes the image (1962: 113). In this image, there is no African goddess, and there are no African gods. The goddess and the gods are all Roman – and although the goddess is black, all the gods are white. The image "Romanizes" and "whitens" the slave trade. There are twelve figures in the image. Eleven of the figures are white – only one of the figures is black. The Sable Venus rides on a scallop shell and sits on a velvet throne. In the sky are six cherubs. Two cherubs fan the Sable Venus with ostrich plumes while one cherub holds peacock feathers. In the sea, two dolphins, with two cherubs, pull the scallop shell, while to the right Triton blows a horn. On the left, Cupid draws a bow and aims an arrow at Neptune, who holds not a trident but a flag, the Union Jack. The Sable Venus eyes the reins and holds them as she guides the dolphins, as if the journey from Africa to the Americas were entirely voluntary – as if it were not a journey by force but a journey by choice.

The Sable Venus is virtually nude. "Except for bracelets, anklets, and a collar of pearls," Mannix says, "she wears nothing but a narrow embroidered girdle" (1962: 112). The obscenity of the image is not the virtual nudity. The perversity of the image is the audacity of the mythological amplification. Roman myth is utterly inappropriate and inapplicable as a parallel to the slave trade. This is not just an incompetent "amplification" – a comparison for which there is no basis. It is a radically disingenuous amplification. The amplification is a euphemism that represses the enormity of the slave trade and conveniently excuses it.

The image reveals even as it conceals. It is obviously not an image that accurately depicts the psychic reality of black African men and women in the transatlantic slave trade. The value of the image is that it accurately depicts the psychic reality of white European men. The image is not a slave narrative but a master narrative. It is a projection, a cultural imposition that serves a quite specific purpose for white European men. The image is an example of how Africa has provided Europe with an opportunity for what Gates calls "the projection of fantasies from its collective unconscious" (1999: 16–17) – or, more accurately, from its cultural unconscious.

The image is not so much a cultural complex as it is a cultural duplex. It is a duplicitous image, an image that, even as it represses what Hugh Thomas calls the "iniquity" of the slave trade (1997: 11), expresses the duplicity of white European men. The image is a certain variety of anima that a certain variety of ego imposes culturally on a scene. It is the exotic, erotic anima of an imperialistic, psychopathic ego. In this image, which is both racist and sexist, the slave is a woman – and not just any woman but a woman no man coerces because she always consents. As a woman, the slave never resists.

The function of the image is aesthetic. The image stylizes an ugly, coercive experience, the slave trade, and revises it into a beautiful, consensual – and sensual – experience. Slavery is lovely. In this stylization and revision, Britain waves the flag, and, like Neptune, rules the waves – and, by Cupid, loves the slave as a woman. The image implies that slaves are like women who, like Venus, just love it. Slaves, however, were not goddesses enthroned on shells. They were women and men, girls and boys, confined on ships. They did not wear bracelets, anklets, and collars of pearls. They wore chains. In the slave trade there were flags – among them, the Union Jack and the Stars and Stripes – but there were no cherubs, dolphins, Triton, Cupid, and Neptune, and there was no Venus. What Marcus Wood calls "the ludicrous panoply of Gods and putti" (2000: 54) is not just the use of an image. It is the abuse of an image.

On the journey of the Sable Venus, there are no white men with horrible looks, red faces, and long hair. There are no bad spirits. There are only white gods. There are no black slaves – much less 600 black slaves. There is only one black goddess – and she is not a black African goddess but a black European goddess. The wealth of classical details does not just embellish the image to demonstrate the erudition of the artist. The mythological amplification converts an atrocity into art. It does not just normalize the slave trade. It idealizes it. It is all royally academic. This is not truth and reconciliation. It is lie and rationalization.

References

Campbell, J. (1968) *The Hero with a Thousand Faces*, Princeton, NJ: Princeton University Press.

Edwards, B. (1801) *The History, Civil and Commercial, of the British West Indies*, 3rd ed., London: John Stockdale, vol. 2.

Equiano, O. (1987) *The Interesting Narrative of the Life of Olaudah Equiano, or Gustavus Vassa, The African*, in H.L. Gates, Jr. (ed.), *The Classic Slave Narratives*, New York: Mentor: 1–182.

Gates, Jr., H.L. (1999) *Wonders of the African World*, New York: Alfred A. Knopf.

Honour, H. (1989) *The Image of the Black in Western Art*, Cambridge, MA: Oxford University Press, vol. 4, pt 1.

Mannix, D.P., with Cowley, M. (1962) *Black Cargoes: A History of the Atlantic Slave Trade, 1518–1865*, New York: Viking Press.

Rawley, J.A. (1981) *The Transatlantic Slave Trade: A History*, New York: W.W. Norton.

Thomas, H. (1997) *The Slave Trade: The Story of the Atlantic Slave Trade: 1440–1870*, New York: Simon & Schuster.

Wood, M. (2000) *Blind Memory: Visual Representations of Slavery in England and America, 1780–1865*, New York: Routledge.

Economic and Political Applications

7

THE INVISIBLE HAND AND THE ECONOMIC UNCONSCIOUS

The Most Important Image of the Last 250 Years

Both Freud and Jung regarded psychoanalysis as a cultural theory and practice. They both analyzed culture psychologically. Except, however, for occasional skeptical remarks about communism and socialism, which they criticized as naïvely utopian, they never had much to say about economics as an aspect of culture. Neither Freud nor Jung ever analyzed capitalism psychologically, and they never interpreted the economic unconscious.

What is the "economic unconscious"? As I define it, it is what economics, as a discipline, is unconscious of both theoretically and practically.

If psychoanalysis has had hardly any relation to economics, economics has had hardly any relation to psychology – much less to psychoanalysis. Albert O. Hirschman conjectures that there is a historical relation between self-interest in economics and a number of discoveries "toward the end of the nineteenth century" – among them, he says, the discovery of "the unconscious." These discoveries, Hirschman says, were examples of "the extraordinary vogue for the nonrational" (1986: 51). In contrast to psychoanalysis, economics emphasized rational motives. By definition, self-interest, or the profit motive, was a perfectly rational pursuit. Economics arbitrarily excluded from consideration – or repressed – any motives that it regarded as nonrational. To continue as a viable theory and practice, Hirschman says, economics retreated from psychology:

> It was out of the question for economics, all based on rationally pursued self-interest, to incorporate the new findings into its own apparatus. So that discipline reacted to the contemporary intellectual temper by withdrawing from psychology to the greatest possible extent, by emptying its basic concepts of their psychological origin – a survival strategy that turned out to be highly successful.
>
> (1986: 51)

This strategic retreat from psychology ensured the success of economics as a discipline. The nonrational motives that were repressed were not eradicated but were relegated to the unconscious, where they continued to exist and

106

continued to exert an influence – an unconscious influence. This repression established the economic unconscious.

Although I am a psychoanalyst, not an economist, I had the opportunity to study economic history with W.W. Rostow, who wrote *The Stages of Economic Growth* (1960). What interested me most, however, was not economic history but the history of economic ideas. One of those ideas was the invisible hand of Adam Smith.

The invisible hand is the most famous idea in the history of economic ideas. It is an affirmation of self-interest as a value. What is "self-interest"? Milton Friedman, recipient of the 1976 Nobel Prize in economics, defines it more expansively than Smith does. Friedman says of self-interest: "It is whatever it is that interests the participants, whatever they value, whatever goals they pursue" (Friedman and Friedman 1980: 27). In this respect, self-interest means any goals that an individual may pursue, even when what the individual values may not be in the economic interest of the individual or may even be in contradiction to it. As Smith defines self-interest, however, it is strictly the economic interest of the individual.

The relation between private interest and public interest, Smith says, is paradoxical and counterintuitive. He says that when individuals intend to promote a private interest, they promote a public interest that they do not intend. What leads them to do so, Smith says, is the invisible hand.

The invisible hand is a version of what William K. Wimsatt, Jr., and Monroe C. Beardsley call the "intentional fallacy" (1954) – the fallacious notion that effects are necessarily derivable from and reducible to intentions. Logically, there is no necessary relation between intentions and effects. Often, if not always, effects exceed intentions – and this is true, Smith says, of self-interest. The invisible hand, he says, leads individuals to effect a public interest when they intend a private interest.

The invisible hand is an example of what Michael Polanyi calls "spontaneous order" in a system. "The most massive example," Polanyi says, "of spontaneous order in society – the prototype of order established by an 'invisible hand' – is that of economic life," defined as the aggregative, competitive activity of individuals in pursuit of self-interest (1951: 160). There is no deliberate imposition of order from without the system. Rather, there is a spontaneous emergence of order from within the system. Order spontaneously emerges when the invisible hand leads individuals who pursue a private interest to promote the public interest unintentionally but effectively.

When Arthur O. Lovejoy defines the discipline of the history of ideas, he mentions as an example the study of "implicit or incompletely explicit *assumptions*, or more or less *unconscious mental habits*". Such mental habits are not necessarily unconscious in the psychoanalytic sense. That is, they may not be a function of repression. What is repressed is radically inaccessible. In contrast, what is assumed is just not immediately available. Assumptions that are implicit or incompletely explicit are uncritical assumptions. Lovejoy says that they "are so much a matter of course that they are rather tacitly presupposed." These tacit presuppositions, he says, "seem so natural and inevitable that they are not scrutinized." Lovejoy says that among these implicit factors, which "may be of various sorts," are "particular types of imagery" (1936: 7).

In this respect, the invisible hand is not only an idea but also an image. It is, in fact, the most important image of the last 250 years. The first time that Smith mentioned the invisible hand in an economic context was two and a half centuries ago, in 1759, when he published *The Theory of Moral Sentiments*. The second time that he mentioned it in an economic context was in 1776, when he published *The Wealth of Nations* – a date that was revolutionary not only for democratic politics but also for capitalist economics.

If there were a discipline of the history of images, as there is a discipline of the history of ideas, the invisible hand would be paramount. The invisible hand is the archetypal image of capitalism (just as the hammer and sickle is the archetypal image of communism). No other image so pervades, so dominates, the modern world. The reach of the invisible hand is now global.

The invisible hand is a most peculiar image. It is difficult to visualize the image, for the hand is, by definition, invisible. Visual images of the invisible hand are rare. Examples do appear, however, in contemporary popular culture. "The Invisible Hand" is the name of a rock and roll band. The band employs a visual image of the invisible hand. To imply invisibility, the band renders the hand with dashes rather than a continuous line around it. Examples also appear in the comic strip *This Modern World* by Dan Perkins, the cartoonist who writes and draws under the name "Tom Tomorrow." In one example, the invisible hand is on the body of a man where the head would normally be. This invisible hand is an addict desperate for an infusion of billions of dollars from the government to preserve the pretense that the market is perfectly rational. George W. Bush shouts a greeting: "Yo, Hand!" In another example, the invisible hand is not on a body – it is a hand at large, a hand on the loose. In a sweat, Paul Krugman, recipient of the 2008 Nobel Prize in economics, mumbles a warning about imminent economic catastrophe. Both examples employ the image of the invisible hand to satirize the economic crisis of 2008.

In a discussion of passions and interests – among them, self-interest – Hirschman reproduces as an illustration an image of a hand in a book of emblems from the seventeenth century (1977: frontispiece). The image, if not exactly an invisible hand, is a celestial, ethereal, immaterial hand – apparently the hand of a god. In the image, an arm emerges from a cloud, and the hand of that arm grips tongs that squeeze a heart. The title of the image, in Latin, is *Affectus Comprime*, which Hirschman translates rather psychoanalytically as an exclamatory imperative: "Repress the Passions!"

The invisible hand is not original with Smith. He did not invent it – it has a history. Gavin Kennedy cites several instances of the invisible hand prior to Smith – in Ovid, Augustine, Shakespeare, Defoe, Voltaire, and other sources

(2009: 242–3). What is original with Smith is that he employs the invisible hand in an economic context.

The first time that Smith mentions the invisible hand, however, he does so not in an economic context but in a mythological context. Smith first mentions the invisible hand in an essay, "The History of Astronomy." Although that essay was not published until 1795, five years after the death of Smith, it was written before 1758. The essay includes a discussion of invisible beings.

In this respect, Lucien Lévy-Bruhl says that the primitive believes that "an infinite number of invisible beings" are "actually real" although they are "not perceptible to sense" (1966: 31). The primitive, he says, immediately regards "any unusual event" as "the manifestation of an invisible force." To the primitive, between "things which are unseen" and "things which are seen," Lévy-Bruhl says, the unseen are "more formidable" than the seen (1966: 61).

Smith says that the savage believes that all irregular natural events "proceed from some intelligent, though invisible causes" (1980: 48). He cites the invisible beings, or gods, of Roman mythology to exemplify – or to amplify – these invisible causes:

> The sea is spread out into a calm, or heaved into a storm, according to the good pleasure of Neptune. Does the earth pour forth an exuberant harvest? It is owing to the indulgence of Ceres. Does the vine yield a plentiful vintage? It flows from the bounty of Bacchus. Do either refuse their presents? It is ascribed to the displeasure of those offended deities. The tree, which now flourishes, and now decays, is inhabited by a Dryad, upon whose health or sickness its various appearances depend. The fountain, which sometimes flows in a copious, and sometimes in a scanty stream, which appears sometimes clear and limpid, and at other times muddy and disturbed, is affected in all its changes by the Naiad who dwells within it. Hence the origin of Polytheism, and of that vulgar superstition which ascribes all the irregular events of nature to the favour or displeasure of intelligent, though invisible beings, to gods, daemons, witches, genii, fairies.
>
> (1980: 49)

In this mythological amplification, invisible causes are attributable to invisible beings – among them gods – all of whom have an invisible hand in irregular natural events. In contrast, Smith says, the savage does not attribute regular natural events to invisible causes:

> For it may be observed, that in all Polytheistic religions, among savages, as well in the early ages of Heathen antiquity, it is the irregular events of nature only that are ascribed to the agency and power of their gods. Fire burns, and water refreshes; heavy bodies descend, and lighter substances fly upwards, by the necessity of their

own nature; nor was the invisible hand of Jupiter ever apprehended to be employed in those matters. But thunder and lightning, storms and sunshine, those more irregular events, were ascribed to his favour, or his anger.

(1980: 49–50)

When Smith first mentions the invisible hand, it is a mythological hand. It is the hand of a god – specifically, the hand of Jupiter – although the implication is that Neptune, Ceres, Bacchus, Dryads, Naiads, and all the other gods also have invisible hands.

The second and third times that Smith mentions the invisible hand it is an economic hand. On both occasions, he says that the invisible hand leads individuals who pursue a private interest to promote the public interest. In *The Theory of Moral Sentiments*, he defines the public interest in terms of the distribution of wealth between the rich and the poor. Smith says that the rich "consume little more than the poor." Although the rich have "vain and insatiable desires," he says, they "divide with the poor" the wealth that they produce (1976b: 184). "They are led," Smith says, "by an invisible hand to make nearly the same distribution of the necessaries of life, which would have been made, had the earth been divided into equal portions among all its inhabitants, and thus without intending it, without knowing it, advance the interest of the society" (1976b: 184–5). In *The Wealth of Nations*, he defines the public interest in terms of the production of wealth. Smith says that the individual who pursues a private interest "neither intends to promote the publick interest, nor knows how much he is promoting it." He says of the individual that "he intends only his own gain, and he is in this, as in many other cases, led by an invisible hand to promote an end which was no part of his intention." The effective means to this unintentional end is self-interest. The individual who pursues a private interest enhances the public interest. "By pursuing his own interest," Smith says, "he frequently promotes that of the society more effectually than when he really intends to promote it" (1976a, 1: 456).

Smith was not only an economist but also a moral philosopher. In that capacity, he perpetrated what Polanyi calls a *moral inversion* (Polanyi and Prosch 1975: 18). That is, when Smith advocated self-interest as a value, he inverted the terms of traditional morality. Before Smith, selflessness was a virtue and selfishness was a vice. It was virtuous to be altruistic, and it was vicious to be avaricious. After Smith, selfishness was a virtue, and selflessness was, if not a vice, at least not as much a virtue as selfishness. What was once immoral (avarice) was now moral, and what had been moral (altruism) was now not as moral as it once had been. William J. Baumol succinctly says that the individual who pursues self-interest "is virtuous in spite of himself" (1991: 1).

It would be difficult, if not impossible, to exaggerate just how radical the implications of this moral inversion were. Hirschman says that the effect was "to assuage any guilt feelings" of individuals who did not "serve the public interest *directly*," for Smith reassured them that by pursuing a private interest they "were doing so *indirectly*" (1986: 39). Now that selfishness was a virtue, there was no need for individuals who pursued a private interest to feel guilty. They could be utterly selfish and feel perfectly innocent.

In addition to the mythological and economic contexts of the invisible hand, there is also a religious context. Freud was an atheist who declared that religion was an illusion with no future. According to Jung, however, Freud unconsciously worshipped a god – not Yahweh but sexuality. Jung says that Freud substituted sexuality in place of the god "whom he had lost." For Freud, he says, sexuality was "a *deus absconditus*, a hidden or concealed god." The substitution of one god for another god was, however, only a change of name. Jung says that "the psychological qualities of the two rationally incommensurable opposites – Yahweh and sexuality – remained the same" (1963: 151). Just as psychoanalysts after Freud have unconsciously worshipped a god, the god of sexuality, so economists after Smith have unconsciously worshipped a god, the god of the market. Smith is the prophet of the market god, and the invisible hand is the hand of the market god. *The Wealth of Nations* is the holy book of capitalism, and self-interest is the article of faith in this religion.

The religious dimension of economics is an example of what Polanyi calls a "tacit dimension" (1966). It is not just that capitalism has a relation to religion, as Max Weber, R.H. Tawney, and others have noted. Rather, John McMurtry emphasizes that classical and neo-classical economics "is *itself* a religion". Although McMurtry is an economist, not a psychoanalyst, he does, at least to a certain extent, interpret the economic unconscious. Capitalism, he says, is "a tacit fundamentalist religion" that operates "beneath consciousness of it" (2004: 152). From this perspective, classical and neo-classical economists are unconscious religious fundamentalists. In the religion of capitalism, the market god is a *deus absconditus*. It is a god that is hidden or concealed in classical and neo-classical economics – a theory and practice that is, tacitly and unconsciously, not just an ideology but a theology. McMurtry says that in the "deification" of the market the invisible hand "exceeds the wonders of Yahweh" (2004: 158). The assumption, he says, is that the invisible hand is "omnipotent, omniscient and benevolent" (2004: 159). McMurtry says that the market god is just as jealous a god as Yahweh is. Yahweh says that no other god may be put before him (Exodus 20: 3). McMurtry says of the invisible hand of the market god: "No other economic idea may be put before it" (2004: 179).

Among all economic ideas, the invisible hand is the most fundamental. The fundamentalist religiosity of economics is, however, tacit and unconscious, just as invisible as the hand of the market god is. As a discipline, economics purports to be strictly secular, but it is fundamentally – and surreptitiously

– religious. With the globalization of capitalism and the repudiation of communism and socialism (or any other alternative that might afford a critical perspective on capitalism), the covert fundamentalism of economics is more influential – and more insidious – than the overt fundamentalism of any religion proper.

When Smith mentions the invisible hand in an economic context, he does not explicitly identify it as the hand of any specific god. Implicitly, however, the hand of the market god is the hand of Yahweh. Just as Freud substitutes the god of sexuality for Yahweh, so Smith substitutes the god of the market for Yahweh.

In the Bible, Yahweh has a body, but only on occasion is that body visible – and, when it is, not the whole of it but only a part of it is visible. Yahweh has a hand, a face, and back parts. For example, a finger of the hand of Yahweh writes the Ten Commandments on the tablets (Exodus 31: 18). To Moses, Yahweh says: "Thou canst not see my face: for there no man shall see me, and live" (Exodus 33: 19). A man who sees the face of Yahweh will die, but a man may see the back parts of Yahweh and live. Yahweh says to Moses that he "will cover thee with my hand while I pass by" (Exodus 33: 22) and that, after he has passed by, he "will take away mine hand, and thou shalt see my back parts, but my face shall not be seen" (Exodus 33: 23).

Not only is Yahweh only occasionally and only partly visible, but there is also, as Freud notes, "the prohibition against making an image of God" (1939 [1934–38], *SE* 23: 112). This stricture privileges the unseen over the seen. Yahweh is an abstract idea rather than a sensory perception. In this respect, Freud mentions "the compulsion to worship a God whom one cannot see" (1939 [1934–38], *SE* 23: 112–13). As Freud analyzes this compulsion psychologically, he says that "it meant that a sensory perception was given second place to what may be called an abstract idea – a triumph of intellectuality over sensuality" (1939 [1934–38], *SE* 23: 113). There is, as Freud emphasizes, a prohibition "against worshipping God in a visible form" (1939 [1934–38], *SE* 23: 115).

The market god is not only a *deus absconditus* but also a *deus ex machina*, which in ancient drama was a god lowered mechanically onto the stage by a crane to decide the final result of the play. More generally, a *deus ex machina* is any contrivance that is introduced abruptly into a situation to provide an *ad hoc* solution to a problem that has no apparent solution. In economics, the market god has an identical function. The manipulation of the economy by the invisible hand is an example of an intervention that is simultaneously divine and mechanistic. The assumption is that the invisible hand is the solution to any economic problem, however difficult, even apparently impossible, it may be.

Thurmond W. Arnold, Assistant Attorney General in the Anti-Trust Division of the Justice Department in the Great Depression, never mentions the invisible hand, but he does discuss self-interest as a value. Arnold criticizes the assumption that the "selfishness of business" ultimately results in "unselfish conduct" if it is "only let alone" (1937: 35). The notion is that any governmental intervention in the economy is governmental interference. In the religion of capitalism, there is not only a market god but also a government devil. "Our Devil is governmental interference," Arnold says. "Thus we firmly believe in the inherent malevolence of government which interferes with business" (1937: 37). From this perspective, governmental intervention is not only unnecessary but also evil, in contrast to the ostensibly inherent benevolence of business and divine intervention by the invisible hand.

Only in contrast to the "divine" intervention of the invisible hand does intervention by the government appear to be "devilish." Of course, in an economic crisis, even if certain economists continue in theory to regard governmental intervention as an evil, they tolerate it in practice as a necessary evil. After an economic crisis, however, they revert to the purist position that governmental intervention is never necessary, in spite of cogent evidence that contradicts that notion. They repress the immediate experience of the economic crisis. The nonrational imperfection of the market is a fact too awkward for them to abide, and, as a result, they consign it to the oblivion of the economic unconscious. To grant the necessity of governmental intervention would require them to revise the paradigm of self-interest that constitutes the very basis of capitalist economics. Rather than commence such an exigent project, they simply reiterate what John Kenneth Galbraith calls the "conventional wisdom" (1958: 9).

Classical and neo-classical economics is a monotheistic religion. In the economic unconscious, the invisible hand of the market god occupies a monopolistic position among images. If there is a wealth of nations, there is also a poverty of images. The invisible hand exerts such a pervasive, dominant influence that it impoverishes the imagination. The image eliminates from competition other, alternative images that might emerge from the economic unconscious. It prevents the emergence of images that might compensate the morality of selfishness with a morality of selflessness.

The invisible hand is an example of what Paul Kugler calls a "god term," which he defines as an "ultimate explanatory principle" that grounds a theory and practice. He says that the "ultimate ground" of psychoanalysis is "the unconscious itself" (1990: 316). In this respect, what ultimately grounds Jungian psychoanalysis is the compensatory function of the unconscious. Compensation is what Jung calls "unconscious self-regulation" (1928, *CW* 7, par. 257). "The unconscious processes that compensate the conscious ego," Jung says, "contain all those elements that are necessary for the self-regulation of the psyche as a whole" (1928, *CW* 7, par. 275). In classical and neo-classical economics, the invisible hand has an identical compensatory function. The invisible hand that compensates the market contains all those elements that are necessary for the self-regulation of the economy as a whole. Divine regulation by the invisible hand, or self-regulation through self-interest, putatively obviates any necessity for governmental regulation – that is, human accountability for the economy.

Certain economists who extol the virtue of the invisible hand and who cite Smith with approval advocate not only deregulation but also, at the extreme, privatization of the economy, on the assumption that there is no public interest that private interest cannot serve. These economists believe that the best government is no government at all. They assert that the market renders the government utterly unnecessary.

It is important to note what Smith says and what he does not say. He does not say that the invisible hand always leads individuals who pursue a private interest to promote the public interest. He says that it often does. In this respect, Smith says that the government has three duties. These are defense, justice, and certain public works and public institutions. It is the responsibility of the government, rather than the market, to perform these duties, for they are in the public interest, not a private interest. The invisible hand does not lead individuals to perform these duties. Self-interest, or the profit motive, is, at least to this extent, inadequate. For example, certain public works and public institutions are, to the individual, so expensive as to be unprofitable. Smith says that the government is responsible for "erecting and maintaining certain publick works and publick institutions, which it can never be for the interest of any individual, or small number of individuals, to erect and maintain; because the profit could never repay the expence to any individual or small number of individuals" (1976a 2: 687–8).

The most influential contemporary proponent of the invisible hand is Friedman. For Friedman, there are two hands, an economic hand and a political hand. Friedman contrasts the invisible hand of economics with "the visible hand of politics." He says that Smith scorned and derided "the operation of the visible hand," which in the eighteenth century was a monarchal, mercantilist, monopolistic hand that, through restraint on trade, prices, and wages, restricted "voluntary transactions" by individuals in pursuit of self-interest (1981: 7). What concerns Friedman is what he considers unnecessary, excessive intervention by the government in the market in the twentieth and twenty-first centuries. Since the political hand is visible and the economic hand is invisible, Friedman says that "we tend to grossly overestimate the importance of the visible hand which we can see, and underestimate the importance of the invisible hand which we cannot see" (1981: 22).

Although Friedman contends that, as a rule, the government should keep the political hand off the market, on the assumption that the economic hand can handle it single-handedly, he does acknowledge exceptions. He believes that the best government is the least government necessary. Friedman says that the market "does not of course eliminate the need for government" (1962: 15). The burden, however, should be on the government, he insists, to prove that the market cannot provide certain goods and services as well as or better than the government can.

Friedman concedes that the government has "essential functions" (Friedman and Friedman 1980: 7). These are identical with those that Smith mentions – defense, justice, and certain public works and public institutions. What Friedman disputes is not general principles but particular policies. He says that the market must "be supplemented by other arrangements." He admits that certain "criticisms of the invisible hand are valid." He says of these criticisms, however, that the decisive issue is "whether the arrangements that have been recommended or adopted to meet them, to supplement the market, are well devised for that purpose" (Friedman and Friedman 1980: 189).

Friedman qualifies considerably the notion that the invisible hand is the perfectly rational solution to every economic problem. He says, quite explicitly, that government is necessary. In spite what of Friedman says, however, certain economists who cite him as the ultimate authority on the market selectively disregard the reservations that he expresses about the invisible hand. To them, government is dispensable, but that is not the opinion of Friedman.

The invisible hand is not just a metaphor. It is also a metaphysic. If the invisible hand were only a metaphor, it would be only an elegantly aesthetic conceit. As a metaphysic, however, it is a tacit, unconscious, uncritical assumption with serious consequences. The notion is that self-interest is the means to an end that is perfectly rational. In accordance with supply and demand, the invisible hand unintentionally but effectively – that is, efficiently – ensures the rational allocation of resources in the production, distribution, and consumption of goods and services.

Ironically, the invisible hand is superfluous. If, as Smith says, individuals who pursue a private interest promote the public interest – that is, if self-interest is the necessary and sufficient condition for the perfectly rational operation of the economy – why posit, in addition, an invisible hand? If self-interest as such suffices, why does the market need a god to handle, invisibly, the economy? Just as evolutionary biology, after Darwin, has no need of a god, so capitalist economics, after Smith, has no need of a god.

From a psychoanalytic perspective, what purpose does the market god serve? Logically, the invisible hand is adventitious and redundant. Rhetorically, however, it is expedient. The invisible hand of the market god provides a convenient excuse – or, in psychoanalytic terms, a rationalization – that perpetuates the arbitrary exclusion of nonrational motives from economics as a theory and practice. Even in a Great Depression – or a Great Recession such as the economic crisis of 2008 – the invisible hand enables economists to ignore or deny the very existence of the economic unconscious. I might call this the "Great Repression." Just as "God's in His heaven – All's right with the world," the invisible hand's in the market and all's right with the economy.

References

Arnold, T.W. (1937) *The Folklore of Capitalism*, New Haven, CT: Yale University Press.

Baumol, W.J., with Blackman, S.A.B. (1991) *Perfect Markets and Easy Virtue: Business Ethics and the Invisible Hand*, Cambridge, MA: Blackwell.

Freud, S. (1939 [1934–38]) *Moses and Monotheism: Three Essays*, SE 23: 1–137.

Friedman, M., with Friedman, R.D. (1962) *Capitalism and Freedom*, Chicago: University of Chicago Press.

Friedman, M., and Friedman, R. (1980) *Free To Choose: A Personal Statement*, New York: Harcourt Brace Jovanovich.

Friedman, M. (1981) *The Invisible Hand in Economics and Politics*, Singapore: Institute of Southeast Asian Studies.

Galbraith, J.K. (1958) *The Affluent Society*, Cambridge, MA: Riverside Press.

Hirschman, A.O. (1977) *The Passions and the Interests: Political Arguments for Capitalism Before its Triumph*, Princeton, NJ: Princeton University Press.

Hirschman, A.O. (1986) "The Concept of Interest: From Euphemism to Tautology," in *Rival Views of Market Society and Other Recent Essays*, New York: Viking Press: 35–55.

Jung, C.G. (1928) *The Relations between the Ego and the Unconscious*, CW 7: 121–241.

Jung, C.G. (1963) *Memories, Dreams, Reflections*, ed. A. Jaffé, trans. R. and C. Winston, New York: Pantheon Books.

Kennedy, G. (2009) "Adam Smith and the Invisible Hand: From Metaphor to Myth," *Economic Journal Watch*, 6, 2: 239–63.

Kugler, P. (1990) "The Unconscious in a Postmodern Depth Psychology," in K. Barnaby and P. D'Acierno (eds.), *C.G. Jung and the Humanities: Toward a Hermeneutics of Culture*, Princeton, NJ: Princeton University Press: 307–18.

Lévy-Bruhl, L. (1966) *Primitive Mentality*, trans. L.A. Clare, Boston: The Beacon Press.

Lovejoy, A.O. (1936) *The Great Chain of Being: A Study of the History of an Idea*, Cambridge, MA: Harvard University Press.

McMurtry, J. (2004) "Understanding Market Theology," in B. Hodgson (ed.), *The Invisible Hand and the Common Good*, Berlin: Springer: 151–82.

Polanyi, M. (1951) "Manageability of Social Tasks," in *The Logic of Liberty: Reflections and Rejoinders*, London: Routledge and Kegan Paul: 154–200.

Polanyi, M. (1966) *The Tacit Dimension*, Garden City, NY: Doubleday.

Polanyi, M., and Prosch, H. (1975) *Meaning*, Chicago: University of Chicago Press.

Rostow, W.W. (1960) *The Stages of Economic Growth: A Non-Communist Manifesto*, Cambridge: Cambridge University Press.

Smith, A. (1976a) *An Inquiry into the Nature and Causes of the Wealth of Nations: Vols. 1 and 2*, ed. R.H. Campbell, A.S. Skinner, and W.B. Todd, Oxford: Clarendon Press.

Smith, A. (1976b) *The Theory of Moral Sentiments*, ed. D.D. Raphael and A.L. Macfie, Oxford: Clarendon Press.

Smith, A. (1980) "The History of Astronomy," in *Essays on Philosophical Subjects*, ed. W.P.D. Wightman and J.C. Bryce, Oxford: Clarendon Press: 33–105.

Wimsatt, Jr., W.K., and Beardsley, M.C. (1954) "The Intentional Fallacy," in W.K. Wimsatt, Jr., *The Verbal Icon: Studies in the Meaning of Poetry*, Lexington, KY: University of Kentucky Press: 3–18.

8

OBAMA AND ICARUS

Political Heroism, "Newspaper Mythology,"
and the Economic Crisis of 2008

From Journalism to Jungian Analysis

Although I am now a Jungian analyst, I once aspired to become a journalist.
So, too, did another Jungian analyst, James Hillman. Hillman says that as a
young man he "thought the way to take on wrongs was through politics and
journalism." That, he says, was "where my ambition was" (1983: 97). Those
were exactly my thoughts at that time in my life. My ambition was to become
a political journalist and to right wrongs by writing about them.

If I were to write a memoir of that period, the title might be *A Portrait of
the Young Man as a Journalist*. I was the editor of my high school newspaper,
and then I was the editor of my university newspaper. As an undergraduate
student, I majored in journalism. In the summer of 1968, I was an intern
reporter on the *Washington Post*. That was before Watergate and "Deep Throat"
but just after the assassinations of Martin Luther King, Jr., and Robert
Kennedy. With other intern reporters, I covered the Poor People's Campaign
of Ralph David Abernathy and the Southern Christian Leadership Conference.
I also covered a racial murder trial (a white man had shot a black boy to death).
Larry L. King – the magazine writer, novelist, and playwright (the Broadway
musical *The Best Little Whorehouse in Texas*) – took me for a "nine-hour lunch"
of Scotch, Bloody Marys, and beer at four different bars on Capitol Hill. King
describes me as eventually getting "real silent" and then, after the usual
catharsis, becoming "pale but lucid" (1999: 134). For me, that was a
memorable initiation into one of the most venerable traditions of journalism.
In New York, I visited Willie Morris, the editor of *Harper's*, who on a previous
occasion had presented me with a copy of *North Toward Home* (1967) and had
inscribed it, "From one editor to another." That was the period of the "New
Journalism" and Tom Wolfe, when journalists were not only reporters of
events but also participants in those events – and when Morris published such
writers as Norman Mailer. In the summer of 1969, I was an intern reporter on
the *Atlanta Constitution*. I covered the Atlanta Pop Festival (not quite
Woodstock but still quite a sex, drugs, and rock and roll experience) and civil
rights protests against the anti-integration tactics of Lester Maddox. In 1970,

I was a reporter on the *Texas Observer*. I covered the case of a black political activist in prison for the ostensible sale of a single marijuana cigarette, and I covered the provision of legal aid to conscientious objectors against the Vietnam War (Adams 2004b).

Soon, however, I realized that journalism was not for me. Events, especially current events, felt superficial. What appealed to me were ideas, which felt deep. Hillman says that he eventually realized that, for him, journalistic life was unsatisfying and that he "was dying for intellectual life" (1983: 98). That was precisely what I, too, realized. As a graduate student, I pursued an interdisciplinary education in the humanities and social sciences. I studied intellectual and cultural history, political and economic history, the history of ideas, literature, the philosophy of science, and psychology. The very first course that I took as a graduate student was "Freud in America," a seminar on the intellectual and cultural history of psychoanalysis in America.

I became a professor, which I continue to be, and eventually I became a Jungian analyst. Psychoanalysis, Freud says, is "a depth-psychology or psychology of the unconscious" (1933 [1932], *SE* 22: 158). The ideas of Freud and Jung felt (and still feel) deep to me. What feels most profound to me about psychoanalysis – and especially Jungian analysis – is the idea that the deepest dimension of the unconscious is mythological.

As a Jungian analyst, I now feel that events, even current events, need not be superficial but can be just as profound as any ideas. From a psychoanalytic perspective, what is decisive is the experience of an event. Ultimately, what most deepens an event is an experience of the unconscious mythological dimension of that event. In this respect, an important recent event was the 2008 American presidential election. The election of Barack Obama was, in the experience of all Americans, an event of mythological proportions.

Politicians as Heroes

Most journalists do not appreciate the relevance of mythology for current events. Maureen Dowd of the *New York Times* is one of the few who do. In a sense, Dowd is a "Jungian" journalist. For several years, she has written articles and columns on political heroism. They are examples of what Jung calls "newspaper mythology" (1977: 75).

Betty Sue Flowers says that "we must to learn to read the news mythologically" (2000: 209). Dowd writes the news mythologically. In effect, she applies to politicians the Jungian method of "amplification," which is a comparative method. When Jungian analysts amplify an image in the psyche (for example, in a dream), they compare it to the same or similar images in other sources (for example, in myths). When Dowd practices newspaper mythology, she compares modern politicians to ancient heroes in order to identify similarities between them. (She also contrasts them in order to identify differences, often for satirical purposes.)

In an article during the 1992 American presidential election between Bill Clinton and George H.W. Bush, Dowd mentioned *The Hero with a Thousand Faces* by Joseph Campbell (1968). "The arc of a political campaign," she said, "traces the standard pattern of mythological adventure, as described by Joseph Campbell." (This standard pattern is, of course, an example of what Jung means by an archetype. In this instance, the archetype is what Jung calls the "hero myth.") The politician, Dowd said, has to become a dragon-slaying or giant-slaying hero. "One important campaign ritual," she said, "comes when the candidate assures the voters that he has completed the 'hero-task,' as it is called by myth experts, that he has slain the dragon or the giant" (1992: A9).

In a column in 2001, Dowd included an allusion to *Joseph Campbell and the Power of Myth* (2001), a series of television interviews that Bill Moyers conducted with Campbell. Jacqueline Kennedy Onassis was the editor who arranged to publish a transcript of those interviews as the book *The Power of Myth* by Campbell (1988). Dowd noted that "Jackie Kennedy understood the power of myth." She recounted that after the assassination of John Kennedy, Jackie Kennedy encouraged Robert Kennedy to read *The Greek Way* by Edith Hamilton (1942). Dowd said that "the great families of Greek mythology" transfixed Robert Kennedy. "He recognized the hubris of the house of Atreus," she said, "with doom seeping down through the generations." In effect, the Kennedy family was a contemporary house of Atreus, which Hamilton described as "an ill-fated house." Dowd quoted Hamilton: "A curse seemed to hang over the family, making men sin in spite of themselves and bringing suffering and death down upon the innocent as well as the guilty." She also quoted Evan Thomas, author of a biography of Robert Kennedy. Thomas applied another myth to the Kennedy family – the myth of Icarus. "The Kennedys," he said, "flew too close to the sun" (Dowd 2001).

During the 2008 American presidential election, Dowd criticized Obama from a mythological perspective. Dowd implied that he needed a new, mythological name – Barack "Jason" Obama. Seeking the Oval Office, she said, was tantamount to seeking the golden fleece. (Previously, William Proxmire employed the myth of Jason for political purposes. Annually, from 1975 to 1988, Proxmire bestowed the "Golden Fleece Awards" on federal agencies that funded grants with tax money, or "gold," for frivolous research projects that "fleeced" the American public.) Obama was not, Dowd declared, sufficiently attentive to the mythological dimension of politics:

> The Illinois senator doesn't pay attention to the mythic nature of campaigns, but if he did, he would recognize the narrative of the classic hero myth: The young hero ventures out on an adventure to seek a golden fleece or an Oval Office; he has to kill monsters and face hurdles before he returns home, knocks off his father and assumes the throne.
>
> (April 30, 2008)

The immediate context for this criticism was the controversial comments of Jeremiah Wright, the African-American minister of the church that Obama attended in Chicago. Obama denounced those remarks and ultimately renounced Wright. This denunciation and renunciation, Dowd said, was for Obama "a painful form of political patricide" (April 30, 2008). In effect, as I have previously noted, Obama became a monster-slaying hero, or at least a "minister-slaying hero" (Adams 2008: 237–8) – or, as Dowd emphasized, a father-slaying hero.

In another column, Dowd said that Obama needed to become a Herculean hero. She said that "he has to swiftly and convincingly perform the political equivalent of the Labors of Hercules." In contrast to Hercules, who had to perform twelve labors, Dowd said that Obama had to perform four labors. The first labor was the most formidable. Dowd implied that George W. Bush had left such a pile of political manure (the euphemism that Harry Truman famously employed) that even a flood would not immediately wash away the mess. "Cleaning the Augean stables in a single day," she said, "seems like a cinch compared with navigating the complexities of Afghanistan, Iraq, Israel, Palestine and Jordan." The second labor that Obama had to perform was to handle Hillary Clinton. "Instead of obtaining the girdle of the Amazon warrior queen Hippolyte," Dowd said, "Obama has to overcome the hurdle of the Amazon warrior queen Hillary." The third labor that Obama had to perform was to handle Bill Clinton, that Arkansas razorback who, Dowd implied, was a real swine. "Obama must capture his own equivalent of the Erymanthian Boar," she said, and decide whether he "will be help or hindrance, or both," and "how to use him, if at all." The fourth and final labor that Obama had to perform, Dowd said, "should be the simplest for him, nailing his Denver convention speech." It would be, she said: "Not half as hard as getting past that 100-headed dragon to steal the Apples of the Hesperides" (July 20, 2008).

In yet another column, Dowd mentioned a comedy sketch that Jon Stewart presented on *The Daily Show*. She noted that Stewart combined allusions to Jason and the Argonauts, the dragon-slaying hero, and Odysseus. "Jon Stewart was poking fun at the grandiosity of the 'Obama Quest' and the 'Obamanauts,'" she said. "He showed film clips of 'our hero' in chain mail fighting off dragons and a Cyclops in his crusade to come home and rule over Dreamerica" (July 30, 2008). She then mentioned a conversation that she had with Obama as he returned to America from a trip to Europe:

> By happenstance, on O-Force One I raised the matter of quests and Cyclops with the candidate. Having read that he had left the trail in early June to go back to Chicago and see his daughter Malia perform in "The Odyssey" for theater class, I wondered if that rang any bells on this trip? The hero on a foreign journey, battling through obstacles to get back home, where more trouble would wait?

"The whole sort of siren thing, the Cyclops, that's interesting," he said.

(July 30, 2008)

What, exactly, was interesting to Obama about the siren thing and the Cyclops (and whether Obama identified himself in any respect with Odysseus), Dowd did not say.

"Obama," Dowd declared, "does not see himself in terms of Greek myth." She did, however, acknowledge that Obama informed Jeff Zeleny, a reporter for the *New York Times*, that "he knew the risks of 'flying too close to the sun.'" The allusion, of course, was to the myth of Icarus. When Obama returned to America from the trip to Europe, more trouble did wait – the economic crisis of 2008. "Sure enough," Dowd said, "'our hero' came home to a passel of economic troubles in Dreamerica, rushing to talk to Bernanke & Paulson" (Ben S. Bernanke, Chairman of the Federal Reserve Board, and Henry M. Paulson, Jr., Secretary of the Treasury). To deal effectively with the economic crisis, she implied, Obama should see himself in terms of the myth of Odysseus rather than the myth of Icarus. "Odysseus's heroic trait," Dowd emphasized, "is his cunning intelligence." In contrast, Icarus's heroic trait (if, in fact, it is heroic at all) is his soaring ambition – his aspiration to fly close to the sun. Much more than soaring ambition, cunning intelligence is a trait that it will be necessary for Obama to possess in abundance, Dowd said, if he is to become a political hero. She said that "even flying close to the sun Obama will need all that he can muster" (July 30, 2008).

The Icarus Myth

Obama is one president who has had personal exposure to the myths of various cultures. In an article that describes how Obama became a Christian, Lisa Miller and Richard Wolffe note that his mother, Ann, although an agnostic, had a special spiritual interest in mythology. "One of Ann's favorite spiritual texts," Miller and Wolffe say, "was 'Joseph Campbell and the Power of Myth,'" which they describe as a television series about "common themes" in mythology (2008: 28). Obama also recounts how he grew up among books of mythology. "In our household," he says, "the Bible, the Koran, and the Bhagavad Gita sat on the shelf alongside books of Greek and Norse and African mythology" (2006: 203–4).

In spite of what Dowd said, Obama does see himself in terms of Greek myth – or at least in terms of one quite specific Greek myth. More than once, he has invoked the myth of Icarus. For example, in a television interview, David Axelrod, Chief Campaign Strategist, recounted how Obama mentioned the myth of Icarus the day after he lost the New Hampshire primary, with only three hours of sleep and with no notes, before a speech in Boston. According to Axelrod (2009), this is what Obama said:

"I know this sounds like spin, but I think it was meant to be that we didn't win the primary. It would have been far too easy." And he said: "Change is never easy. Change is something you have to fight for. And this would have come too easily." He said: "I think we were a little bit like Icarus, flying too close to the sun." And he said: "We're going to have to work for every vote from this point on. And let me tell you why it's worth the struggle, why it's worth the fight."

In this anecdote, Obama sees himself not in terms of Jason, Hercules, or Odysseus but in terms of Icarus.

In mythology, there is not just one hero – there are many heroes. (As Campbell says, the hero has a thousand faces.) As an archetype, the hero is a general, abstract concept, of which there are many particular, concrete images. An archetype is a theme, and there are many variations on that theme. All heroes have to perform tasks, but the specific tasks and the specific styles in which specific heroes perform them vary considerably. Different heroes have very different styles.

For example, not all heroes are monster-slaying heroes, or at least they are not always monster-slaying heroes. Even Hercules is only occasionally a monster-slaying hero. Most famously, he slays the Nemean lion and the Lernaean Hydra, but most frequently he is a monster-capturing hero. Similarly, in only some versions of the myth of the golden fleece is Jason a monster-slaying hero. In most versions, he does not slay the dragon that guards the golden fleece but enlists the aid of Medea, who, with a magic spell and potion, charms the dragon to sleep so that Jason can steal the golden fleece. Odysseus is not a monster-slaying hero. He does not slay the Cyclops. He blinds the Cyclops with a fiery stake in the eye so that he can escape the cave. With the assistance of Medea, Jason is a monster-charming hero. Odysseus is a monster-blinding hero.

Icarus is also not a monster-slaying hero. He does not slay – he flies. He is a high-flying hero (if he is, by any definition, a hero). The expressions to "fly high" and "flying high" are idioms. To "fly high" means to be "ambitious" (Cowie, Mackin, and McCaig 1983: 193), or it means to be "elated" (Ammer 1997: 215). "Flying high" means "very successful" either "in one's ambitions" or "in an important or powerful position," frequently "with the implication that this is not the usual situation or will change" (Spears 2004: 223), or it means "doing well" or "very excited or happy" (Heacock 2003: 135).

What does the myth of Icarus actually say? It is a myth about a father and son, Daedalus and Icarus. Some heroes go on what Jung calls the "night sea journey." In contrast, Daedalus and Icarus go on a "day sky journey." Daedalus is artisan and architect to Minos and Pasiphae, king and queen of the island of Crete. Pasiphae orders Daedalus to create a model of a cow that enables her to have sexual intercourse with the bull of Poseidon. The result of this bestial perversion is a monstrous birth, the Minotaur. Minos then orders Daedalus to create the labyrinth, in which he confines the Minotaur. (There is a monster-slaying hero, but it is Theseus, not Icarus, who enters the labyrinth, slays the Minotaur, and then, with the assistance of Ariadne, exits the labyrinth.) Minos also confines Daedalus and Icarus in the labyrinth, but Pasiphae releases them. Then, to escape the island of Crete, Daedalus creates two pairs of wings. He sews the larger feathers with thread and glues the smaller feathers with wax. Daedalus warns Icarus not to fly too high. He also warns him not to fly too low. If Icarus soars too high, the sun will melt the wax, and he will fall from the sky and drown. If he swoops too low, the sea will wet the feathers, and he will fall from the sky and drown. Daedalus then warns Icarus to fly close behind and not to fly off. Icarus, however, flies up, up, and away, flies too high, flies too close to the sun, burns and crashes, and then drowns (Figure 8.1).

The myth of Icarus is what I would call an "admonitory" myth. Although the myth includes an admonition not to fly too low, what it emphasizes is the admonition not to fly too high – and, more specifically, not to fly too close to the sun. As a myth of excessive ambition, the myth of Icarus is also what I would call a "transgressive" myth. In this transgression, exuberance carries Icarus away – carries him way beyond the upper limit of endurance. In the index that Stith Thompson provides of typical (or archetypal) motifs, the high-flying hero is type "F1021.2. *Extraordinary effect of high flight*," and Icarus is an image of subtype "F1021.2.1. *Flight so high that sun melts glue of artificial wings*" (1955, 3: 260). The myth of Icarus graphically illustrates the catastrophic consequence of flying too high, too close to the sun. The hero who does so suffers a "meltdown."

In terms of physical energy, the sun is radiantly, radioactively hot. From a Jungian perspective, the sun is a quite specific image of the archetype of libido, or psychic energy. In 1992, at the "Festival of Archetypal Psychology

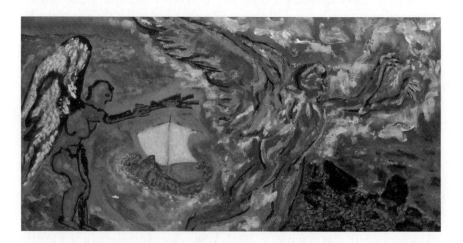

Figure 8.1 Push/Jump!, painting by Michael P. Jenkins, 2008.

in Honor of James Hillman" at Notre Dame University, I delivered a presentation on several of my dreams of Hillman (Adams 1992). After the presentation,
a Jungian analyst recounted to me one of her dreams of Hillman. In the dream,
she was at Versailles, and Hillman was in the palace of Louis XIV, the "Sun
King." As the Jungian analyst interpreted the dream, it cautioned her not to
get too close to Hillman, for, among Jungian analysts, he was a "sun hero"
who radiated such hot psychic energy that he could incinerate her. To her, the
dream implied that if Jungian analysts could not stand the heat of Hillman,
they should get out of the palace.

The Icarus Complex (and the Phaethon Complex)

The *DSM-IV*, the fourth edition of the *Diagnostic and Statistical Manual of
Mental Disorders*, includes only one mythological diagnosis – "Narcissistic
Personality Disorder" (American Psychiatric Association 1994: 658–61).
The allusion, of course, is to the myth of Narcissus. If there were a "Jungian"
manual of mental disorders, it would include many more mythological
diagnoses – among them, "Icarian Personality Disorder." Although currently
there is no Icarian personality disorder, there is an "Icarus complex." Henry
A. Murray, who directed the Psychological Clinic at Harvard University
and, with the assistance of Christiana Morgan, developed the Thematic
Apperception Test, or "TAT," originally proposed the diagnosis. As Murray
defines the Icarus complex, it comprises an "ascension–descension sequence"
(1979: 95). The individual with an Icarus complex rises (or flies) and then
falls – calamitously.

Although Murray calls this diagnosis the Icarus complex, he might just as
well have called it the "Phaethon complex." When Murray discusses the myth
of Icarus, he also mentions the myth of Phaethon. That myth is also about a
father and son, Phoebus and Phaethon. Phoebus is Apollo, the sun god who
drives the chariot of the sun across the sky. In the myth, Phaethon persuades
Phoebus to permit him to drive the chariot. Phaethon is a teenager who, in
effect, drives a "hot rod" across the sky, loses control, careens across the sky,
flies too fast, flies both too high and too low. When he scorches the earth, Zeus
strikes him with a lightning bolt, and Phaethon burns and crashes. Phaethon
is what Jung calls a *puer aeternus*, an eternal youth. Michael Perlman observes
that the tragedy of Phaethon is similar to "that of other high-flying pueri such
as Icarus" (1983: 91). Just as Daedalus warns Icarus not to fly too high or too
low, Phoebus warns Phaethon, Perlman emphasizes, "to keep a safe, middle
course" (1983: 96).

As I have previously noted, the tendency of modern corporations to advertise
products by an appeal to ancient gods or heroes is cogent evidence that what
I call the *mythological unconscious* remains just as relevant as ever (Adams 2004a:
60; Adams 2010). For example, in 2002, Volkswagen introduced a new luxury
sedan and named it after Phaethon (although the corporation spelled it

"Phaeton"). As Diana Winstanley remarks, there was a certain irony in the decision to name the vehicle after the victim of the first car crash in history. A representative of Volkswagen attempted to justify the decision. He argued, Winstanley says, that it was perfectly appropriate to name the vehicle after Phaethon, for, although the driver had died, "the car had survived without damage" – as if this would reassure customers! The death of Phaethon, Winstanley says, did not imply to Volkswagen any "failure of the vehicle" (2004: 183).

The myths of Icarus and Phaethon are both myths of a father and son. Both myths involve the sun. Both Icarus and Phaethon are sun heroes. Icarus flies too close to the sun, and Phaethon flies out of control in the chariot of the sun. Both Icarus and Phaethon are adolescents who fly and then burn and crash. They both experience exhilaration. Icarus flies too high, and Phaethon flies too fast and both too high and too low. Murray says that the individual with an Icarus complex (or a Phaethon complex) "belongs with the adolescent, overreaching, would-be solar heroes, Icarus and Phaethon – father-superseding enthusiasts with unstructured ego systems" (1979: 95).

Although the adage says that if humans had been meant to fly, they would have been given wings, flying is not intrinsically an impossible, inappropriate, or psychopathological activity. (I do not mean literal, physical flying, like Orville and Wilbur Wright or Charles Lindbergh. I mean metaphorical, psychic flying – imaginal flying: the flight of the imagination.) When Hillman discusses the *puer aeternus*, he notes that there is a "winged godlike imago in us each." (An imago is a psychic, or intrapsychic, image.) As examples, Hillman cites "Icarus on the way to the sun, then plummeting with waxen wings," and "Phaethon driving the sun's chariot out of control, burning up the world" (1979: 65). Each and every individual has what I might call an "inner Icarus" or an "inner Phaethon."

Icarian Flight versus Daedalian Flight

Both Icarus and Phaethon are examples of the high-flying hero as the *puer aeternus*. "The *puer* flies because he has to," Peter H. Tatham says. "It is, inescapably, his way of going through the world: of transcension." Tatham also notes, however, that "the dream of flight brings with it a fear of falling that easily and often prevents take-off." Some heroes never even get off the ground, he says, "for, to anyone but *puer*, falling is seen only as death and extinction." What goes up must come down. Some heroes land safely, but other heroes fall. The consequence of transcension (or the ascension–descension sequence) may be a downfall that is, ironically, a comeuppance (as in the myths of Icarus and Phaethon), but this need not be the case. Tatham says that "since the vertical dimension works both ways, a 'coming-down' is inevitable, whether that be seen as a fall or as safe landing." What distinguishes the *puer aeternus* is a risky attitude that defies and denies death. "The fall," Tatham says, "is something he is dying to risk: a risking to die, because for him there is also 'life in death'" (1992: 27).

Tatham says that Icarus "lives, it seems, but to fly and to fall, which is the sum of his whole existence" (1992: 43). What is problematic is not flying as such but flying too high and then falling. "It often seems," Tatham says, "as if it is only young men aspiring to flight in general and approaching the overbright sun in particular who come to a fiery end." In this respect, he notes that Daedalus "flew on to safety." He says that "it is only Icarian flight that falls and kills" (1992: 44). Daedalian flight has a very different trajectory and a very different conclusion. In contrast to Icarus, who flies and dies, Daedalus flies and lives. Daedalus, Tatham emphasizes, epitomizes the capacity for "flying-without-falling" (1992: 131).

Dreams of Flying (and Falling) and the Dream of Flight

Among what Freud calls "typical dreams" are dreams of flying and falling. He says that these are dreams "in which the dreamer finds himself flying through the air to the accompaniment of agreeable feelings or falling with feelings of anxiety." Freud notes that one interpretation of such dreams is purely physical – dreams of flying and falling ostensibly derive from the sensation of the rising and falling of the lungs during sleep. He rejects that interpretation and, as an alternative, proposes that such dreams derive from games that adults play with children. "There cannot be a single uncle," Freud says, "who has not shown a child how to fly by rushing across the room with him in his outstretched arms, or who has not played at letting him fall by riding him on his knee and then suddenly stretching out his leg, or by holding him up high and then suddenly pretending to drop him" (1900, *SE* 4: 271).

Subsequently, however, Freud offers a different interpretation of dreams of flying. He wonders why "so many people dream of being able to fly." From a psychoanalytic perspective, he says, the wish to fly is "only a disguise for another wish" (1910, *SE* 11: 125) – quite predictably, a sexual wish. Freud asserts that "in dreams the wish to be able to fly is to be understood as nothing else than a longing to be capable of sexual performance." Finally, he contends that "aviation, too, which in our day is at last achieving its aim," also derives from sexual wishes (1910, *SE* 11: 126).

Jung also notes that there are typical dreams, "such as of flying" (1945/1948, *CW* 8: par. 535). As examples, he mentions dreams in which the dreamer is "flying through space" or is actually "the sun" (1928, *CW* 7: par. 250). Jung does not, as Freud does, interpret these dreams in sexual terms. Nor does Jung interpret them in mythological terms. He does not amplify them – that is, compare dreams of flying to myths of flying. It is not Jung but G.S. Kirk, a specialist in Greek mythology, who relates dreams of flying to the myth of Icarus. Kirk observes that modern studies have established that "dreams about flying are surprisingly common." He says that although the implication of such dreams is "arguable," they do demonstrate why the myth of Icarus "flying towards the sun" is so evocative (1974: 87).

If Jung does not relate dreams of flying to the myth of Icarus, at least one Jungian analyst does. Stanton Marlan recounts the following dream of a woman:

> I am standing on the Earth. I think: "Why should I do this when I can fly?" As I am flying I think I would like to find my spiritual guide. Then I notice, clinging to my waist, a person. I think this may be my guide. I reach behind me and pull the figure to the front so I can look it in the face. It is a young, borderline schizophrenic girl. I know this is not my guide. I put her aside and continue on my journey to the sun. Just before I get there, a wind comes and carries me back to Earth.
>
> (2005: 30)

Like Icarus, the woman flies toward the sun, but, unlike him, she does not fly too close to the sun and then fall. She does not burn and crash. Just before she gets to the sun, a wind comes and carries her back to the earth – where, apparently, she lands safely.

Just as there are dreams of flying, there is also what Gaston Bachelard calls "the dream of flight" (1988: 26–7). Bachelard relates the myth of Icarus to the history of aviation and recounts an anecdote about flying and falling:

> If we read the history of efforts to imitate Icarus, we will find many examples of materialistic thinkers who believe that participating in the nature of feathers is the same thing as participating in flight. For example, Father Damian, an Italian living at court in Scotland, tried to fly in 1507 using wings made out of feathers. He took off from the top of a tower, but fell and broke his legs. He attributed his fall to the fact that some rooster feathers had been used to make the wings.
>
> (1988: 37)

Unlike Icarus, Father Damian does not fly too close to the sun. In fact, he does not fly at all – he just falls. In an effort to imitate Icarus, he tries to fly, but the feathers fail him, and he suffers fractures in a painfully funny pratfall.

Not all dreams of flying are about flying to the sun. Some are about flying to the moon. Some are simply about flying in the sky. Some are about flying through space. For example, Lauren Lawrence quotes a dream that occupies a quite special position in the history of aviation – it is a dream of Wally Schirra, commander of Apollo 7 in 1968:

> During my youth my best dream recurred frequently, where I would just lift off from the ground and start flying in the sky. I would fly

higher and faster and farther than could be imagined. It was a wonderful dream of mine that was accomplished in reality by the NASA space program. Once I became an astronaut these dreams stopped.

(2002: 52)

This dream of flying is not only a recurrent dream but also what Jung calls a "prospective dream" – a dream that is "an anticipation in the unconscious of future conscious achievements" (1916/1948, *CW* 8: par. 493). In this example of the prospective function of the unconscious, imagination coincides with reality, and a dream of flying coincides with the dream of flight. For Schirra, becoming an astronaut and flying through space is quite literally a dream come true.

Mania and Depression in Psychology and Economics

Jungian analysts caution against what they call an "inflation" of the ego, but an "elation" of the ego is equally problematic. Only one psychoanalyst, Bertram D. Lewin, not a Jungian but a Freudian, has specifically studied elation. One explanation for this dearth of studies, Lewin says, is that "mild forms" of elation are not "apt to bring persons into analysis, or once they are there to provoke much desire for change or therapeutic effort" (1950: 15). It is not happy individuals but sad individuals who tend to enter analysis. In extreme, or psychopathological, forms of elation, Lewin mentions "the illusory sense of reality that attaches to the mood" (1950: 171). In such instances, there is, he notes, a disparity, or incongruity, between the sense of elation and the sense of reality. The manic ego is a radically unrealistic ego.

In the diagnosis of "Bipolar Disorder," mania is a "high" and depression is a "low." In terms of mood, a manic individual is "up" and a depressive individual is "down." As the *DSM-IV* says, in a manic episode, the elated individual experiences a mood that is "persistently elevated" and may experience a "flight of ideas." The mood of the manic individual is "euphoric," or "high" (American Psychiatric Association 1994: 328). In this respect, the myth of Icarus is about elation and elevation, attitude and altitude – and psychoanalysis is not only a depth psychology but also a "height psychology."

The word "depression" is not only a psychological term but also an economic term, as in the phrase "Great Depression." Hillman notes that the word "'depression' combines both economics and psychology, suggesting that any downward trend in economics points toward disease and any melancholic phase in personal psychology could herald economic disaster" (2001: 13–14).

So, too, are the words "mania" and "panic" both psychological and economic terms. As Charles P. Kindleberger says, "Speculative excess, referred to concisely as a mania, and revulsion from such excess in the form of a crisis, crash, or panic can be shown to be, if not inevitable, at least historically common" (1989: 4). Although Kindleberger does not mention the myth of

Icarus, he does employ an idiom about flight. After a mania that ends in a crisis, he says, "some time must elapse" before investors are "willing to take a flyer again" (1989: 17). The expression to "take a flyer" is an idiom that means to "take an ambitious gamble; take a risky chance or chancy risk," especially "financially" (Chapman 1995: 547).

Hyman P. Minsky and John Kenneth Galbraith also discuss the relation between economics and psychology (or between economics and psychopathology). Both cite euphoria as a factor in economic crises. Minsky says that "the fundamental instability of a capitalist economy" is a tendency to enter a "'euphoric' state" (1982: 118). He says that "euphoria is a necessary prelude to a financial crisis" and that "euphoria is almost an inevitable result of the successful functioning of an enterprise economy" (1982: 145). Galbraith emphasizes the "speculative mood" and the concomitant "retreat from reality or, more precisely, perhaps, from sanity." The economy, he says, is historically episodic. Periodically, it becomes so euphoric as to be psychotic. "Euphoria leading on to extreme mental aberration is a recurring phenomenon," Galbraith says, "and one that puts the affected individual, the particular enterprise, and the larger economic community at risk" (1990: 1). He calls these episodes "flights into what must conservatively be described as mass insanity" (1990: 3). The implication is that, diagnostically, capitalism is intrinsically bipolar, a recurrent cycle of manias and depressions, or economic mood swings.

The Rational and the Irrational

Economists assume that the allocation of resources in the production, distribution, and consumption of goods and services is a rational function of supply and demand. This model arbitrarily excludes from consideration any factor that is putatively irrational. In this respect, Jung says that the irrational is "an existential factor" that "may be pushed further and further out of sight by an increasingly elaborate rational explanation." He notes that science (which presumably would include economics as a social science) "posits objects that are confined within rational bounds, because by deliberately excluding the accidental it does not consider the actual object as a whole, but only that part of it which has been singled out for rational observation" (1921, *CW* 6: par. 775). When economists arbitrarily exclude irrational factors from consideration, on the assumption that such factors are merely accidental (not necessary to the model), they comprehend only a part, not the whole, of the object (which, in this instance, is the economy). Only occasionally – when some event that does not strictly conform to this model occurs – do economists momentarily ponder the implications and, even then, they tend to dismiss such an event as an anomaly that does not oblige them to revise the model permanently. If there is a psychology of economics, it is a psychology of rational motives (for example, the profit motive).

Psychoanalysis is what I call an *affective–attitudinal psychology*. It is a psychology that comprises rational and irrational factors. In contrast, the psychology of economics is a "cognitive-behavioral psychology" that omits irrational factors. (A psychology adequate to economics would be one that scrutinizes affects and attitudes – among them, irrational ones – not just cognitions and behaviors.) What is problematic about the psychology of economics is not just that the exclusion of irrational motives is arbitrary. The problem is also that what economists regard as rational may, in fact, be irrational.

Epistemologically, what is rational and what is irrational is no simple matter. For example, Jung observes that apparent rationality may be mere rationalization, or bias:

> The very rationality of the judgment may even be the worst prejudice, since we call reasonable what appears reasonable to us. What appears to us unreasonable is therefore doomed to be excluded because of its irrational character. It may really be irrational, but may equally well merely appear irrational without actually being so when seen from another standpoint.
>
> ([1916]/1957, *CW* 8: par. 137)

Similarly, Max Weber says that "what is rational from one point of view may well be irrational from another" (1992: 26).

It is an exceptional economist who is enough of a psychologist to include any consideration of irrational motives. Robert J. Shiller is one such economist. He employs the term "irrational exuberance," which he derives from remarks by Alan Greenspan, Chairman of the Federal Reserve Board, in 1996. Shiller defines the term as "wishful thinking on the part of investors" (2006: xvii). (This is similar to the Freudian notion that all dreams are wish-fulfillments.) Shiller says that irrational exuberance is a "useful name" for those historically recurrent instances when the economy rises "up to unusually high and unsustainable levels under the influence of market psychology" (2006: 1). Not all economic excesses are a function of economic crazes. For example, the irrational exuberance of the 1990s, Shiller says, is "not the kind of investor euphoria or madness" that economists have ascribed to previous "speculative excesses." Investors who are irrationally exuberant are not insane. "Irrational exuberance," Shiller emphasizes, "is not *that* crazy." It is merely, he says, "the kind of bad judgment we all remember having made at some point in our lives when our enthusiasm got the best of us" (2006: 2). Irrational exuberance is a recurrent factor in what Shiller calls the "ups and downs" of the economy (2006: 172).

The Icarus Paradox and the Icarus Effect

It is not just individuals who may fly too high and then crash. So may institutions – for example, the stock market, as in the "Wall Street Crash" of

1929. So, too, may corporations fly too high and then crash. In this respect, two recent books by economists explicity invoke the myth of Icarus.

In *The Icarus Paradox*, Danny Miller notes that it was the wings of Icarus that "gave rise to the abandon that so doomed him." Paradoxically, Miller says, "his greatest asset led to his demise." As Miller defines the "Icarus paradox," corporations frequently experience a crash when success leads to excess and then to failure. Miller says that "their victories and their strengths often seduce them into the excesses that cause their downfall." This tendency, he says, leads to "falling sales, plummeting profits, even bankruptcy" (1990: 3). Miller says that "overconfident, complacent executives extend the very factors that contributed to success to the point where they cause decline." He says that "Icarus flew so well that he got cocky and overambitious" (1990: 18) – and so do corporations.

In *Icarus in the Boardroom*, David Skeel describes Icarus as a "risk-taker" (2005: 4). In this respect, Icarus is not only a high-flying hero but also a risk-taking hero. Skeel calls this tendency the "Icarus effect." He says that when an entrepreneur emulates Icarus and risks everything – for example, "puts every dollar he or she has or can borrow into an Internet innovation" – and then "loses everything," the effect may not extend "much further than a few family and friends." When, however, an executive risks all the assets of a corporation and then loses them all, the effect extends much, much further. "Put Icarus in the boardroom and everything changes," Skeel says. "The ability to tap huge amounts of capital in enterprises that adopt the corporate form, together with the large number of people whose livelihood depends in one way or another on the business, means that the stakes are extraordinarily high if Icarus is running a major corporation." The executive who emulates Icarus and "who takes excessive or fraudulent risks with a large corporation," he notes, "may jeopardize the financial lives of thousands of employees, investors, and suppliers of the business" (2005: 5). Skeel says that not only "excessive and sometimes fraudulent risks" but also "competition" and "size and complexity" are the three factors that lead to the failure of corporations (2005: 6). He refers to "crashes that fit this pattern as Icarus Effect failures" (2005: 7).

As a scandalous instance of corporate excess, Skeel mentions Enron and Kenneth L. Lay. He cites Lay as a notorious example of an executive with Icarian tendencies. After the bankruptcy of Enron, Lay was convicted of fraud but died before he could be sentenced. In an obituary, Vikas Bajaj and Kurt Eichenwald say that Bill Burton, an attorney who had known Lay for over a decade, "compared Mr. Lay to Icarus, the figure in Greek mythology who was given wings made of feather and wax but fell into the sea when he flew too close to the sun." In the mythological narratives of Enron and Lay, Burton said, the tragic flaw was pride. "'The Enron and Ken Lay stories are best told in an English literature class, or a classics class,' Mr. Burton told an interviewer in 2002, 'where you are trying to explain what hubris is all about'" (2006).

The Icarus Allusion and the Economic Crisis of 2008

A politician who is "high on himself" (or, if he is an ideologue, so high on ideas that he experiences a flight of ideas) is susceptible to flying too close to the sun. In this respect, Obama aspires to become a hero stylistically different not only from politicians who slay monsters, giants, dragons, and fathers but also from politicians who fly too high and then burn and crash.

Icarus is an example of what Michael Balint calls a "philobat." A philobat is a thrill-seeker. Icarus is not only a high-flying hero but also a thrill-seeking hero. What thrills the philobat is danger. As Balint says, "We understand now why the thrill is the greater the farther we dare get away from safety – in distance, in speed, or in exposure; that is to say, the more we can prove our independence" (1959: 29). In just this way, Icarus is a son who distances himself from his father in order to prove his independence. As a philobat, Icarus also assumes that he possesses the necessary skill to experience the thrill and not to suffer any disastrous consequences. "The philobat apparently firmly believes," Balint says, "that his skill will be sufficient to cope with all hazards and dangers, and that everything will turn out all right in the end" (1959: 83).

Although Obama sees himself in terms of Icarus, he does not identify himself with Icarus. In fact, he disidentifies himself from Icarus – quite consciously. To Obama, Icarus is no hero to emulate. For him, the myth of Icarus is a cautionary tale about the exercise of restraint. It is about moderation, not extremism. As a politician, Obama does not appear to be either a risk-taking hero or a thrill-seeking hero. He does not believe that "the sky's the limit" – an idiom that means there is "no upper limit" (Makkai, Boatner, and Gates 2004: 324), or "no limit (to ambition, aspirations, expense, or the like)" (Ammer 1997: 589).

Obama does not aspire to become an Icarus, and it is improbable that he will get carried away on the wings of ambition, fly too close to the sun, and then burn and crash. He is ambitious, but not excessively so. In what I might call the "Icarus allusion," Obama is quite conscious that "Icarus can be alluded to as someone who fails because of excessive ambition" (Delahunty, Dignen, and Stock 2001: 11).

The myth of Icarus does not say not to fly – it says not to fly too high (or too low). The moral of the story is to fly just high enough and not fall. The myth emphasizes what Hillman calls "the inherent difficulties of flying" (1995: 141). In this respect, it remains to be seen whether Obama will be a too-high-flying hero, a too-low-flying hero, or a high-enough-flying hero.

When Obama assumed the office of president on January 20, 2009, he immediately addressed the economic crisis of 2008. He tried to get off to a "flying start" – an idiom that means an "initial advantage" or a "good beginning" that "takes one some way towards the completion of a race, journey, or any other enterprise" (Cowie, Mackin, and McCaig 1983: 193).

A month and a half later, however, on March 5, 2009, the Dow Jones Industrial Average fell 281.40 points to close at 6,594.44 – 53 per cent lower than the record high on October 9, 2007. The *New York Times* described the situation as "A Continuing Free Fall" (Anonymous, 2009).

To address the economic crisis, Obama authorized the expenditure of $787 billion and proposed an additional expenditure of $275 billion. The total was over $1 trillion – a very high figure but a figure that, even so, some economists worried might be too low. Paul Krugman, recipient of the 2008 Nobel Prize in economics, wondered whether Obama would be, in effect, "up" to what was necessary under the circumstances. The situation was so extreme, Krugman argued, that moderate measures simply would not suffice. In such dire circumstances, he said, only a radical intervention would be effective. Krugman worried that the program that Obama advocated to address the economic crisis "isn't going to fly" (2009).

Obama obviously wants the program to succeed, or to "fly." In this respect, there are two political "wings" in America, the "right wing" of conservative Republicans and the "left wing" of liberal Democrats. Obama wants the program to fly not on one wing but on two wings, on both political wings. He wants the effort to address the economic crisis to be bipartisan. He does not want just to "wing it" with liberal Democrats. What Obama prefers is pragmatic consensus, not ideological conflict. (In spite of this preference, it is a fact that, at least so far, no conservative Republicans have supported the effort by Obama to address the economic crisis. Not one Republican in the House of Representatives and only three moderate or liberal Republicans in the Senate voted to approve the $787 billion expenditure.)

Regulation and Restraint

Half a century ago, Daniel Bell proclaimed the "end of ideology." He declared that "there is today a rough consensus among intellectuals on political issues." For example, Bell said, few conservatives still insisted that the government "should play no role in the economy." He said that both conservatives and liberals now concurred that "a system of mixed economy" was necessary (1960: 373). Since then, however, there has been a resurgence of radical (or reactionary) ideology among conservatives.

Since Ronald Reagan, Republicans have tried to abolish the system of mixed economy that Franklin Roosevelt introduced to address the economic crisis of the Great Depression. They have advocated privatization of the economy, on the assumption that there is no public interest that the private sector cannot serve (and serve much more efficiently than the public sector can). The notion is that the government should play no role in the economy – that, at least in terms of the economy, the best government is not just the least government but no government at all, that business is no business of government. The most radical version of this position is not just conservative but libertarian or even anarchistic.

Republicans have also advocated deregulation of the economy, on the supposition that any intervention by the government in the economy is, by definition, interference – an intrusion that is not only utterly unnecessary, superfluous, and gratuitous but also invariably detrimental. Democrats – among them, liberal Democrats – have colluded with conservative Republicans in this effort. (An especially egregious example of this collusion was the repeal, in 1999, of the Glass-Steagall Act of 1933, which had separated commercial banks from investment banks.) In this deregulation of the economy, both Republicans and Democrats have been negligently permissive. (In recent years, the Securities and Exchange Commission, the most important agency accountable for regulation of the stock market, has also been irresponsibly lenient. For example, it did not properly investigate complaints about Bernard L. Madoff, who for twenty years operated a $50–65 billion Ponzi scheme and finally pleaded guilty to committing fraud, theft, and perjury and laundering money. Madoff, of course, opposed regulation.)

The definition of "regulation" is "restraint." Republicans (with the complicity of Democrats) have systematically tried to remove every restraint on the economy. The consequence has been a high-flying economy – one that has flown too high, flown too close to the sun, and that, if it has not yet burned and crashed, has fallen perilously low.

Galbraith says that intrinsic to "the speculative episode is the euphoria, the mass escape from reality, that excludes any serious contemplation of the true nature of what is taking place." He identifies two factors that contribute to euphoria. The first factor, he says, is "the extreme brevity of the financial memory." Galbraith says that "financial disaster is quickly forgotten," with the result that the errors of the past tend to be repeated in the present. "There can be few fields of human endeavor," he says, "in which history counts for so little as in the world of finance." The second factor, Galbraith says, is "the specious association of money and intelligence" (1990: 12). The fallacy is, the more money, the more intelligence. The assumption, Galbraith says, is that the mere possession of money necessarily implies "some special genius" (1990: 13). In combination, these two factors tend recurrently to render an economy unconscious – or, as Galbraith says, euphoric and insane. "Recurrent descent into insanity is not," he sardonically remarks, "a wholly attractive feature of capitalism" (1990: 79).

Merely to state, as Galbraith does, that the financial memory is extremely brief is not to analyze the problem psychologically. I would emphasize that, from a psychoanalytic perspective, when financial disaster is not remembered, it may not just be "forgotten" – it may be *repressed*. Financially, there is no apparent profit in remembering economic crises. In fact, there is every incentive to repress that history – to relegate it to the unconscious, to consign it to oblivion.

The solution, Galbraith says, is not regulation. "Regulation outlawing financial incredulity or mass euphoria is not a practical possibility," he says. "If applied generally to such human condition, the result would be an impressive, perhaps oppressive, and certainly ineffective body of law." Ultimately, Galbraith says, the only practical solution is "skepticism that would resolutely associate too evident optimism with probable foolishness" (1990: 80).

Although a vigilantly skeptical attitude as a deterrent against folly is a splendid notion, it does not seem to me to be a viable alternative to regulation. Just as it is not feasible to legislate morality, it is not feasible to legislate mood (for example, to outlaw euphoria). As Galbraith says, any such attempt would be an exercise in futility. That, however, is not the issue. Rather, the issue is whether and, if so, how to regulate (or restrain) certain economic activities so as to mitigate the cyclical highs and lows of what W.W. Rostow (who famously employs an image of flight, the "take-off," to describe the dynamics of economic growth) calls "the upswing and the downswing" (1962: 19). Regulation is simply a moderation of economic extremism by the imposition of restraint on the conduct of individuals (as well as institutions and corporations) who episodically experience such exhilaration that they exhibit radically Icarian tendencies. The purpose of regulation is not to "clip the wings" of the economy but to curtail moody excesses.

The Apollonian Maxims: "Know Thyself" and "Nothing in Excess"

In this respect, it is fortuitous that in the current economic crisis America has a president who does not identify himself with the archetype of the high-flying hero but who quite consciously disidentifies himself from it. Obama appears to have an ego that is more Apollonian than Icarian (or Phaethonian).

The maxims of Apollo are "Know thyself" and "Nothing in excess." Obama seems to know himself (or, from a psychoanalytic perspective, to be quite conscious of himself). He also seems not to be especially prone, even under stress, to anything in excess. Jung notes that the Apollonian style entails an appreciation "of measure, of controlled and proportioned feelings" (1921, *CW* 6: par. 236). In this respect, Obama appears to be prudent rather than impulsive or compulsive. Temperamentally, he seems to have a disposition (and the discipline) to explore practical solutions to actual problems. He seems to have an ego that is more pragmatic than ideological – more heuristic than hubristic. (Perhaps Obama has a tragic flaw, but, if so, pride does not seem to be it.) Obama exudes poise. He appears to possess the equanimity necessary to address a crisis. Of course, composure is no substitute for competence – and it remains to be seen just how capable as a president Obama will ultimately be.

In the pantheon of what Hillman aptly calls "polytheistic psychology" (1981), Apollo is neither the only god nor the god for every occasion. Different gods have different specializations and different proficiencies. The expertise of one god may be very different from that of another god. From a Jungian perspective, a god is not a literal, metaphysical entity in a supernatural dimension but a "god," a metaphorical, psychic factor – an archetypal image in the mythological unconscious. In the current economic crisis, however, Apollo may be the most apposite god (or archetypal image) for Obama to invoke as he attempts to perform a political task of truly heroic proportions. As Phoebus, Apollo does, after all, know how to drive the chariot of the sun across the sky.

"The road of excess," William Blake says, "leads to the palace of wisdom" (1976: 150). Perhaps, in this instance, it also leads, ironically, from Wall Street and the New York Stock Exchange to Pennsylvania Avenue and the White House. In contrast to the high-flying heroes who indulged in such speculative excess in recent years, Obama now has an opportunity to be wise – to deal with the current situation in ways that, not only in style but also in substance, differ radically from the unwise practices that led to what is, by all accounts, the most serious economic crisis since the Great Depression.

References

Adams, M.V. (1992) "My Imaginal Hillman; or, 'James, I'll See You in My Dreams,'" Boulder, CO: Sounds True Recordings: audiotape.

Adams, M.V. (2004a) *The Fantasy Principle: Psychoanalysis of the Imagination*, Hove: Brunner-Routledge.

Adams, M.V. (2004b) "An Interview with Maury Maverick, Jr.," in C. Miller (ed.), *Fifty Years of the Texas Observer*, San Antonio, TX: Trinity University Press: 54–61.

Adams, M.V. (2008) "Imaginology: The Jungian Study of the Imagination," in S. Marlan (ed.), *Archetypal Psychologies: Reflections in Honor of James Hillman*, New Orleans: Spring Journal Books: 225–42.

Adams, M.V. (2010) *The Mythological Unconscious*, 2nd rev. ed., Putnam, CT: Spring Publications.

American Psychiatric Association (1994) *The Diagnostic and Statistical Manual of Mental Disorders: Fourth Edition*, Washington, DC: American Psychiatric Association.

Ammer, C. (ed.) (1997) *The American Heritage Dictionary of Idioms*, Boston: Houghton Mifflin.

Anonymous (March 6, 2009) "A Continuing Free Fall," *The New York Times*: B7.

Axelrod, D. (January 26, 2009) *Charlie Rose*, PBS/WNET.

Bachelard, G. (1988) *Air and Dreams: An Essay on the Imagination of Movement*, trans. E.R. Farrell and C.F. Farrell, Dallas: Dallas Institute Publications.

Bajaj, V., and Eichenwald, K. (July 6, 2006) "Kenneth L. Lay, 64, Enron Founder and Symbol of Corporate Excess, Dies," *The New York Times*: C7.

Balint, M. (1959) *Thrills and Regressions*, New York: International Universities Press.

Bell, D. (1960) *The End of Ideology: On the Exhaustion of Political Ideas in the Fifties*, Glencoe, IL: The Free Press.

Blake, W. (1976) *The Marriage of Heaven and Hell*, in *Blake: Complete Writings with Variant Readings*, ed. G. Keynes, London: Oxford University Press: 148–60.

Campbell, J. (1968) *The Hero with a Thousand Faces*, Princeton, NJ: Princeton University Press.

Campbell, J., with Moyers, B. (1988) *The Power of Myth*, ed. B.S. Flowers, New York: Doubleday.

Chapman, R.L. (ed.) (1995) *Dictionary of American Slang*, New York: HarperCollins.

Cowie, A.P., Mackin, R., and McCaig, I.R. (eds.) (1983) *Oxford Dictionary of Current Idiomatic English: Volume 2: Phrase, Clause & Sentence Idioms*, Oxford: Oxford University Press.

Delahunty, A., Dignen, S., and Stock, P. (2001) *The Oxford Dictionary of Allusions*, Oxford: Oxford University Press.

Dowd, M. (1992) "Of Knights and Presidents: Race of Mythic Proportions," *The New York Times*: A1 and A9.

Dowd, M. (January 7, 2001) "Pappy and Poppy," *The New York Times*, Week in Review Section: 17.

Dowd, M. (April 30, 2008) "Praying and Preying," *The New York Times*: A19.

Dowd, M. (July 20, 2008) "Ich Bin Ein Jet-Setter," *The New York Times*: Week in Review Section: 13.

Dowd, M. (July 30, 2008) "Cyclops and Cunning," *The New York Times*: A17.

Flowers, B.S. (2000) "Practicing Politics in the Economic Myth," in T. Singer (ed.), *The Vision Thing: Myth, Politics and Psyche in the World*, London and New York: Routledge: 207–12.

Freud, S. (1900) *The Interpretation of Dreams*, SE 4.

Freud, S. (1910) *Leonardo da Vinci and a Memory of His Childhood*, SE 11: 63–137.

Freud, S. (1933 [1932]) *New Introductory Lectures on Psycho-Analysis*, SE 22: 1–182.

Galbraith, J.K. (1990) *A Short History of Financial Euphoria*, Knoxville, TN: Whittle Direct Books.

Hamilton, E. (1942) *The Greek Way*, New York: W.W. Norton.

Heacock, P. (ed.) (2003) *Cambridge Dictionary of American Idioms*, Cambridge: Cambridge University Press.

Hillman, J. (1979) "Peaks and Vales: The Soul/Spirit Distinction as Basis for the Differences between Psychotherapy and Spiritual Discipline," in J. Hillman (ed.), *Puer Papers*, Irving, TX: Spring Publications: 54–74.

Hillman, J. (1981) "Psychology: Monotheistic or Polytheistic," in D.L. Miller, *The New Polytheism: Rebirth of the Gods and Goddesses*, Dallas: Spring Publications: 109–42.

Hillman, J., with Pozzo, L. (1983) *Inter Views: Conversations with Laura Pozzo on Psychotherapy, Biography, Love, Soul, Dreams, Work, Imagination, and the State of the Culture*, New York: Harper & Row.

Hillman, J. (1995) "Oedipus Revisited," in K. Kerényi and J. Hillman, *Oedipus Variations: Studies in Literature and Psychoanalysis*, Woodstock, CT: Spring Publications: 87–169.

Hillman, J. (2001) *Farewell Welfare*, Buffalo, NY: Analytical Psychology Club of Western New York.

Joseph Campbell and the Power of Myth (2001), Mystic Fire Video: DVD.

Jung, C.G. (1916/1948) "General Aspects of Dream Psychology," *CW* 8: 237–80.

Jung, C.G. ([1916]/1957) "The Transcendent Function," *CW* 8: 67–91.

Jung, C.G. (1921) *Psychological Types*, *CW* 6.

Jung, C.G. (1928) *The Relations between the Ego and the Unconscious*, *CW* 7: 121–241.

Jung, C.G. (1945/1948) "On the Nature of Dreams," *CW* 8: 281–97.

Jung, C.G. (1977) "Does the World Stand on the Verge of a Spiritual Rebirth?" in *C.G. Jung Speaking: Interviews and Encounters*, ed. W. McGuire and R.F.C. Hull, Princeton, NJ: Princeton University Press: 67–75.

Kindleberger, C.P. (1989) *Manias, Panics, and Crises: A History of Financial Crises*, New York: Basic Books.

King, L.L. (1999) *Larry L. King: A Writer's Life in Letters, or Reflections in a Bloodshot Eye*, ed. R.A. Holland, Fort Worth, TX: TCU Press.

Kirk, G.S. (1974) *The Nature of Greek Myths*, Harmondsworth: Penguin Books.

Krugman, P. (March 6, 2009) "The Big Dither," *The New York Times*: A27.

Lawrence, L. (2002) *Private Dreams of Public People*, New York: Assouline.

Lewin, B. (1950) *Psychoanalysis of Elation*, New York: W.W. Norton.

Makkai, A., Boatner, M.T., and Gates, J.E. (eds.) (2004) *A Dictionary of American Idioms*, Hauppauge, NY: Barron's.

Marlan, S. (2005) *The Black Sun: The Alchemy and Art of Darkness*, College Station, TX: Texas A&M University Press.

Miller, D. (1990) *The Icarus Paradox: How Exceptional Companies Bring about Their Own Downfall*, New York: Harper Business.

Miller, L. and Wolffe, R. (July 21, 2008) "Finding His Faith," *Newsweek*: 27–32.

Minsky, H.P. (1982) "Financial Instability Revisited: The Economics of Disaster," in *Can "It" Happen Again? Essays on Instability and Finance*, Armonk, NY: M.E. Sharpe: 117–61.

Morris, W. (1967) *North Toward Home*, Boston: Houghton Mifflin.

Murray, H.A. (1979) "American Icarus," in J. Hillman (ed.), *Puer Papers*, Irving, TX: Spring Publications: 77–99.

Obama, B. (2006) *The Audacity of Hope: Thoughts on Reclaiming the American Dream*, New York: Crown Publishers.

Perlman, M. (1983) "Phaethon and the Thermonuclear Chariot," *Spring: An Annual of Archetypal Psychology and Jungian Thought*: 87–108.

Rostow, W.W. (1962) *The Process of Economic Growth*, New York: W.W. Norton.

Shiller, R.J. (2006) *Irrational Exuberance*, Princeton, NJ, and Oxford: Princeton University Press.

Skeel, D. (2005) *Icarus in the Boardroom: The Fundamental Flaws in Corporate America and Where They Came From*, New York: Oxford University Press.

Spears, R.A. (ed.) (2004) *McGraw-Hill's Dictionary of American Idioms and Phrasal Verbs*, New York: McGraw-Hill.

Tatham, P. (1992) *The Makings of Maleness: Men, Women, and the Flight of Daedalus*, New York: New York University Press.

Thompson, S. (1955) *Motif-Index of Folk Literature*, Bloomington, IN: Indiana University Press, 6 vols.

Weber, M. (1992) *The Protestant Ethic and the Spirit of Capitalism*, trans. T. Parsons, London: Routledge.

Winstanley, D. (2004) "Phaethon: Seizing the Reins of Myth," in Y. Gabriel (ed.), *Myths, Stories, and Organization: Premodern Narratives for Our Times*, Oxford: Oxford University Press: 176–91.

Literary and Artistic Applications

9

GETTING A KICK OUT OF
CAPTAIN AHAB

The Merman Dream in *Moby-Dick*

Interpreting a literary dream might seem merely an idle exercise. Freud, however, expresses a special interest in "the class of dreams that have never been dreamt at all – dreams created by imaginative writers and ascribed to invented characters in the course of a story." Although he acknowledges that "submitting this class of dreams to an investigation might seem a waste of energy and a strange thing to undertake," he says that "from one point of view it could be considered justifiable" (1907 [1906], *SE* 9: 7). What is this point of view?

"It is far," Freud says, "from being generally believed that dreams have a meaning and can be interpreted" (1907 [1906], *SE* 9: 7). To demonstrate that literary dreams have a meaning, he asserts, would tend to corroborate the psychoanalytic proposition that dreams have a meaning. Exactly why this should be so, Freud never explicitly says. Logically, the notion is a *non sequitur*. Even if a literary dream – a dream that has been created by an imaginative writer and ascribed to an invented character – has a meaning, it does not necessarily follow, as a matter of course, that a dream that has been dreamed has a meaning.

Freud, however, contends that literary dreams provide independent evidence that dreams have a meaning and can be interpreted. In this respect, he says that "creative writers are valuable allies and their evidence is to be prized highly, for they are apt to know a whole host of things between heaven and earth of which our philosophy has not yet let us dream." According to Freud, creative writers have anticipated what psychoanalysts have only begun to discover by another, more systematic method. "In their knowledge of the mind," he says, "they are far in advance of us everyday people, for they draw upon sources which we have not yet opened up for science." What so impresses Freud also exasperates him: "If only this support given by writers in favour of dreams having a meaning were less ambiguous!" (1907 [1906], *SE* 9: 8).

One writer who does give unambiguous support to dreams (or at least literary dreams) having a meaning is Herman Melville. *Moby-Dick*, which Jung considers "the greatest American novel" (1930/1950, *CW* 15: par. 137), includes an especially impressive example of a literary dream. Shortly before

Captain Ahab vows to dismember the White Whale as the White Whale has dismembered him, Stubb, the second mate, has a dream. The next morning, Stubb recounts the dream to Flask, the third mate. This is what I call the "Merman Dream":

Such a queer dream, King-Post, I never had. You know the old man's ivory leg, well I dreamed he kicked me with it; and when I tried to kick back, upon my soul, my little man, I kicked my leg right off! And then, presto! Ahab seemed a pyramid, and I, like a blazing fool, kept kicking at it. But what was still more curious, Flask – you know how curious all dreams are – through all this rage that I was in, I somehow seemed to be thinking to myself, that after all, it was not much of an insult, that kick from Ahab. "Why," thinks I, "what's the row? It's not a real leg, only a false leg." And there's a mighty difference between a living thump and a dead thump. That's what makes a blow from the hand, Flask, fifty times more savage to bear than a blow from a cane. The living member – that makes the living insult, my little man. And thinks I to myself all the while, mind, while I was stubbing my silly toes against that cursed pyramid – so confoundedly contradictory was it all, all the while, I say, I was thinking to myself, "what's his leg now, but a cane – a whalebone cane. Yes," thinks I, "it was only a playful cudgelling – in fact, only a whaleboning that he gave me – not a base kick. Besides," thinks I, "look at it once; why, the end of it – the foot part – what a small sort of end it is; whereas, if a broad footed farmer kicked me, *there's* a devilish broad insult. But this insult is whittled down to a point only." But now comes the greatest joke of the dream, Flask. While I was battering away at the pyramid, a sort of badger-haired old merman, with a hump on his back, takes me by the shoulders, and slews me round. "What are you 'bout?" says he, 'Slid! man, but I was frightened. Such a phiz! But, somehow, next moment I was over the fright. "What am I about?" says I at last. "And what business is that of yours, I should like to know, Mr. Humpback? Do *you* want a kick?" By the lord, Flask, I had no sooner said that, than he turned round his stern to me, bent over, and dragging up a lot of sea-weed he had for a clout – what do you think, I saw? – why thunder alive, man, his stern was stuck full of marlinspikes, with the points out. Says I, on second thoughts, "I guess I won't kick you, old fellow." "Wise Stubb," said he, "wise Stubb;" and kept muttering it all the time, a sort of eating of his own gums like a chimney hag. Seeing he wasn't going to stop saying over his "wise Stubb, wise Stubb," I thought I might as well fall to kicking the pyramid again. But I had only just lifted my foot for it, when he roared out, "Stop that kicking!" "Halloa," says I, "what's the matter now, old fellow?" "Look ye here," says he; "let's

argue the insult. Captain Ahab kicked ye, didn't he?" "Yes, he did," says I – "right *here* it was." "Very good," says he – "he used his ivory leg, didn't he?" "Yes, he did," says I. "Well then," says he, "wise Stubb, what have you to complain of? Didn't he kick with right good will? it wasn't a common pitch pine leg he kicked with, was it? No, you were kicked by a great man, and with a beautiful ivory leg, Stubb. It's an honor; I consider it an honor. Listen, wise Stubb. In old England the greatest lords think it great glory to be slapped by a queen, and made garter-knights of; but, be *your* boast, Stubb, that ye were kicked by old Ahab, and made a wise man of. Remember what I say; *be* kicked by him; account his kicks honors; and on no account kick back; for you can't help yourself, wise Stubb. Don't you see that pyramid?" With that, he all of a sudden seemed somehow, in some queer fashion, to swim off into the air. I snored; rolled over; and there I was in my hammock! Now, what do you think of that dream, Flask?
(Melville 1988: 131–2)

Flask replies that he does not know what to think of the dream, although "it seems a sort of foolish to me." Be that as it may, Stubb says that "it's made a wise man of me." What would be wise, he advises Flask, is to avoid Ahab – "to let that old man alone; never speak quick to him, whatever he says" (Melville 1988: 132).

The night of the dream, Stubb has an altercation with Ahab. What occasions the incident is a suggestion, which Stubb intends as a joke but which Ahab interprets as an insult. Most nights – out of consideration for the sailors sleeping below deck, "within six inches of his ivory heel" – Ahab refrains from pacing up and down, Ishmael says, for "such would have been the reverberating crack and din of that bony step, that their dreams would have been of the crunching teeth of sharks." This night, however, the sound of Ahab's heel so disturbs the sailors' sleep that Stubb approaches Ahab and, "with a certain unassured, deprecating humorousness," suggests that "there might be some way of muffling the noise." He hints that Ahab might insert his heel into "a globe of tow" (Melville 1988: 127). From the perspective of a cripple, this attempt at comic relief is incredibly cruel ridicule. To Ahab, the loss of his leg is no laughing matter. What to Stubb is a joke is to Ahab an insult.

Ahab orders Stubb to go below deck. He curses and threatens him. "Down, dog, and kennel!" Ahab shouts. Stubb replies: "I am not used to be spoken to in that way, sir; I do but less than half like it, sir." Ahab again orders him to go below deck. "No, sir, not yet," Stubb replies, "I will not tamely be called a dog, sir." In spite of the polite form of address, what Stubb says infuriates Ahab. "Then be called ten times a donkey, and a mule, and an ass," Ahab shouts, "and begone, or I'll clear the world of thee!" (Melville 1988: 127). As Stubb goes below deck, he compulsively repeats the experience: "But how's that? Didn't he call me a dog? blazes! he called me ten times a donkey, and piled a lot of jackasses on top of *that*! He might as well have kicked me, and done with it. Maybe he *did* kick me, and I didn't observe it." The entire affair seems unreal to Stubb. "I must," he says, "have been dreaming." Finally, he resolves to forget it, or "stash it," and go to sleep (Melville 1988: 128). As Stubb sleeps, however, he dreams. In a return of the repressed, the dream elaborates the traumatic experience of being kicked by Ahab, being cursed and threatened by him – that is, being insulted by him – and being too intimidated to kick back.

For Freud, dreams have a meaning, and that meaning is a wish-fulfillment. From a Freudian perspective, this dream fulfills a wish to kick Ahab back. The consequence of kicking back, however, is that Stubb kicks his own leg off. A Freudian interpretation would regard this amputation as a castration. Such an interpretation is plausible to the extent that the humiliation of Stubb by Ahab is an emasculation – but there is more to the dream than that. The dream serves another purpose than the fulfillment of a wish – it is an ironic commentary on the wisdom of being kicked and the folly of kicking back.

The moral of the dream is that *whatever the intent may be, an insult is not, in effect, an insult unless it is considered to be an insult.* This logic is not immediately evident to Stubb. He has to argue the insult with the merman before he finally accepts the proposition that *interpretation is a consideration.* When is a joke a joke, when is an insult an insult? When is a joke an insult, a curse, a threat, and a kick? What does it mean to get a kick out of a joke, out of an insult?

In the first part of the dream, Stubb is implicitly identified with Ahab – and Ahab with the White Whale. That is, as Ahab is to the White Whale, so Stubb is to Ahab. Stubb occupies precisely the same position in relation to Ahab that Ahab occupies in relation to the White Whale. Stubb is kicked by Ahab, and when Stubb kicks Ahab back, he kicks his own leg off. Ahab does not bite Stubb's leg off as the White Whale has bitten Ahab's leg off, but Stubb loses his leg just as Ahab has lost his leg. Like Ahab, Stubb loses his leg, but only because he kicks back and kicks his leg off. In the dream, Ahab suddenly becomes a pyramid, and Stubb starts kicking the pyramid – with ludicrous agility, kicking simultaneously with and on only one leg. Although in kicking the pyramid he does not kick his other leg off, Stubb does stub his toes.

What follows is an attempt at rationalization. Stubb reasons that the kick from Ahab was an insult but not much of an insult. It was not a real leg, only a false leg – not a live kick, only a dead kick. A blow from a live member – a hand, for example, and also presumably a leg – is much harder to bear than a blow, say, from a cane. Ahab's leg is a dead member, a whalebone. Stubb was not properly kicked or insulted – he was sportively caned or whaleboned. That is, the insult is a false or dead issue. Similarly, Stubb reasons that the kick from Ahab was an insult but not a broad insult. It was not a broad kick because the end of Ahab's leg is not a broad foot but a point only – a moot point.

In the second part of the dream, when the merman appears, he has a hump on his back. He asks Stubb why he is kicking the pyramid. Stubb tells the merman to mind his own business. Again, Stubb is implicitly identified with Ahab, for earlier, when Stubb suggests that Ahab might insert his ivory heel into a globe of tow, Ahab tells Stubb, in so many words, to mind his own business. Like the exchange between Ahab and Stubb, the exchange between Stubb and the merman includes a curse and a threat. Stubb calls the merman "Mr. Humpback" and asks: "Do *you* want a kick?" He makes fun of the merman, who is deformed, just as he has made fun of Ahab, who is disabled. Unlike Ahab and Stubb, however, the merman does not consider the curse and the threat an insult. The merman merely turns around and bends over – as if to say, kick me and see what you get out of it. His rear is full of marlinspikes, with the points sticking out. Rather than kick the merman and spike his foot, Stubb falls to kicking the pyramid again. At that, the merman insists that he stop kicking and "argue the insult."

What follows is another attempt at rationalization. The kick by Ahab was not, the merman reasons, an insult at all. Rather, it was an aesthetic experience. Stubb was not kicked by an ordinary wooden leg – he was kicked by a beautiful ivory leg. Not only that, it was a royal honor. Being kicked by Ahab was like being knighted by the queen of England. The merman says: "It's an honor; I consider it an honor." That is, whatever Ahab may have intended, all that really matters is how Stubb considers it. The merman gives Stubb some advice – be kicked and never kick back, "for you can't help yourself." By kicking back, Stubb can only hurt himself. He will only kick his leg off, stub his toes, or spike his foot.

Similarly, after Stubb recounts the dream, he advises Flask to avoid Ahab, "to let that old man alone; never speak quick to him, whatever he says." That advice, which Stubb says has made him a wise man, is the moral of what seems to Flask only a rather foolish dream. Stubb should leave Ahab well enough alone, or worse will happen to him. Injury will be added to insult, and the responsibility, or fault, will not be Ahab's – it will be Stubb's for kicking back. Stubb should not kick back at Ahab – that is, should not talk back to him, whatever he may say.

It is possible to interpret the dream as Freud would have, as a dream in which Stubb fulfills a wish to kick Ahab back. At least one literary dream would have a meaning – and not just any meaning but the very meaning, the fulfillment of a wish, that Freud contends all dreams always have. From this perspective, Melville would have anticipated, half a century before Freud, how wishes are fulfilled in dreams. It is also possible, however, to interpret the dream as Jung would have – not as a wish-fulfillment but as an attitude-compensation. According to Jung, dreams emerge from the unconscious to compensate a partial, prejudicial, or defective attitude of the ego. From a Jungian perspective, the dream does not fulfill a wish to kick Ahab back but compensates that attitude. In the dream, the unconscious presents various alternative perspectives for Stubb to consider. Stubb could, if he only would, consider the kick by Ahab not an insult but a false or dead issue, a moot point, an aesthetic experience, or a royal honor – and not kick back.

To demonstrate how the dream functions as a literary device in *Moby-Dick* and what the dream contributes to the plot of the novel, it is necessary to interpret specific images in the dream – for example, the images of the pyramid and the merman. Why a pyramid, and why a merman? A pyramid is an especially apt image of the futility – and the folly – of kicking back. Kicking a pyramid is tantamount to butting a wall. In this respect, Ahab says that the White Whale "is that wall, shoved near to me" (Melville 1988: 164). But there is, again, more to the dream than that. The White Whale has a "pyramidical white hump" on its back (Melville 1988: 183). When, in the dream, Ahab is suddenly transformed into a pyramid, he is implicitly identified with the White Whale. The White Whale is, of course, a sperm whale, not a humpback whale – yet, it is, in another sense, a humpback whale. The pyramidical hump on the White Whale's back is identified with the hump on the merman's back. Ahab, too, has a hump on his back. At one point in the novel, Ahab disparages Starbuck, the first mate, who does not respect him as the captain of a whaling ship but "takes me for the hunchbacked skipper of some coasting smack" (Melville 1988: 509). ("Hunch" and "hunchback" are synonyms for "hump" and "humpback.") The White Whale, which is identified with Ahab by means of the image of the pyramid, is also implicitly identified, by means of the image of the humpback, not only with Ahab but also with the merman.

The image of the merman appears again when Pip, the cabin boy, jumps overboard, in a panic, from one of the whaleboats. In pursuit of a whale that they have harpooned, Stubb and the other sailors leave Pip far behind. Pip experiences what Freud calls "a sensation of 'eternity', a feeling as of something limitless, unbounded – as it were, 'oceanic'" (1930 [1929], *SE* 21: 64). Ishmael remarks that, "in calm weather, to swim in the open ocean" is easy enough. "But the awful lonesomeness is intolerable," he says. "The intense concentration of self in the middle of such a heartless immensity, my God! who can tell it?" (Melville 1988: 414). Surely not Pip. For Pip, all alone on the vast expanse of the sea and desperately uncertain of rescue, the feeling is not only oceanic but also traumatic – so much so that it renders him insane. Physically, Pip floats on the surface of the sea, but, psychically, he sinks to incredible depths, to the very bottom of the ocean – or, Jung would say, the collective unconscious. Ishmael says of Pip:

> The sea had jeeringly kept his finite body up, but drowned the infinite of his soul. Not drowned entirely, though. Rather carried down alive to wondrous depths, where strange shapes of the unwarped primal world glided to and fro before his passive eyes; and the miser-merman, Wisdom, revealed his hoarded heaps.
>
> (Melville 1988: 414)

From a Jungian perspective, the hoarded heaps that the miser-merman, in the name of Wisdom, reveals to Pip are an image of the archetype of "value." (By definition, a "miser" is someone who hoards what is valuable.) Jung mentions "the hoard, the 'treasure hard to attain,'" when he discusses the myth of the hero (1955–56, *CW* 14: par. 756). "An archetypal content," Jung says, "expresses itself, first and foremost, in metaphors." Among the metaphors that he mentions is "the hoard of gold" (1940, *CW* 9, 1: par. 267).

In *Moby-Dick*, the image of the hoard of gold is identified with the gold doubloon that Ahab nails to the mast as a reward for the first sailor to sight the White Whale. Ishmael says of Ahab that "one morning, turning to pass the doubloon, he seemed to be newly attracted by the strange figures and inscriptions stamped on it, as though now for the first time beginning to interpret for himself in some monomaniac way whatever significance might lurk in them" (Melville 1988: 430). On the gold doubloon are images of three mountains – one with a flame on it, another with a tower on it, and another with a cock on it. These images are all, Ahab says, "egotistical." It is irrelevant to Ahab what specific images are minted on the gold doubloon, for, as he interprets them, "all are Ahab." He says of the doubloon that "this round gold is but the image of the rounder globe." The doubloon is an image of the world, which, he says, "to each and every man in turn but mirrors back his own mysterious self" (Melville 1988: 431). That is, to Ahab, all interpretation is merely a solipsistic reflection of the ego of the interpreter.

Stubb watches not only Ahab but also the other sailors as they attempt to interpret what the gold doubloon might mean. "Shall I," Stubb asks, "call that wise or foolish, now; if it be really wise it has a foolish look to it; yet, if it be really foolish, then it has a sort of wiseish look to it" (Melville 1988: 433). As he looks at the sailors who look at the gold doubloon, Stubb articulates *a psychological theory of relativity in the interpretation of texts*. "There's another rendering now; but still one text," he says. "All sorts of men in one kind of world, you see" (Melville 1988: 434). That is, *any interpretation of a text is relative to the perspective of the interpreter*, to what sort of man the interpreter is. Since there are, as Stubb says, all sorts of men, there are all sorts of interpretations, all sorts of perspectives from which to interpret a text – be it a gold doubloon or a White Whale. There is not just one meaning of any text but many meanings, as many as there are interpreters and perspectives.

Pip, who Stubb says "has been watching all of these interpreters – myself included," also attempts to interpret what the gold doubloon might mean. As Pip looks at the gold doubloon, he conjugates the verb "to look." Three times, he repeats: "I look, you look, he looks; we look, ye look, they look" (Melville 1988: 434). This grammatical exercise – in the present tense, with pronouns in the first, second, and third person, singular and plural – is a satirical commentary on the interpreters who look at the gold doubloon. Look, look, look, Pip says, look, look, look. When Pip looks, what he sees is, tautologically, what he sees. That is, it is all in who looks at the gold doubloon – *there is no perception that is not a projection*.

Stubb can tolerate the rest of the sailors, "for they have plain wits," but, as for Pip, Stubb says that "he's too crazy-witty for my sanity" (Melville 1988: 435). If Ahab ever had a sense of humor, he lost it when he lost his leg. In contrast, when Pip loses his wits, he gains wit – a facetious sense of humor. Pip is crazy, but he is also witty. There is sense in his nonsense, sanity in his insanity, wisdom in his folly.

Pip says that "when aught's nailed to the mast it's a sign that things grow desperate." He laughs: "Ha, ha! old Ahab! the White Whale; he'll nail ye!" Pip says that "when they come to fish up this old mast, and find a doubloon lodged in it," they will wonder how it got there. "Oh," he exclaims, "the gold! the precious, precious gold! – the green miser'll hoard ye soon!" (Melville 1988: 435). The miser who Pip says will soon hoard the gold doubloon is the miser-merman, Wisdom, who has previously revealed his hoarded heaps to Pip.

Pip is an image of the archetype of the fool as a wise man. Enid Welsford says that it is "the Fool who suggests that there is ambiguity in the words wisdom and folly" (1935: 256). In this respect, *Moby-Dick* is a novel of very wise follies. It epitomizes what Welsford calls "the reversal of wisdom and folly" (1935: 263–4). For Melville, what seems foolish is, paradoxically, wise. Pip is an example of what Welsford calls "the Fool who speaks the truth" (1935: 267). The question is, as Welsford says: "Which is the wise man, and which is the fool?" (1935: 268).

In *Moby-Dick*, wisdom consists in an appreciation of the folly of privileging one interpretation over all others, as if it were the one and only necessary interpretation rather than merely one possible interpretation among many. This is precisely what Stubb concludes when he argues the insult with the merman and resolves not to talk back to Ahab, no matter what Ahab may say. The implication of the dream is that Stubb could consider the kick a false or dead issue, a moot point, an aesthetic experience, or a royal honor – and decide not to kick back at Ahab. To do so, Stubb would have to be another sort of man than he is. He would have to be a wise man instead of a fool.

Melville derives and adapts the image of the merman from *Indian Antiquities*, a late-eighteenth-century study in comparative mythology by Thomas Maurice. In the late 1940s, on the basis of internal evidence, Howard P. Vincent established *Indian Antiquities* as an important source of images in *Moby-Dick* (1949: 278–80). *Indian Antiquities* includes an illustration (Figure 9.1) that Maurice identifies as "the MATSE AVATAR, or first incarnation of Veeshnu, in a form composed of man and fish" (1794, 1: 108). Maurice describes the form of the Matse Avatar as "*half man, half fish*" (1794, 1: 109). Similarly, in *Moby-Dick*, Ishmael mentions what he calls "the Hindoo whale" and describes "the incarnation of Vishnu in the form of leviathan, learnedly known as the Matse Avatar," as "half man and half whale" (Melville 1988: 261). (The first incarnation of Vishnu is conventionally spelled "Matsya Avatar," but in both *Indian Antiquities* and *Moby-Dick* it is idiosyncratically spelled "Matse Avatar.")

In *Moby-Dick*, the merman is a fishman that is a whaleman. In this respect, Ishmael mentions "Vishnoo, who, by the first of his ten earthly incarnations, has for ever set apart and sanctified the whale." He asks: "Was not this Vishnoo a whaleman, then?" (Melville 1988: 363). The incarnation of Vishnu as the Matse Avatar (or Matsya Avatar) is half man, half fish, and is, in that sense, a fishman. A whaleman is not, however, in that sense, a fishman – not, that is, half man, half fish (or half whale) – but a man who hunts, harpoons, and kills whales. When Ishmael says that Vishnu is a whaleman, he humorously conflates the two senses in a pun that is simultaneously verbal and visual.

The merman is a composite image. The upper body is that of a man, the lower body that of a fish. In *The Origin of Pagan Idolatry*, an early-nineteenth-century study in comparative mythology that I argue is another important source of images in *Moby-Dick*, George Stanley Faber says: "In the Hindoo delineation of this Avatar, Vishnou does not appear simply as a fish, but as a man issuing out of the mouth of a fish" (1816, 2: 116). Faber explicitly identifies this image as formally equivalent to a "merman" (1816, 2: 117).

In *Moby-Dick*, the image of the merman is equivalent to a man (Captain Ahab) in the act of being swallowed by a fish (the White Whale). In the composite image of the merman, Melville ingeniously epitomizes the conflict that motivates the plot. The merman in *Moby-Dick* is a version of what Jung calls the "'Jonah-and-the-Whale complex,' which," he says, "has any number of variants." Jung says that in the Jonah-and-the-Whale complex the libido, or psychic energy, regresses to the collective unconscious "where Jonah saw the 'mysteries' ('représentations collectives') in the whale's belly" (1911–12/1952, *CW* 5: par. 654). Although only a part of Ahab is swallowed, while the whole of Jonah is swallowed, the one is, *pars pro toto*, equivalent to the other.

Both Pip and Ahab are insane, and, in both instances, insanity is the result of trauma. The insanity of Ahab is, however, very different from the insanity of Pip. Ahab is monomaniacal. Monomania, the most popular diagnosis in nineteenth-century psychiatric nosology, is a fixation on one object. In this respect, the monomania of Ahab is a psychopathological preoccupation with the White Whale to the exclusion of all other objects. "It is not probable," Ishmael says of Ahab, "that this monomania in him took its instant rise at the precise time of his bodily dismemberment" (Melville 1988: 184). Rather, he says, it was probably only later, "after the encounter, that the final monomania seized him" (Melville 1988: 185). Had there been a *Diagnostic and Statistical Manual of Mental Disorders* in the early nineteenth century, Ahab would have been a paradigmatic case of "Posttraumatic Stress Disorder" (American Psychiatric Association 1994: 424–9).

From a Jungian perspective, the White Whale is an image of the archetype of the "monster," and Ahab is an image of the archetype of the "monster-slaying hero." Jung says that "if a man is a hero, he is a hero because, in the final reckoning, he did not let the monster devour him, but subdued it, not

Figure 9.1 The Matse Avatar, Thomas Maurice, *Indian Antiquities*, 1794 (illustration in vol. 1, pt. 1, opposite p. 260).

once but many times." According to Jung, "Victory over the collective psyche alone yields the true value – the capture of the hoard" (1928, *CW* 7: par. 261). The hoard is an image of the archetype of what Jung calls "the 'treasure hard to attain,' which the hero wrests from the monster" (1911–12/1952, *CW* 5: par. 482). The treasure hard to attain is, Jung says, "the highest value" (1943, *CW* 11: par. 931). In *Moby-Dick*, Ahab does not subdue the White Whale. It devours him (not physically but psychically). "Anyone," Jung says, "who identifies with the collective psyche – or, in mythological terms, lets himself be devoured by the monster – and vanishes in it, attains the treasure," although "he does so in spite of himself and to his own greatest harm" (1928, *CW* 7: par. 261).

The identification of Ahab with the White Whale is an identification with the collective psyche, or the monster. "Probably no one who was conscious of the absurdity of this identification would have the courage to make a principle of it," Jung says. "But the danger is that very many people lack the necessary humour, or else it fails them at this particular juncture; they are seized by a sort of pathos, everything seems pregnant with meaning, and all effective self-criticism is checked" (1928, *CW* 7: par. 262). The monomaniacal pursuit of the White Whale by Ahab, who lost his sense of humor when he lost his leg, is pathetic in just this sense. It is a psychotically uncritical, unconscious identification with the White Whale.

As Ahab interprets his dismemberment, it is not only an injury but also an insult. It is not so much the injury that traumatizes him as it is the interpretation of that injury as an insult. To Ahab, the loss of his leg epitomizes the idiom to "add insult to injury," a cliché that means to "make harm worse by adding humiliation" (Ammer 1992: 3). What is so insane about this interpretation is that it is so arbitrary. An injury is not *per se* an insult. The White Whale does not insult Ahab – it is Ahab who adds insult to the injury that the White Whale has inflicted.

Moby-Dick is a novel of insult and revenge. Ahab insanely interprets the loss of his leg as an insult and, as a result, monomaniacally vows revenge against the White Whale. "The prophecy was that I should be dismembered; and – Aye! I lost this leg," Ahab says. "I now prophesy that I will dismember my dismemberer" (Melville 1988: 168). (This is, of course, an example of *lex talionis* – an eye for an eye, a tooth for a tooth – or, in this instance, a member for a member.) Jung says of the prophet:

> I would not deny in general the existence of genuine prophets, but in the name of caution I would begin by doubting each individual case; for it is far too serious a matter for us lightly to accept a man as a genuine prophet. Every respectable prophet strives manfully against the unconscious pretensions of his role. When therefore a prophet appears at a moment's notice, we would be better advised to contemplate a possible psychic disequilibrium.
>
> (1928, *CW* 7: par. 262)

The psychic disequilibrium that Ahab experiences is radically psychopathological. Ahab is not a genuine prophet – he is the fanatic as a psychotic. "Uncultivated people who feel insulted," Nietzsche says, "are accustomed to set the degree of insultingness as high as possible and to recount the cause of the insult in strongly exaggerated terms, so as to be able really to revel in the feeling of hatred and revengefulness thus engendered" (1986: 43). This is a perfect description of Ahab, who feels insulted by the White Whale, revels in the feeling of hatred and revengefulness, and retaliates against the White Whale.

That the White Whale swallowed Ahab's leg is what John R. Searle calls a "brute fact," which he defines as a fact "totally independent of any human opinions" (1995: 2). Ahab, of course, has a quite specific, very personal opinion about the injury he has suffered. He considers the injury an insult. It is a brute fact that the White Whale bit his leg off. In addition, however, Ahab is of the opinion that the White Whale intended to bite his leg off. He commits what William K. Wimsatt, Jr., and Monroe C. Beardsley call the "intentional fallacy" (1954). Ahab fallaciously imputes to the White Whale a malicious intention – and, as a result, vows revenge. Starbuck protests that the injury was not intentional but instinctive. The notion that the White Whale intended to bite Ahab's leg off, he says, is an insane, anthropocentric projection. Starbuck exclaims: "Vengeance on a dumb brute!" (Melville 1988: 163). Similarly, Bunger, the surgeon on another ship, insists that the injury was not intentional but accidental. He says to Ahab that "what you take for the White Whale's malice is only his awkwardness." The White Whale, Bunger says, "never means to swallow a single limb" (Melville 1988: 441). Just as the merman argues the insult with Stubb, so Starbuck and Bunger argue the insult with Ahab – but to no avail. As an interpreter of the White Whale, Ahab is not a relativist but an absolutist.

The moral of the dream – which is to be kicked and not kick back – is the moral of the novel. The issue is the same in both the dream and the novel – whether to strike back after being insulted. Stubb answers this question one way, Ahab another way. As Stubb goes below deck after being insulted, after being cursed and threatened by Ahab, he mutters: "I was never served so before without giving a hard blow for it." He wonders whether "to go back and strike him" (Melville 1988: 128). In contrast to Stubb, striking back presents absolutely no problem for Ahab, who has been not only injured but also insulted by the White Whale. When Ahab says that he will dismember the White Whale just as the White Whale has dismembered him, he swears – in words that allude to what Stubb has said about striking back – that he would "strike the sun if it insulted me." Ahab says that "could the sun could do that, then could I do the other" (Melville 1988: 164). Unlike Stubb, who has qualms about striking back, Ahab does not quibble about what he should or should not do. He simply does it. What Ahab can do, he will do. To suppose that the sun, which is an inanimate object, could insult him is, of course, an even more extreme notion than to suppose that the White Whale, which is at least an animate object, could insult him.

Ahab also threatens Starbuck. When the oil in the hold springs a leak, Starbuck suggests to Ahab that they should pause in pursuit of the White Whale to repair the ship. "Devils!" Ahab shouts. "Dost thou then so much as dare to critically think of me?" He orders Starbuck to get back on deck. Starbuck politely refuses to comply immediately: "Nay, sir, not yet" (Melville 1988: 474). At that, Ahab points a musket at Starbuck and threatens to shoot him unless he gets back on deck. Starbuck obeys Ahab but not before he interprets the threat: "Thou has outraged, not insulted me, sir" (Melville 1988: 474–5). Like Stubb, Starbuck denies that he has been insulted, much less injured, although he has been threatened. As Starbuck interprets the confrontation, he has simply been outraged by Ahab. The implication is that Ahab, too, could interpret events in such a way as to consider that he was not insulted but merely outraged by the White Whale.

The dream complicates the plot of *Moby-Dick* and anticipates the climax of the novel. The purpose that the dream serves is to contrast Stubb's and Ahab's positions toward the activity of interpretation – toward being insulted and striking back. As Stubb interprets the dream, a wise man will let Ahab alone and never talk back, say what he may. If Ahab were like Stubb, he would leave the White Whale alone and not strike back, whatever the White Whale has done or may do. Ahab, however, is not a wise man but a fool – "a forty years' fool – fool – old fool" (Melville 1988: 544).

"A strictly critical eye might object that writers take their stand," Freud says, "neither for nor against particular dreams having a psychical meaning" (1907 [1906], *SE* 9: 8–9). In this instance, Melville does take a stand for a particular literary dream having such a meaning. Just as the White Whale pulls Ahab's leg – and pulls it off – so Melville pulls the reader's leg. Ultimately, the joke is on the reader. The "Merman Dream" implies that if readers of *Moby-Dick* would only turn around and bend over, they would get a kick out of Captain Ahab and be the wiser for it.

References

American Psychiatric Association (1994) *The Diagnostic and Statistical Manual of Mental Disorders: Fourth Edition*, Washington, DC: American Psychiatric Association.

Ammer, C. (1992) *Have a Nice Day – No Problem! A Dictionary of Clichés*, New York: Dutton.

Faber, G.S. (1816) *The Origin of Pagan Idolatry*, London: A.J. Valpy for F. and C. Rivingtons, 3 vols.

Freud, S. (1907 [1906]) *Delusions and Dreams in Jensen's Gradiva*, SE 9: 1–95.

Freud, S. (1930 [1929]) *Civilization and its Discontents*, SE 21: 57–145.

Jung, C.G. (1911–12/1952) *Symbols of Transformation: An Analysis of the Prelude to a Case of Schizophrenia*, CW 5.

Jung, C.G. (1928) *The Relations between the Ego and the Unconscious*, CW 7: 121–241.

Jung, C.G. (1930/1950) "Psychology and Literature," *CW* 15: 84–105.

Jung, C.G. (1940) "The Psychology of the Child Archetype," *CW* 9, 1: 151–81.

Jung, C.G. (1943) "The Psychology of Eastern Meditation," *CW* 11: 558–75.

Jung, C.G. (1955–56) *Mysterium Coniunctionis: An Inquiry into the Separation and Synthesis of Psychic Opposites in Alchemy, CW* 14.

Maurice, T. (1794–1800) *Indian Antiquities*, London: Richardson, 7 vols.

Melville, H. (1988) *Moby-Dick; or The Whale*, eds. H. Hayford, H. Parker, and G.T. Tanselle, *The Writings of Herman Melville*, Evanston, IL, and Chicago: Northwestern University Press and Newberry Library, vol. 6.

Nietzsche, F. (1986) *Human, All Too Human: A Book for Free Spirits*, trans. R.J. Hollingdale, Cambridge: Cambridge University Press.

Searle, J.R. (1995) *The Construction of Social Reality*, New York: The Free Press.

Vincent, H. (1949) *The Trying-Out of Moby-Dick*, Boston: Houghton Mifflin.

Welsford, E. (1935) *The Fool: His Social and Literary History*, London: Faber and Faber.

Wimsatt, Jr., W.K., and Beardsley, M.C. (1954) "The Intentional Fallacy," in W.K. Wimsatt, Jr., *The Verbal Icon: Studies in the Meaning of Poetry*, Lexington, KY: University of Kentucky Press: 3–18.

10

"IT WAS ALL A MISTAKE"

Jung's Postcards to Ernest Jones and
Kipling's Short Story "The Phantom 'Rickshaw"

In May 2003, I purchased two postcards that Jung wrote to Ernest Jones in late 1913 (Figures 10.1 and 10.2). A week or two earlier, I had attended the New York Autograph Show. I had thought it might be fun to own an autograph of Jung. I had asked several dealers whether they had for sale any autographs of Jung, and a few had said yes. They had given me copies of their catalogs and had invited me to visit their offices so that I could inspect the autographs. I had identified myself as a Jungian psychoanalyst, and one dealer

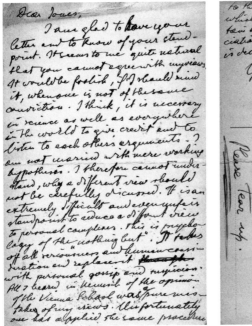

Figure 10.1 Postcard from Jung to Ernest Jones, November 25, 1913.

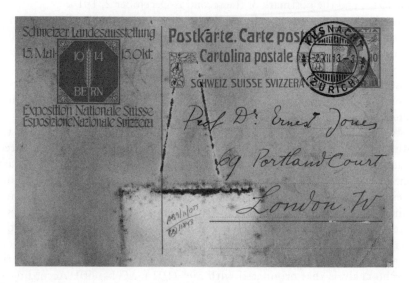

Figure 10.2 Postcard from Jung to Ernest Jones, December 2, 1913.

had informed me that his wife was a Freudian psychoanalyst. Later, I remembered his first name as "David." I could not remember his last name.

One of the catalogs was from a dealer with the name "David." I made an appointment with him to visit his office. On his wall was a framed photograph of Jung with a typed, autographed letter from Jung. The photograph and letter were too expensive for me to afford. I again identified myself as a Jungian psychoanalyst, and David informed me that his wife was a Freudian psychoanalyst.

I had, however, an odd feeling that something was not quite right, although I could not say what it was. I left the dealer's office and walked down the hall toward the elevator. Then I turned around and walked back to his office. I asked him, "By any chance is there another dealer with the name 'David' and with a wife who is a Freudian psychoanalyst?" He looked at me quizzically and said, "Yes." In fact, he said, both their wives had trained at the same psychoanalytic institute.

It was all a mistake. I had confounded two different dealers with the name "David." The one David then kindly told me the last name of the other David. Subsequently, I made an appointment with the other David to visit his office. He showed me a number of autographs of Jung, including the two postcards that I eventually purchased.

The postcards that Jung wrote to Ernest Jones in late 1913 are significant documents in the early history of psychoanalysis. At the time, Jung was president of the International Psychoanalytical Association. Jung wrote the postcards shortly after the Fourth International Psychoanalytic Congress in Munich, September 7–8, 1913. The postmark of the first postcard is November 25, 1913, and the postmark of the second is December 2, 1913.

At the Munich Congress, Freud read a paper entitled "The Disposition to Obsessional Neurosis: A Contribution to the Problem of Choice of Neurosis," and Jung read a paper entitled "A Contribution to the Study of Psychological Types." Jung was reelected president of the International Psychoanalytical Association, but of the 52 psychoanalysts who voted, 22 loyal to Freud submitted blank ballots. They abstained in a partisan protest against Jung (Freud and Jung 1974: 549–50).

In *On the History of the Psycho-Analytic Movement*, Freud said that the Munich Congress "was conducted by Jung in a disagreeable and incorrect manner." As a result, Freud said, the proceedings were "fatiguing and unedifying" (1914, *SE* 14: 45). In addition, Jung and the Zürich School had presented new views so different from the views of Freud and the Vienna School that there was confusion over the very definition of psychoanalysis. "At the Munich Congress," Freud said, "I found it necessary to clear up this confusion, and I did so by declaring that I did not recognize the innovations of the Swiss as legitimate continuations and further developments of the psycho-analysis that originated with me" (1914, *SE* 14: 60). According to Freud, the Swiss were, in effect, no longer psychoanalysts. The Munich

Congress was the last time, John Kerr notes, that Freud and Jung "were ever in the same room" (1993: 457).

Seven months later, in a letter of April 20, 1914, Jung resigned as president of the International Psychoanalytical Association. "The latest developments," he said, "have convinced me that my views are in such sharp contrast to the views of the majority of the members of our Association that I can no longer consider myself a suitable personality to be president" (Freud and Jung 1974: 551). That was effectively the end of relations between Jung and Freud.

The postcard that Jung wrote to Jones on November 25, 1913, reads as follows:

Dear Jones,

I am glad to have your letter and to know of your standpoint. It seems to me quite natural that you cannot agree with my views. It would be foolish, if I should mind it, when one is not of the same conviction. I think, it is necessary in science as well as everywhere in the world to give credit and to listen to each other's arguments. I am not married with mere working hypotheses. I therefore cannot understand, why a different view should not be carefully discussed. It is an extremely difficult and even unfair standpoint to reduce a different view to personal complexes. This is psychology of the "nothing but". It takes off all seriousness and human consideration and replaces it with personal gossip and suspicion. All I heard in Munich of the opinions of the Vienna School was a pure mistake of my views. Unfortunately one has applied the same procedure to the views of Adler's which deserve a certain amount of appreciation. This isolation is decidedly unhappy.

Yours sincerely
Dr Jung

Jung described psychoanalysis as a science in which different views deserved to be "carefully discussed" and not reduced to "personal complexes." The reduction of different views to personal complexes, Jung said, was an example of "psychology of the 'nothing but.'" This was a reference to William James. In the paper that Jung had read at the Munich Congress, he had cited James, who defined reductive explanations as follows: "What is higher is explained by what is lower and treated for ever as a case of 'nothing but' – nothing but something else of a quite inferior sort" (1913a, *CW* 6: par. 867; James 1975: 15). Jung regarded the opinions that the Vienna School had expressed about the different views that he had presented at the Munich Congress as reductive in exactly that sense. Those opinions, he said, were "a pure mistake of my views."

The postcard that Jung wrote to Jones on November 25, 1913, was not the first occasion on which Jung had expressed repugnance at the reduction of different views to personal complexes. For example, in a letter of November 11, 1912, Jung had declared to Freud that he refused "to be treated like a fool riddled with complexes." He had said: "I think I have objective reasons for my views" (Freud and Jung 1974: 516). Similarly, in a letter of December 3, 1912, Jung had complained to Freud that "I am forced to the painful conclusion that the majority of ψAsts [psychoanalysts] misuse ψA [psychoanalysis] for the purpose of devaluing others and their progress by insinuations about complexes (as though that explained anything. A wretched theory!)" (Freud and Jung 1974: 526). According to Jung, what was so problematic about this reductive procedure was that psychoanalysts employed it as a convenient excuse to avoid thinking. "Anything," he had said, "that might make them think is written off as a complex" (Freud and Jung 1974: 527).

In the last sentence of the postcard that Jung wrote to Jones on November 25, 1913, Jung said that the same reductive procedure that had been applied to his views had also, unfortunately, been applied to Alfred Adler's views, which he said, "deserve a certain amount of appreciation." The paper that Jung had read at the Munich Congress included just such an appreciation of Adler's views. In the final three paragraphs of that paper, Jung compared Freud and Adler as two different "psychological types" with two different theories. The adjectives that Jung employed to describe Freud's theory were "causal," "pluralistic," and "sensualistic"; the adjectives that he employed to describe Adler's theory were "finalistic," "monistic," and "intellectualistic" (1913a, *CW* 6: par. 880). Jung noted that Freud emphasized "pleasure" and that Adler emphasized "power" (1913a, *CW* 6: par. 881). He concluded: "The difficult task of creating a psychology which will be equally fair to both types must be reserved for the future" (1913a, *CW* 6: par. 882). Jung did not privilege Freud's theory; he did not describe Freud's theory as true and Adler's theory as false; he relativized Freud's and Adler's theories as merely different views. In effect, he envisaged a "general theory" of psychoanalysis in which Freud's and Adler's views would both be "special cases."

Any comparison to Adler was certain to be anathema to Freud. Adler had been one of the original members of the Vienna Psychoanalytic Society – and, next to Freud, the most prominent. When Adler eventually articulated views different from those of Freud, Freud, in effect, expelled Adler from the Society. In a letter of October 12, 1911, Freud informed Jung that "yesterday I forced the whole Adler gang (six of them) to resign from the Society." Adler had established the "Society for Free Psychoanalytic Investigation" – in contrast, Freud sarcastically remarked, "to our unfree variety" (Freud and Jung 1974: 447). On October 11, 1911, Freud had reported to the members of the Vienna Psychoanalytic Society that Adler had resigned. A resolution had then been passed, by a vote of eleven to five, that membership in the Society for Free

Psychoanalytic Investigation was "incompatible" with membership in the Vienna Psychoanalytic Society (Nunberg and Federn 1974: 282–3).

Edward Hoffman speculates that Adler's different views must have distressed Freud because they constituted "irrefutable evidence that his basic system was going to be challenged, and rejected, by other cogent explorers of human personality." He says that Freud must have intuited that the departure of Adler "would not be the only one, and that others must certainly follow." Hoffman notes that "many would eventually quit their association with Freud, including formerly close colleagues" – among them, Jung. He contends that "none would arouse such lifelong implacable enmity as Adler" (1994: 74).

In 1932, E.A. Bennet asked Freud why he and important colleagues in the early history of psychoanalysis "were on such bad terms with each other." Freud replied that some separations were inevitable, "cannot be avoided and need not be objected to." He said that the departure of Adler was "not a loss" and that he had "no regrets" because Adler was "never an analyst." Bennet then inquired about Jung. According to Bennet, "Freud, after a pause, said very quietly, 'Jung was a great loss'" (1961: 56).

For Jung to compare Freud to Adler at the Munich Congress – and to envisage a psychology that would be "equally fair" to both Freud and Adler – was utterly intolerable to Freud. In the early history of psychoanalysis, it proved extremely difficult, even impossible, for Freud to tolerate others' views when they differed from his views.

In a letter of June 13, 1912, Freud wrote to Jung that "Adler's book *On the Nervous Character* [*The Neurotic Constitution* (1916)] appeared a few days ago." Freud remarked: "I am unlikely to read it but I have been made acquainted with parts of it" (Freud and Jung 1974: 511). In a letter of December 7, 1912, Jung wrote to Freud that "I would like you to know that I have designs on reviewing Adler's book." Jung continued: "I have succeeded in descending into its depths, where I found some delightful things that deserve to be hung aloft. The man really is slightly dotty" (Freud and Jung 1974: 531). In this instance, Jung engaged in the same *ad hominem* devaluation that Freud indulged in. To describe Adler as "slightly dotty" was not exactly to reduce different views to personal complexes, but it was to pathologize Adler. In a letter of December 9, 1912, Freud replied: "Your intention of attacking Adler's book has my entire approval" (Freud and Jung 1974: 532). Freud reiterated that he had not read Adler's book. Adler had not sent him a copy, and, Freud said, "I am too stingy to spend my good money on such a product" (Freud and Jung 1974: 533). Jung never wrote a review of Adler's book. In fact, in the foreword to *The Theory of Psychoanalysis*, the lectures that Jung delivered at Fordham University in September 1912, Jung said that only after he had prepared those lectures in the spring of 1912 did Adler's book "become known to me." He said of Adler: "I recognize that he and I have reached similar conclusions on various points" (1913b, *CW* 4: 87).

In a letter of May 23, 1912, Freud had mentioned what he regarded as "a disastrous similarity" between the views of Adler and the views of Jung (Freud and Jung 1974: 507). In a letter of June 8, 1912, Jung replied: "The parallel with Adler is a bitter pill; I swallow it without a murmur. Evidently this is my fate. There is nothing to be done about it, for my reasons are overwhelming." The similarity that Freud regarded as disastrous was a new view of incest. "I set out with the idea of corroborating the old view of incest," Jung said, "but was obliged to see that things are different from what I expected" (Freud and Jung 1974: 509).

Jung had published *Wandlungen und Symbole der Libido* (*Transformations and Symbols of the Libido*) in two parts in 1911–12. (In 1916, he published it in an English translation with the title *Psychology of the Unconscious: A Study of the Transformations and Symbolisms of the Libido*.) Freud had expressed a positive opinion of the first part of the book. In a letter of November 12, 1911, Freud wrote to Jung: "One of the nicest works I have read (again), is that of a well-known author on the 'Transformations and Symbols of the Libido.'" He continued: "In it many things are so well-expressed that they seem to have taken on definitive form" (Freud and Jung 1974: 459). In the second part of the book, however, Jung argued that "the sexualism of neuroses is not to be taken literally but as regressive phantasy and symbolic compensation" for a recent failure to achieve an effective adaptation to reality and that "the sexualism of the early infantile fantasy, especially the incest problem," is also not to be taken literally but as "a regressive product." Jung declared that he did not regard incest as "a gross sexual inclination." The ultimate significance of incest, he concluded, was not physical but strictly psychological. Jung said that "the mother has acquired incestuous significance only psychologically" (1916, *CW* B: par. 675). In the letter of May 23, 1912, Freud noted that Adler had said that "the neurotic has no desire at all for his mother." This was the "disastrous similarity" between Jung and Adler. About the parallel with Adler, Freud said to Jung: "I have no doubt that your derivation of the incestuous libido will be different. But there is a certain resemblance" (Freud and Jung 1974: 507). In effect, both Adler and Jung had deliteralized incest – and, to Freud, they had "desexualized" psychoanalysis.

In a letter of April 27, 1912, Jung had previously said to Freud: "Like you, I am absorbed in the incest problem and have come to conclusions which show incest primarily as a fantasy problem" (Freud and Jung 1974: 502). In a letter of May 17, 1912, Jung noted that Freud had originally taken "the so-called sexual trauma" literally and had mistaken fantasies for realities. "The trauma," Jung said, "is *seemingly important* or real," but "*cum grano salis* it doesn't matter whether a sexual trauma really occurred or not, or was a mere fantasy" (Freud and Jung 1974: 506). Similarly, Jung now argued that to take incest literally was to mistake it. It was all a mistake. In the letter of May 23, 1912, Freud acknowledged the original mistake about the sexual trauma: "I value your letter for the warning it contains, and the reminder of my first big error, when

I mistook fantasies for realities" (Freud and Jung 1974: 507). Freud never, however, acknowledged that it was a mistake to take incest literally.

On the front of the postcard that Jung wrote to Jones on November 25, 1913, Jung wrote: "Please tear up." Jones did not tear up the postcard; he immediately mailed it to Freud. Freud read the postcard and then returned it to Jones in a letter of December 4, 1913. In that letter, Freud said to Jones (in imperfect English):

> I cannot abstain from sending back Jungs letter [Jung's postcard], it
> may be interesting for you after some time. He has learned ψA
> [psychoanalysis] in order to bring forward the demand that personal
> complexes ought to be overlooked. A very nice result. "It is all a
> mistake" reminds me of something similar recurring saying in
> Kipling's Phantom Rickshaw.
>
> (Freud and Jones 1993: 246)

What was at issue between Jung and Freud was the very definition of psychoanalysis. Both Freud and Jung regarded psychoanalysis as a science. As scientists, psychoanalysts presented for consideration different views that, Jung said, deserved to be "carefully discussed" and not reduced to "personal complexes." As Freud defined psychoanalysis, it was a procedure that reduced a manifest content to a latent content in order to expose ulterior, unconscious motives. In this instance, the manifest content was different views, and the latent content was personal complexes. What was problematic to Jung about this procedure was that it reduced objective propositions to subjective motives – or, as James said, reduced the "higher" to "nothing but" the "lower." According to Jung, to reduce different views to personal complexes was to misuse psychoanalysis in order to devalue others. It was, as Jung exclaimed in exasperation: "A wretched theory!" In contrast, according to Freud, for Jung to "demand that personal complexes ought to be overlooked," was, in effect, to repudiate psychoanalysis. It was, as Freud sarcastically said: "A very nice result."

Jung said that at the Munich Congress the opinions of the Vienna School were "a pure mistake of my views." Freud said that the complaint by Jung "It is all a mistake" reminded him of a similar, recurrent saying in Rudyard Kipling's "The Phantom 'Rickshaw." In that short story, Theobald Jack Pansay, a British civil servant in India, has an affair with Agnes Keith-Wessington, the wife of a British officer. The affair begins on a voyage from Gravesend to Bombay and resumes three or four months later in Simla. Pansay says that "Agnes's passion was a stronger, a more dominant, and – if I may use the expression – a purer sentiment than mine." Eventually, Pansay loses interest in Agnes: "From my own lips, in August, 1882, she learnt that I was sick of her presence, tired of her company, and weary of the sound of her voice." Most women, Pansay says, "would have wearied of me as I wearied of them," and many women "would have promptly avenged themselves by active and obtrusive flirtation with other men." Agnes, however, was the exception to the rule. "On her," Pansay says, "neither my openly-expressed aversion nor the brutalities with which I garnished our interviews had the least effect." Agnes simply says: "I'm sure it's all a mistake – a hideous mistake; and we'll be good friends again some day. *Please* forgive me, Jack, dear" (1987: 29).

Pansay knows that he is "the offender," and that knowledge, he says, "transformed my pity into passive endurance, and, eventually into blind hate." The next year, in 1883, he and Agnes meet again in Simla. Agnes utters the same words: "Still the unreasoning wail that it was all a 'mistake'; and still the hope of eventually 'making friends'" (1987: 29). Pansay says: "I might have seen, had I cared to look, that that hope only was keeping her alive. She grew more wan and thin month by month" (1987: 29–30). The next year, in 1884, again in Simla: "The same weary appeals, and the same curt answers from my lips." Pansay becomes engaged to another woman, Kitty Mannering. On horseback, he encounters Agnes in a 'rickshaw: "'So I hear you're engaged, Jack, dear.' Then, without a moment's pause: 'I'm sure it's all a mistake – a hideous mistake. We shall be as good friends some day, Jack, as we ever were'" (1987: 30). Pansay cruelly spurns her again, and a week later Agnes dies.

In 1885, again in Simla, Pansay and Kitty decide to marry at the end of June, and he buys her a sapphire ring with two diamonds. Subsequently, Pansay begins to suffer hallucinations – to "hear" and "see" things. Again and again, Pansay "sees" Agnes in a 'rickshaw and "hears" her say that it is all a mistake and that they will be friends again. In effect, Agnes is a "ghost" who "haunts" Pansay.

The phantom 'rickshaw with Agnes in it Pansay calls "It." In this respect, perhaps it is not irrelevant to note that Freud also employed the term "It" (in German, *das Es*, which James Strachey translated as the "id"). Freud appropriated the term from Georg Groddeck, who said of patients that "the It, the unconscious, drives them into illness against their conscious will" (1976: 31). This is an accurate description of the experience of Pansay, who is driven into illness against his conscious will. From this perspective, the hallucination of the phantom 'rickshaw with Agnes in it would be a projection of the id, or It. "I have an indistinct idea," Pansay says, "that I dragged Kitty by the wrist along the road up to where It stood, and implored her for pity's sake to speak to It; to tell It that we were betrothed" (1987: 41).

I do not mean that Kipling derived the term "It" from Groddeck or Freud. This would have been impossible. Kipling published a first version of "The Phantom 'Rickshaw" in 1885. He then revised the short story and published a second, final version in 1888. Groddeck published *The Book of the It* in 1923, the same year that Freud published *The Ego and the Id*. That is, Kipling employed the term "It" more than three decades before Groddeck and Freud. Freud said that "Groddeck himself no doubt followed the example of Nietzsche, who habitually used this grammatical term for whatever in our nature is impersonal" (1923, *SE* 19: 23n.). It is possible that Kipling also derived the term "It" from Nietzsche – although it is also possible that he employed the term independent of any influence.

Pansay continues: "As I talked I suppose I must have told Kitty of my old relations with Mrs. Wessington, for I saw her listen intently with white face and blazing eyes." In reply, Pansay says, Kitty strikes him with "her riding-whip across my face from mouth to eye" (1987: 42). Later, a doctor who has been treating Pansay and trying, without success, to cure him, tells him what Kitty has said: "Says that a man who would have behaved to a woman as you did to Mrs. Wessington ought to kill himself out of sheer pity for his kind … Says she'll die before she ever speaks to you again" (1987: 43).

Jung's complaint that the opinions of the Vienna School were "a pure mistake of my views" reminded Freud of Agnes's refrain that "it's all a mistake." In effect, Freud free associated to the word "mistake" in Jung's postcard, and it reminded him of the word "mistake" in Kipling's short story. Freud merely mentioned the comparison. He did not elaborate the basis for the comparison. Nor did he analyze it psychologically or interpret what it meant unconsciously. Freud remained unconscious of what the comparison essentially implied. If Jung was comparable to Agnes and if Freud was comparable to Pansay, then Freud positioned Jung as a lover whom he had cruelly spurned. What the comparison essentially implied was that Freud, like Pansay in the affair with Agnes, was "the offender" in the affair with Jung. Had Freud been conscious of the implication, he would never have made the comparison between Agnes and Jung. The comparison is tantamount to a "Freudian slip," which is, of course, a "mistake." Ironically, in a way that Freud never consciously knew or acknowledged, "It was all a mistake."

If Agnes was a ghost who haunted Pansay, Jung was a ghost who haunted Freud – and psychoanalysis. Jung analyzed ghosts psychologically. He said that "we are dealing with a fact of experience, and one so general that everyone knows what is meant by 'ghost.'" In such cases, Jung said, "we are confronted with a definite complex of psychic facts" (1926, *CW* 8: par. 625). That is, from a psychoanalytic perspective, a ghost was a complex. In this sense, just as Pansay had an "Agnes complex," so Freud had a "Jung complex." What was the Jung complex? For Freud, it was the specter of a psychoanalysis in which Jung's views might supersede his views.

The postcard that Jung wrote to Jones on December 2, 1913, reads as follows:

Dear Jones,

You can order Prof. Freud's photo from Camill Ruf, Photograph, Bahnhofstrasse, Zürich. (with reference to me – in case of doubt!)
    Thank you for your kind invitation to write an article for the Zeitschrift, but I cannot repeat myself, having said everything in my

book and my lectures. And what would be the use of it? München has shown, what the attitude of the Vienna School is. I dislike advertising even in science. If people don't understand what I have said, they may work until they begin to understand, if not – tant pis pour eux.

With best regards
Yours sincerely
Jung

Jung declined to repeat in yet another article what he had already said in his book and in his lectures. To do so would be no use, he said, for the Munich Congress had abundantly exposed the irreconcilably negative opinions of the Vienna School toward the different views that he had presented. Jung was finally in a defiant mood: "If people don't understand what I have said, they may work until they begin to understand, if not – tant pis pour eux" – too bad for them. If the Vienna School misunderstood what he had said, so much the worse for them.

It may or may not have been a mistake for Freud to take the sexual trauma and incest literally. It may or may not have been a mistake for Freud to reduce different views to personal complexes. It was certainly a mistake for him to be so intolerant of different views. In *On the History of the Psycho-Analytic Movement*, a polemic against Adler and Jung, Freud emphasized that "psycho-analysis is my creation." He acknowledged that "it is a long time now since I was the only psycho-analyst," but he maintained that "even to-day no one can know better than I do what psycho-analysis is, how it differs from other ways of investigating the life of the mind, and precisely what should be called psycho-analysis and what would better be described by some other name" (1914, *SE* 14: 7).

Freud intended to demonstrate that certain views (the views of Adler and Jung) "controvert the fundamental principles of analysis (and on what points they controvert them) and that for this reason they should not be known by the name of analysis" (1914, *SE* 14: 50). He said: "I am of course perfectly ready to allow that everyone has a right to think and to write what he pleases; but he has no right to put it forward as something other than what it really is" (1914, *SE* 14: 60–1). According to Freud, psychoanalysis was simply – or, as James might have said, "nothing but" – what he said it was. As the creator of psychoanalysis, Freud reserved the right to define it – and to expel those with views that differed from his views. In *An Autobiographical Study*, Freud described the criticism that he had presented of "the two heretics" Adler and Jung as "a mild one." He said: "I only insisted that both Adler and Jung should cease to describe their theories as 'psycho-analysis'" (1925 [1924], *SE* 20: 53).

Michael Polanyi says that in science one of the "main principles underlying the process of free discussion" is "tolerance" (1964: 68). Science, Polanyi says, is a community that "effectively practices free discussion" (1964: 71). In

1913, psychoanalysis was not, in this sense, a science, because it was not a community that tolerated different views and effectively practiced free discussion. Freud noted that the departure of colleagues "has often been brought up against me as a sign of my intolerance." He said, however, that "I think I can say in my defence that an intolerant man, dominated by an arrogant belief in his own infallibility, would never have been able to maintain his hold upon so large a number of intellectually eminent people" (1925 [1924], *SE* 20: 53). This comment is, as Freud said, defensive. It begs the question of why such intellectually eminent people as Adler and Jung departed under circumstances that proved so perpetually acrimonious and detrimental to the progress of psychoanalysis as a science.

As a science, psychoanalysis was unique. It was the creation of an individual, Freud. In science, however, no individual, not even the creator of a science, has the exclusive right to say which different views are legitimate and which are illegitimate. Yet this is exactly what Freud did. Adler resigned from the Vienna Psychoanalytic Society, and Jung resigned from the International Psychoanalytical Association, but, in effect, Freud expelled them. He did so because he could not tolerate different views that (at least as he defined psychoanalysis) did not continue and develop the views that had originated with him. If, however, psychoanalysis was a science, such a proprietary attitude was a grave error. It was all a mistake.

References

Adler, A. (1916) *The Neurotic Constitution: Outlines of a Comparative Individualistic Psychology and Psychotherapy*, trans. B. Glueck and J.E. Lind, New York: Moffat, Yard and Company.

Bennet, E.A. (1961) *C.G. Jung*, London: Barrie and Rockliff.

Freud, S. (1914) *On the History of the Psycho-Analytic Movement*, *SE* 14: 1–66.

Freud, S. (1923) *The Ego and the Id*, *SE* 19: 1–66.

Freud, S. (1925 [1924]) *An Autobiographical Study*, *SE* 20: 1–74.

Freud, S., and Jones, E. (1993) *The Complete Correspondence of Sigmund Freud and Ernest Jones, 1908–1939*, ed. R.A. Paskauskas, Cambridge, MA: Belknap Press of Harvard University Press.

Freud, S., and Jung, C.G. (1974) *The Freud/Jung Letters: The Correspondence between Sigmund Freud and C.G. Jung*, ed. W. McGuire, trans. R. Manheim and R.F.C. Hull, Princeton, NJ: Princeton University Press.

Groddeck, G. (1976) *The Book of the It*, trans. V.M.E. Collins, New York: International Universities Press.

Hoffman, E. (1994) *The Drive for Self: Alfred Adler and the Founding of Individual Psychology*, Reading, MA: Addison-Wesley.

James, W. (1975) *Pragmatism*, Cambridge, MA: Harvard University Press.

Jung, C.G. (1913a) "A Contribution to the Study of Psychological Types," *CW* 6: 499–509.

Jung, C.G. (1913b) *The Theory of Psychoanalysis*, *CW* 4: 83–226.

Jung, C.G. (1916) *Psychology of the Unconscious: A Study of the Transformations and Symbolisms of the Libido*, *CW* B.

Jung, C.G. (1926) "Spirit and Life," *CW* 8: 319–37.

Kerr, J. (1993) *A Most Dangerous Method: The Story of Jung, Freud, and Sabina Spielrein*, New York: Alfred A. Knopf.

Kipling, R. (1987) "The Phantom 'Rickshaw," in R. Kipling, *The Man Who Would Be King and Other Stories*, ed. L.L. Cornell, Oxford: Oxford University Press: 26–48.

Nunberg, H, and Federn, E. (eds.) (1974) *Minutes of the Vienna Psychoanalytic Society: Volume 3: 1910–1911*, trans. M. Nunberg with H. Collins, New York: International Universities Press.

Polanyi, M. (1964) *Science, Faith and Society*, Chicago: University of Chicago Press.

11

WILLIAM BLAKE, VISIONARY ART, AND THE RETURN OF ODYSSEUS

Homeric Mythology, Neoplatonic Philosophy, and Jungian Psychology

In the late 1940s, the National Trust of England acquired a country house, Arlington Court, and discovered in it a painting, as Kathleen Raine says, "among the broken glass and rubbish on top of a pantry cupboard." Raine describes it as "one of Blake's most beautiful paintings" (1977: 3). The painting bore an 1821 date but no title. Subsequently, it was provisionally entitled *The Sea of Time and Space* or, alternatively, *The Cycle of the Life of Man*. (The painting is now known as *The Arlington Court Picture*.)

Blake completed the painting only six years before his death. It is, Raine says, "a fine example of Blake's late and mature style" (1968, 1: 75). The painting is a marvel of compositional complexity and coherence. The relation of the parts to the whole is ingeniously intricate. Although the size of the painting is small, its theme is large. In an area only 16 × 19½ inches, Blake vividly depicts a narrative scene replete with exquisite figural images in a vast scape of sea, land, and sky. *The Sea of Time and Space* may be the most beautiful of all Blake's paintings (Figure 11.1).

It was Raine, one of the most important Blake scholars of the twentieth century, who identified the sources of the painting. In *Blake and Tradition*, the A.W. Mellon Lectures in the Fine Arts that she delivered in 1962 at the National Gallery of Art in Washington, DC, Raine established that the painting "is based upon Porphyry's treatise on Homer's *Cave of the Nymphs*, to which Blake has added details from the *Odyssey* and from Platonic sources" (1968, 1: 75).

The identification of these sources enabled Raine to interpret *The Sea of Time and Space* accurately. In that interpretation, she demonstrated that the painting is "a profoundly considered representation of the essentials of Neoplatonism" (1968, 1: 75). The painting comprises images from Homeric mythology, specifically from the *Odyssey* – and more generally from Greek mythology – to which Blake applies Neoplatonic philosophy.

Thomas Taylor, a friend of Blake, translated Porphyry's treatise on Homer's *Cave of the Nymphs* and published it in 1788. Taylor was the most prominent Neoplatonist in England in the late eighteenth and early nineteenth centuries. I met Kathleen Raine in London in 1973. On that occasion, Raine gave me a book that she had edited with George Mills Harper – *Thomas Taylor the Platonist* (1969), which includes Taylor's translation of Porphyry's treatise. She kindly inscribed it: "This book has been waiting for the right recipient, and I now give it in the belief that you are that one." At the time, I knew neither Blake's *The Sea of Time and Space* nor Raine's identification of the sources of the painting nor her Neoplatonic interpretation of the painting. I had yet to read *Blake and Tradition*. Only after I had done so did I appreciate the magnitude of what Raine had accomplished.

Among the sources of *The Sea of Time and Space*, Raine mentions details from the *Odyssey*. The two most prominent images in the painting are a man and a woman. The man is Odysseus, and the woman is the goddess Athena. The scene depicts the return of Odysseus. Through the divine intervention of Athena, Odysseus has come home to Ithaca.

Odysseus, in a red robe, kneels and extends his arms and hands out to sea, and Athena, in a white dress, stands behind him and extends her left arm and hand up to the sky. (The red color indicates that Odysseus is a mortal, and the white color indicates that Athena is an immortal.) Athena looks at Odysseus, while he looks neither at her nor at the sea but directly at us. The stare of Odysseus is a dare – it is as if he challenges us to interpret what the scene means.

Odysseus is not only extending his arms and hands out to sea but also, Raine says, "throwing something out to sea, with his face averted" (1968, 1: 75). What is he throwing out to sea, and why is his face averted?

In the left half of the painting, out at sea, is a woman with four horses. She extends her right arm and hand up to a cloud in the shape of a circle in the sky. Raine says that these images are also details from the *Odyssey*. The woman is the goddess Leucothea, or Ino. On the voyage home to Ithaca, Odysseus survives storm and shipwreck through the divine intervention of Leucothea. As he struggles not to drown, she tells him to take off his clothes, jump from his raft, and swim to Phaeacia. She lends him her girdle and tells him to put it on and, once safe on land, to take it off and throw it out to sea, back to her – and, when he does so, to avert his face.

Raine contends that Blake read three translations of the *Odyssey* – George Chapman's, Alexander Pope's, and William Cowper's. She argues that, in this instance, he employed Cowper's translation of 1791 (Homer 1920), for, in contrast to Chapman's and Pope's, it includes all of the details that Blake depicts in this scene. Raine quotes this passage, in which Leucothea advises Odysseus:

> Thus do (for I account thee not unwise)
> Thy garments putting off, let drive thy raft
> As the winds will, then, swimming, strive to reach
> Phaeacia, where thy doom is to escape.
> Take this. This ribbon bind beneath thy breast,

Celestial texture. Thenceforth ev'ry fear
Of death dismiss, and, laying once thy hands
On the firm continent, unbind the zone,
Which thou shalt cast far distant from the shore
Into the Deep, turning thy face away.
                              (Book V, Lines 412–21)

As Blake depicts this passage in the painting, Odysseus does exactly as
Leucothea advises. As soon as he lands on Phaeacia, he throws her girdle back
to her and averts his face.

Raine then quotes this passage, in which Leucothea, or Ino, catches her
girdle when Odysseus throws it back to her:

... loosing from beneath
His breast the zone divine, he cast it far
Into the brackish stream, and a huge wave
Returning bore it downward to the sea,
Where Ino caught it ...
                              (Book V, Lines 553–7)

How does Blake render Leucothea catching her girdle in the painting? He
depicts her out at sea with four horses, extending her right arm and hand up
to a cloud in the shape of a circle in the sky. In Cowper's translation, the
texture of her "zone" (an archaic synonym for "girdle" and also a synonym for
"circle") is "Celestial" – which means that it relates to the sky. What more apt
image of this relation than a cloud in the shape of a circle?

In the left half of the painting, Blake has combined two episodes from the
Odyssey. These are, Raine says, "two accounts" that describe Odysseus "coming
safe to land" (1968, 1: 76). In one account, from Book V, he lands on Phaeacia.
In the other account, from Book XIII, he lands on Ithaca. As different as the
two episodes are, they are variations on the same theme – coming safe to land
through the divine intervention of a goddess, Leucothea or Athena.

The image of four horses at sea is also a detail from the *Odyssey*. In Book
XIII, Odysseus comes home to Ithaca from Phaeacia on a ship. Raine quotes
this passage, which personifies the ship as a woman:

She, as four harness'd stallions o'er the plain
Shooting together at the scourge's stroke,
Toss high their manes, and rapid scour along,
So mounted she the waves ...
                              (Book XIII, Lines 96–9)

In the painting, Blake depicts the ship, or woman, as Leucothea with four
horses out at sea.

If the left half of the painting is an illustration of how Odysseus comes safe to land on both Phaeacia and Ithaca, the right half of the painting is an illustration of where he comes safe to land on Ithaca from Phaeacia. In the right half of the painting, Blake depicts the cave of the nymphs. At the bottom of the painting, he depicts the port of Phorcys.

The first six lines of the relevant passage from Cowper's translation of the *Odyssey* describe the port of Phorcys:

> There is a port sacred in Ithaca
> To Phorcys, hoary ancient of the Deep,
> Form'd by converging shores, prominent both
> And both abrupt, which from the spacious bay
> Exclude all boist'rous winds; within it, ships
> (The port once gain'd) uncabled ride secure.
> (Book XIII, Lines 112–17)

The next twelve lines describe the cave of the nymphs:

> An olive, at the haven's head, expands
> Her branches wide, near to a pleasant cave
> Umbrageous, to the nymphs devoted named
> The Naiads. In that cave beakers of stone
> And jars are seen; bees lodge their honey there;
> And there, on slender spindles of the rock
> The nymphs of river weave their wond'rous robes.
> Perennial springs water it, and it shows
> A twofold entrance; ingress one affords
> To mortal man, which Northward looks direct,
> But holier is the Southern far; by that
> No mortal enters, but the Gods alone.
> (Book XIII, Lines 118–129)

Phorcys is an ancient sea god, and the nymphs are Naiads, river goddesses. Near to the port of Phorcys is the cave of the nymphs. The port of Phorcys is where the ship on which Odysseus comes home to Ithaca from Phaeacia lands. In the cave of the nymphs are jars and spindles. On the spindles, the nymphs weave robes.

Raine does not quote Cowper's translation of the passage that describes the cave of the nymphs. Instead, she quotes Taylor's translation of the passage from Porphyry's treatise on Homer's *Cave of the Nymphs*:

> High at the head a branching olive grows,
> And crowns the pointed cliffs with shady boughs.
> A cavern pleasant, though involv'd in night,

Figure 11.1 William Blake, *The Sea of Time and Space* (*The Arlington Court Picture*), 1821.

Beneath it lies, the Naiades delight:
Where bowls and urns, of workmanship divine
And massy beams in native marble shine;
On which the Nymphs amazing webs display,
Of purple hue, and exquisite array.
The busy bees, within the urns secure
Honey delicious, and like nectar pure.
Perpetual waters thro' the grotto glide,
A lofty gate unfolds on either side;
That to the north is pervious by mankind;
The sacred south t'immortals is consign'd.

(1968, 1: 78)

What Cowper translates as "jars" and "spindles," Taylor translates as "urns" and "beams." (A spindle is a device around which yarn is twisted in spinning, and a beam is a device on which the warp of yarn is wound in weaving.) Why, in this instance, does Raine quote Taylor's translation rather than Cowper's? She does so as she prepares to interpret *The Sea of Time and Space* as a representation of the essentials of Neoplatonism.

In the right half of the painting, Raine says, Blake depicts "each detail" in the passage that describes the cave of the nymphs (1968, 1: 78). Among these details is the olive grove on the cliff. At the top of the painting on the right is the cave, in which nymphs are bearing urns on their heads. Under them, other nymphs are weaving webs on the beams of a loom. Three of them are holding spindles in their hands. On the left, a nymph is holding a skein of yarn on her wrists. Other nymphs unwind the yarn, pass it, and measure it.

At the bottom of the painting is the port of Phorcys. Blake depicts Phorcys lying on his back in the sea and extending, left and right, his arms and hands. In his right hand, he holds a spindle of yarn. In the sea with Phorcys are the Fates. In the painting, right to left, Clotho unwinds the yarn, Lachesis measures it with her fingers, and Atropos cuts it with her shears. What purpose do the Fates serve in *The Sea of Time and Space*?

As Raine notes, there is no mention of the Fates either in the *Odyssey* or in Porphyry's treatise on Homer's *Cave of the Nymphs*. The Fates are an image from Greek mythology but not from Homeric mythology. Why does Blake include the Fates in *The Sea of Time and Space*? Apparently, he adds them for emphasis.

What the Fates in the sea with Phorcys emphasize is the image of weaving that Porphyry's treatise on Homer's *Cave of the Nymphs* describes. In Neoplatonic philosophy, the image of weaving is a symbol – but of what? Porphyry asks "what symbol is more proper to souls descending into generation, and the tenacious vestment of body, than as the poet says, 'Nymphs weaving on stony beams purple garments wonderful to behold?'" He says that "the purple garments plainly appear to be the flesh with which we are invested; and which

171

is woven as it were and grows by the connecting and vivifying power of the blood." He adds that "the body is a garment with which the soul is invested" (1969: 305). In Neoplatonic philosophy, the image of weaving symbolizes the descent of immortal souls from an eternal, spiritual dimension into a temporal and spatial, material dimension and into mortal bodies. In this respect, the presence of the Fates at the bottom of the painting is tantamount to a *memento mori*. They are a remembrance of the mortality of the body, in contrast to the immortality of the soul.

In Cowper's translation of the *Odyssey*, the passage that describes the cave of the nymphs mentions a "twofold entrance." (In Taylor's translation of this passage, this twofold entrance is a "gate" that "unfolds on either side" of the cave of the nymphs.) That is, there is not just one entrance, but, on either side of the cave, there are two entrances – one to the north, the other to the south. The northern entrance is reserved exclusively for "mortal man" (in Cowper's translation") or for "mankind" (in Taylor's translation), while the southern entrance is reserved exclusively for "Gods" (in Cowper's translation) or for "immortals" (in Taylor's translation).

In Cowper's translation, the northern entrance is where men descend from the spiritual dimension into the material dimension, while the southern entrance is where gods descend (as in divine intervention) from the spiritual dimension into the material dimension. In contrast, in Taylor's translation of Porphyry's treatise on Homer's *Cave of the Nymphs*, the northern entrance is where men descend from the spiritual dimension into the material dimension, but the southern entrance is where immortals ascend from the material dimension into the spiritual dimension. From the perspective of Neoplatonic philosophy, Cowper's translation is a mistranslation. Porphyry says that "the gates of the cave which look to the north are with great propriety said to be pervious to the descent of men: but the southern gates are not the avenues of the gods, but of souls ascending to the gods" (1969: 310–11). He continues: "On this account the poet does not say it is the passage of the gods, but of immortals; which appellation is also common to our souls, whether in their whole essence or from some particular and most excellent part only they are denominated immortal" (1969: 311–12). In Neoplatonic philosophy, gods are not the only immortals. Men – or the souls of men – are also immortals.

The immortal souls of men descend into the material dimension, where they live in mortal bodies temporally and spatially. When those mortal bodies die, the immortal souls of men ascend into the spiritual dimension where they live eternally. From the perspective of Neoplatonic philosophy, the soul of man is, symbolically, an Odysseus who returns home. The temporal and spatial return of Odysseus to Ithaca symbolizes the eternal return of the soul of man to the spiritual dimension.

The voyage of Odysseus over the sea of time and space is a symbol of the cycle of the life of man in the material dimension. (In this respect, *The Sea of Time and Space* and *The Cycle of the Life of Man* are equally apt titles for Blake's painting.) Porphyry says that Odysseus symbolizes "to us a man who passes in a regular manner over the dark and stormy sea of generation; and thus at length arrives at that region, where tempests and seas are unknown" (1969: 321). That region is the spiritual dimension to which the immortal soul of man, at death, returns.

Where in the painting are the northern entrance through which souls descend into the material dimension and the southern entrance through which they ascend into the spiritual dimension? On the far right side of the painting, Blake depicts the northern entrance as stairs with steps on which immortal souls descend into the material dimension, as the nymphs weave mortal bodies for them. At the top of the painting, in the sky, he depicts the southern entrance as stairs with steps on which immortal souls ascend into the spiritual dimension. Athena stands behind Odysseus and extends her left arm and hand up to the sky. As she looks down at him, she points up to the steps of the stairs. In that gesture, Athena indicates the spiritual dimension to which Odysseus, symbol of the immortal soul of man, must ultimately return. She shows him the way "home."

In the upper left corner of the painting, Blake adds another detail from Greek mythology. Above, in the sky, is a man with four horses. The man is the god Apollo in the chariot of the sun. Below, in the sea, is a woman, the goddess Leucothea, with four horses. If Leucothea is a symbol of the return home of Odysseus in the temporal and spatial, material dimension, Apollo is a symbol of the return home of the immortal soul of man in the eternal, spiritual dimension.

The Sea of Time and Space is not only, in terms of form, one of Blake's most aesthetically beautiful paintings but also, in terms of content, one of his most philosophically profound paintings. As a representation of the essentials of Neoplatonism, the painting, Raine says, is an illustration of "the perpetual cycle of the descent and return of souls between an eternal and a temporal world," as well as "the journey through life, under the symbol of a crossing of the sea," of which, she says, "the voyage of Odysseus, his dangers and his adventures, his departure and his home-coming to Ithaca, is the type and symbol" (1968, 1: 75).

The Sea of Time and Space is a magnificent example of the interest that Blake has in what he calls "mythological and recondite meaning" (1976: 566). In the painting, Blake employs images from Homeric mythology to depict the return of Odysseus to Ithaca. This is the mythological meaning of the painting. To these images, Blake applies Neoplatonic philosophy to depict the return of the immortal soul of man to the spiritual dimension. This is the recondite meaning of the painting. *The Sea of Time and Space* has both an exoteric, mythological meaning and an esoteric, philosophical meaning.

Does the painting also have an unconscious, psychological meaning? Jung says that "William Blake's paintings" are examples of visionary art (1930/1950, *CW* 15: par. 142). He says of artists such as Blake that "what appears in the vision is the imagery of the collective unconscious" (1930/1950, *CW* 15: par. 152). For Jung, the images in visionary art are archetypal images.

Jung does not say much about Blake, and what he does say tends to be critical. "I am," he says, "no particular friend of Blake, whom I am always inclined to criticize" (1975: 17). Jung asserts that Blake "has compiled a lot of half- or undigested knowledge in his fantasies" (1973: 513). Although Jung categorizes Blake as a visionary artist, he depreciates Blake's fantasies as "an artistic production rather than an authentic representation of unconscious processes" (1973: 514).

This opinion is a projection onto Blake of the notorious prejudice that Jung, as a psychologist, has against art. For example, on one occasion, in active imagination, when a voice from the unconscious insists to Jung that his fantasies are art, he vehemently and adamantly protests that his fantasies have "nothing to do with art" (1963: 185). Why does Jung have a bias against art? When Jung discusses active imagination, he acknowledges that content and form are equally necessary and that each is "compensatory" to the other ([1916]/1957, *CW* 8: par. 177), but, as a psychologist, he tends to value content over form. What most interests Jung is what the content means psychologically, and what concerns him is that the imposition of a form on that content may aesthetically compromise the pristine purity of the content. It is this position that Jung assumes when he characterizes Blake's fantasies not as an authentic representation of unconscious processes but as a mere artistic production.

Jung recorded his fantasies in *The Red Book* (2009). He transcribed them in calligraphic gothic script and embellished them with illustrations in the style of illuminations in medieval manuscripts. Sonu Shamdasani notes that Jung's "combination of text and image" in *The Red Book* is reminiscent of Blake's art (2009: 203). Are Jung's fantasies in *The Red Book* also art? "In the Red Book," Jung says, "I tried an esthetic elaboration of my fantasies, but never finished it." He says that he abandoned "this estheticizing tendency" in order to ground fantasy in reality, which meant to him not artistic production but, he emphasizes, "scientific comprehension" (1963: 188). To Jung, the psychological content of his fantasies was much more important than the aesthetic form – ultimately, science was much more important than art.

There is no evidence that Jung knew *The Sea of Time and Space*. Had he known it, how might he have interpreted it? How might he have applied Jungian psychology to the painting?

From the perspective of Jungian psychology, the voyage of Odysseus is an image of the archetype of the journey of the hero. As Joseph Campbell describes it, the journey of the hero is a mythological journey in three stages: separation, initiation, and return (1968: 30). The return of Odysseus is an example of the third and final stage, after the first stage of separation and the second stage of initiation.

Jungians interpret the mythological journey of the hero as the psychological journey of the ego in relation to the unconscious. In Jungian terms, Odysseus is an image of the ego, the sea is an image of the unconscious, and Athena is an image of the anima. Psychologically, the voyage of Odysseus is a journey of individuation. On what Jung calls "the sea of the unconscious" (1948, *CW* 18: par. 754), the ego experiences an initiation in preparation for the return.

Athena is an image of the anima who, as a psychopomp, is the guide of the ego on the journey of individuation. When the anima "appears as the psychopomp," Jung says, she is "the one who shows the way" (1936, *CW* 12: par. 74). In *The Sea of Time and Space*, when Athena extends her left arm and hand up to the sky, she shows Odysseus the way "home." In Neoplatonic philosophy, this is the spiritual dimension to which the soul returns. In Jungian psychology, it is the archetypal dimension to which the ego returns.

Just as it is possible to apply Neoplatonic philosophy retroactively to Homeric mythology, as Blake does, it is possible to apply Jungian psychology retroactively to *The Sea of Time and Space*, and to interpret Odysseus, the sea, and Athena as the ego, the unconscious, and the anima. To do so, however, is to commit the fallacy of *post hoc, ergo propter hoc* (after this, therefore because of this). Such an *ex post facto* interpretation is, if not arbitrary, adventitious.

Raine acknowledges that Blake's visionary art is similar to Jung's analytical psychology. She says, however, that "all psychological elucidations" (and that includes Jungian interpretation) are inaccurate to the extent that they regard the sources of Blake's visionary art as subjective rather than "objective and traditional." Blake's art would not be visionary, she says, if it "were no more than a projection of his own psychological states." Raine says that "a very great part of Blake's affinity with Jung may be explained without recourse to analytical psychology." What does she mean? Blake and Jung, Raine notes, knew many of the same sources – among them, mythological sources. Although she acknowledges that what "Jung calls the collective unconscious" is the ultimate source of "all mythologies" (1968, 1: xxvi), in *Blake and Tradition* she documents just how extensive Blake's knowledge of mythology was and proves conclusively that the mythological sources of his visionary art are traditional. Blake knew just as much mythology as Jung knew. As Raine says, Blake was not an "untaught original" (1977: 4) but a learned traditionalist.

Raine quite properly cautions that "not even Jung has said the last word" about the unconscious (1967: 90) – especially, I would emphasize, in relation to art. When Jung discusses "the secret of great art," he says that the creative process "consists in the unconscious activation of an archetypal image," which the artist then elaborates and shapes into a work of art (1922, *CW* 15: par. 130). True as that may be for some art, it is not true for all art – and certainly not for Blake's art. *The Sea of Time and Space* is a great work of art that employs what are, in a sense, archetypal images, but Blake does not activate those images unconsciously. On the contrary, he consciously derives them from traditional sources and adapts them to serve a mythological, philosophical, and, ultimately, aesthetic purpose.

Was Blake a Jungian, or was Jung a Blakean? Blake did not just anticipate Jung. Blake and Jung studied many of the same traditional sources, although they employed those sources for different purposes – the one aesthetic, the other psychological. As a result, it should be no surprise and no wonder that a retroactive application of Jungian psychology to *The Sea of Time and Space* is not only possible but also plausible – that is, superficially persuasive although specious. From the perspective of the traditional sources contemporaneous with and available to Blake, a Jungian interpretation of the painting is a misinterpretation. Such an interpretation erroneously assumes that *The Sea of Time and Space* is a spontaneous expression of archetypal images from the collective unconscious when, in actuality, it is a deliberate, quite conscious, superbly erudite allusion to traditional knowledge.

Jungian psychology is a valuable method of interpretation. It is not, however, the perfect method for every purpose. As impressive as Jungian psychology is, it is presumptuous to apply it retroactively – and reductively – to *The Sea of Time and Space*. To reduce the concrete mythological and philosophical images in the painting to abstract psychological concepts – for example, to archetypes – is to perpetrate a complacently facile, formulaic interpretation. After Raine's identification of Blake's traditional sources, ignorance is no longer an excuse for such condescension. In no serious sense was Blake unconscious. On the contrary, he was extraordinarily conscious. As an example of visionary art, *The Sea of Time and Space* is a work of genius, a masterpiece by a master artist. No other artist has ever depicted the return of Odysseus with such consummate artistry and such mythological and philosophical sophistication.

References

Blake, W. (1976) "A Descriptive Catalogue," in *Blake: Complete Writings with Variant Readings*, ed. G. Keynes, London: Oxford University Press: 562–86.
Campbell, J. (1968) *The Hero with a Thousand Faces*, Princeton, NJ: Princeton University Press.
Homer (1920) *The Odyssey of Homer*, trans. William Cowper, London: J.M. Dent & Sons and New York: E.P. Dutton & Co.
Jung, C.G. ([1916]/1957) "The Transcendent Function," *CW* 8: 67–91.
Jung, C.G. (1922) "On the Relation of Analytical Psychology to Poetry," *CW* 15: 65–83.
Jung, C.G. (1930/1950) "Psychology and Literature," *CW* 15: 84–105.
Jung, C.G. (1936) "Individual Dream Symbolism in Relation to Alchemy," *CW* 12: 39–223.
Jung, C.G. (1948) "Psychology and Spiritualism," *CW* 18: 312–16.
Jung, C.G. (1963) *Memories, Dreams, Reflections*, ed. A. Jaffé, trans. R. and C. Winston, New York: Pantheon Books.

Jung, C.G. (1973) *Letters 1: 1906–1950*, ed. G. Adler and A. Jaffé, trans. R.F.C. Hull, Princeton, NJ: Princeton University Press.

Jung, C.G. (1975) *Letters 2: 1951–1961*, ed. G. Adler and A. Jaffé, trans. R.F.C. Hull, Princeton, NJ: Princeton University Press.

Jung, C.G. (2009) *The Red Book: Liber Novus*, ed. S. Shamdasani, trans. M. Kyburz, J. Perk, and S. Shamdasani, New York and London: W. W. Norton.

Porphyry (1969) "Concerning the Cave of the Nymphs: A Translation of Porphyry's *De Antro Nympharum* from *The Commentaries of Proclus*," in K. Raine and G.M. Harper (eds.), *Thomas Taylor the Platonist: Selected Writings*, Princeton, NJ: Princeton University Press: 295–342.

Raine, K. (1967) *Defending Ancient Springs*, London: Oxford University Press.

Raine, K. (1968) *Blake and Tradition*, Princeton, NJ: Princeton University Press, 2 vols.

Raine, K. (1977) *Blake and Antiquity*, Princeton, NJ: Princeton University Press.

Raine, K., and Harper, G.M. (eds.) (1969) *Thomas Taylor the Platonist: Selected Writings*, Princeton, NJ: Princeton University Press.

Shamdasani, S. (2009) "Liber Novus: The 'Red Book' of C.G. Jung," in C.G. Jung, *The Red Book: Liber Novus*, ed. S. Shamdasani, trans. M. Kyburz, J. Peck, and S. Shamdasani, New York and London: W.W. Norton: 194–221.

Part III

THE 2011 MOSCOW LECTURES ON JUNGIAN PSYCHOANALYSIS

12

THE MYTHOLOGICAL
UNCONSCIOUS IN MOSCOW

A Dream of a Russian-American Woman in New York

A Mythological Dream

When I was considering a topic for this first lecture at the 2011 Conference of the Moscow Association for Analytical Psychology on the theme of "The Mythological Unconscious," it occurred to me that a dream of a Russian-American woman in New York might be of special interest to Jungians in Russia. It is a dream that she recounted to me not quite three years earlier. This is the dream:

> My husband and I are in Moscow. He's in a car. I'm following him on foot. I'm supposed to go where he's going, but I don't. He turns left. I turn right. I walk down to the end of this path. I cross the road and enter a park. There I see a five-story Khrushchev-style apartment building. I see the bottom of the building. Then, suddenly, I see, coming out of the top of the building, a statue of horses drawing a chariot. Then, to the left, I see another statue of horses and other mythological creatures. The statues are marble, white, and massive. The scene blows my mind. Other people walking in the park stop and stare and talk in awe about how beautiful the statues are. No human could have put them there – they're so colossal, so "alive." They're a blessing to all of us in this park, coming out of the top of this horrible, depressing Soviet building. The statues are ancient Greek, imaginative and inspirational – the opposite of socialist realism. I think that my husband will be angry that I'm late. I try to call him on my cell phone. The light's flashing red. My battery is low, so I can't call him. Then I see that it's 1:15. I think: "Oh, it's been only an hour, so it's OK." I think that once I tell my husband what I saw, he'll understand. Then I wake up. I think: "No, he'd never understand."

This dream is a mythological dream – that is, a dream in which mythological images figure prominently.

In the fourth lecture that Jung delivered at the Tavistock Clinic in London in 1935, he announced that he would interpret a mythological dream. Before he presented the dream, however, he asked – and answered – a question:

> Under what conditions does one have mythological dreams? With us they are rather rare, as our consciousness is to a great extent detached from the underlying archetypal mind. Mythological dreams therefore are felt by us as a very alien element. But this is not so with a mentality nearer to the primordial psyche. Primitives pay great attention to such dreams and call them "big dreams" in contradistinction to ordinary ones.
>
> (1935, *CW* 18: par. 250)

Contrary to what Jung says, I am personally dubious that modern people have mythological dreams any less frequently than ancient people. Be that as it may, the people in psychoanalysis with me do have mythological dreams.

I am a Jungian analyst, but I am also a Hillmanian analyst. James Hillman is as important to me as Jung is. What is it to be a Jungian–Hillmanian analyst? To me, it means to have a special interest in mythology and imagination – myths and images – especially in dreams.

I shall now present a Jungian–Hillmanian interpretation of the dream of the Russian-American woman. What is a Jungian–Hillmanian interpretation? Jung says that in order to interpret a dream accurately, "I must stick as close as possible to the dream images" (1934, *CW* 16: par. 320). Hillman formulates this procedure as the basic principle of imaginal psychology: "Stick to the image" (2004: 21). In accordance with this dictum, I shall stick closely to the images in this dream – among them, the mythological images. "We have to keep it very simple," Jung says, "and stick to the image" (2008: 332). In addition, as I interpret these images, I shall amplify them – that is, compare them to (and contrast them with) images from other sources – in order to identify important similarities (and differences) between them.

Ernest Jones says that the one question Freud could never answer was "What does a woman want?" (1955, 2: 421). If I, as a mere man, may presume to say so, we all now know the answer to that question. A woman wants to be understood – that is, a woman wants a man, especially a man she loves, to understand her, especially to understand how she feels. We also know that it is difficult for a man to understand a woman – and also for a woman to understand a man. Deborah Tannen, in the book *You Just Don't Understand* (1990), provides numerous impressive examples of just how difficult it is for men and women to understand each other.

This dream ends with the dreamer thinking that once she tells her husband what she has seen, he will understand. Immediately, however, when she wakes up, she thinks that he would never understand. The dreamer is utterly pessimistic. It would not just be difficult for her husband to understand. It would be impossible.

What is it that her husband would never understand? It is how she feels about what she has seen. What has she seen? She has seen ancient Greek statues – a statue of horses drawing a chariot and another statue of horses and other mythological creatures – coming out of the top of a Khrushchev-style apartment building. The statues are marble, white, massive, colossal, beautiful, imaginative, and inspirational. How does the dreamer feel about what she has seen? She feels that she, as well as the other people who have seen these statues, have been blessed.

In *The Mythological Unconscious* (Adams 2010), I reaffirm what Jung argues – that the ancient gods and goddesses, heroes and heroines, and creatures are not dead but are "alive" (not literally, of course, but metaphorically) as images in the psyches of modern men and women. This dream of a contemporary woman confirms the enduring, abiding vitality of the mythological unconscious.

The dream is an archetypal "journey" dream. The journey, as George Lakoff and Mark Johnson note, is one of those "metaphors we live by" (1980: 89–95). For this Russian-American woman, the journey is a metaphor she dreams by. The dreamer departs on a journey and arrives at a destination. Metaphorically, the dream is an archetypal "destiny" dream.

Lakoff notes that among the metaphors we dream by is the metaphor "love is a journey" (2001: 265–8). The dreamer was a woman in her 30s. She was, as the dream indicates, married, but it should be no surprise that she was in the process of obtaining a divorce, for the beginning of the dream says that, although at first she is following her husband and is supposed to go where he is going, he in a car, she on foot, she does not go where he is going. Instead, she goes another, separate way to the end of a path. (Archetypally, this separation is necessary for the arrival at a destination that is the individuation of the dreamer.)

Then, in a modern city park, the dreamer suddenly sees ancient statues. The experience is similar to one that Jung describes. Imagine, he says, "the uncanny feeling which would steal over us if, amid the noise and bustle of a modern city street, we were suddenly to come upon an ancient relic." Instantly, the past is present. "A moment ago, and we were completely absorbed in the hectic, ephemeral life of the present; then, the next moment, something very remote and strange flashes upon us, which directs our gaze to a different order of things," Jung says. "We turn away from the vast confusion of the present to glimpse the higher continuity of history" (1911–12/1952, *CW* 5: par. 1). There is, Jung concludes, a continuous historical – that is, an archetypal – connection between antiquity and modernity.

What is the "different order of things" that Jung mentions? It is what I call the *mythological unconscious*. This order is a mythic reality that is a psychic reality – not an external reality but an internal reality. After Freud and Jung, we now know, as Kathleen Raine says, that 'the mythological order is an interior order" (1967: 138).

Imagination and Socialist Realism

The dreamer is vouchsafed a vision of images emerging from the mythological unconscious. In this dream, the unconscious has a revelatory function. The images that come out of the top of a Khrushchev-style apartment building come upon the dreamer as a revelation. These images are not only ancient but also quite specifically Greek.

Hillman advocates what he calls the "return to Greece" (1975: 27). This dream, however, is not so much a return *to* Greece as it is a return *of* Greece. It is an example of what Freud calls the "return of the repressed." The dreamer does not return to Greece. Rather, Greece returns to her.

The Greece in this dream is not the external Greece but an internal Greece. It is, as Hillman says, an "inscape" (1975: 30). It is a mythological order as an interior order. As Ginette Paris says, "Now, turning within, we must see that *we are Greeks*" (1986: 3).

Freud emphasizes sexual repression. In this dream, however, what has been repressed – and what is returned – is not sex but imagination. More specifically, it is what Hillman calls the "inner Greece of the imagination" (1975: 30). The Greece in this dream is not the real Greece but an imaginal Greece.

What is it that represses imagination? It is realism that represses imagination. Why does it do so? It does so from an apprehensive conviction that imagination perpetrates a distortion of reality, a result that is unrealistic. This position is a bias that devalues the imaginal – that reduces the imaginative to the imaginary, in the pejorative sense of the unreal.

In this respect, the dreamer remarks that the Greek images in the dream are the "opposite of socialist realism." Realism purports to render reality as it is. From a psychoanalytic perspective, realism is an aesthetic that exemplifies what Freud calls the "reality principle." Socialist realism is a special variety of realism. As realism does, socialist realism assumes that a mimetically accurate rendition of reality is perfectly possible. Both realism and socialist realism attempt to imitate reality. Socialist realism, however, purports to render reality not only as it is but also as it will be – in fact, as it must be – the culmination of the ostensibly inevitable revolutionary trend of socialism toward communism. The reality in socialist realism is not only a perception of a present reality but also a projection of a future reality, a reality that is not yet real – that is, a real that is an ideal. Ironically, socialist realism includes socialist idealism. In this, as well as other respects, socialist realism is, as Régine Robin says, "an impossible aesthetic" (1992).

The dreamer describes the Khrushchev-style apartment building as "this horrible, depressing Soviet building." To the dreamer, the building is psychopathological. Diagnostically, it is depressive. It is as if the *DSM-IV*, the fourth edition of the *Diagnostic and Statistical Manual of Mental Disorders*, had the category "Architectural Depressive Disorder." At the sight of the Khrushchev-style apartment building, the dreamer feels depressed, but at the sight of the ancient Greek statues, she feels blessed.

What is a "Khrushchev-style apartment building"? Nikita Khrushchev became premier of the Soviet Union in 1955. Immediately, he implemented an ambitious plan to build millions of apartments. Every family was to have an apartment. The project was to build blocks of cheap, concrete, five-story apartment buildings on a mass scale. Khrushchev emphasized prefabrication and standardization. Aesthetically, the apartment buildings were a Soviet version of the "international style" of modernist architecture and the dictum that "form follows function." This was socialist realism as socialist functionalism.

The apartment buildings were strictly utilitarian and notoriously ugly. Residents nicknamed them "khrushchoby" – a homonymic pun on the Russian word "trushchoby," which means "slums" (Atwood 2000: 155). Khrushchev excluded any architectural ornamentation or decoration, which he considered superfluous, extravagant, excessively expensive, and ideologically reactionary. Ancient Greek statues coming out of the top of a Khrushchev-style apartment building would have been unimaginable.

In Greek mythology, horses draw the chariots of gods and goddesses. This dream, however, does not say whether there is any god or goddess in the chariot. The emphasis in the dream is on the horses and other creatures. Jung says that creatures in general and horses in particular are images of libido, or psychic energy. He notes that "energy is even measured in terms of 'horse power'" and says that "the horse signifies a quantum of energy that stands at man's disposal" (1911–12/1952, *CW* 5: par. 658). Jung defines images as "*transformers*, their function being to convert libido from a 'lower' into a 'higher' form" (1911–12/1952, *CW* 5: par. 344).

In this dream, ancient Greek images of horses and other creatures emerge from the mythological unconscious to energize the psyche of a modern Russian-American woman. The dreamer says that the scene of ancient Greek images coming out of the top of the Khrushchev-style apartment building "blows my mind." This dream is a mind-blowing experience – or, I prefer to say, an ego-exploding experience. The libido that the images of horses and other creatures express is psychically so energetic as to be explosive. An explosion is the result of a large, rapid, and spectacular expansion. The scene of the ancient Greek images coming out of the top of the Khrushchev-style apartment building expands and explodes the ego – that is, the attitudes, the assumptions and expectations, of the dreamer.

What are these assumptions and expectations? They are notions, I would say, about what is imaginable and what is unimaginable – that is, what is possible and what is impossible. Edward S. Casey defines imagination as "pure possibility," which he describes as an orientation "to what *might* be rather than to what must be, or to what is, has been, or will be" (1976: 231). In this respect, imagination is, as the dreamer says, "the opposite of socialist realism," which purports to render accurately not only what is but also what will be – and, ultimately, as a revolutionary imperative, what *must* be.

The scene juxtaposes, although not side-by-side but top-by-bottom, elements that are radically, ironically incongruous. Aesthetically, ancient Greek statues and a Khrushchev-style apartment building are utterly incompatible. They are mutually exclusive. To the dreamer, the combination is unimaginable or impossible. The scene is not just "politically incorrect" but psychically incomprehensible.

Marx on Mythology and Technology

Marx provides an account of the relation between Greek mythology and Greek art. "It is a well-known fact," he says, "that Greek mythology was not only the arsenal of Greek art, but also the very ground from which it had sprung." Mythology – gods as supernatural forces – appeared when natural forces dominated man. If man could not dominate nature, then man imagined gods that could. This mythological perspective on nature, Marx notes, "shaped Greek imagination and art" (1971: 44).

Is, however, Marx asks, such a mythological perspective still "possible in the age of automatic machinery and railways and locomotives and electric telegraphs?" How can ancient mythology possibly compete with modern technology? "Where," Marx asks, "does Vulcan come in as against Roberts & Co? Jupiter, as against the lightning conductor? and Hermes, as against the *Crédit Mobilier*?" (1971: 45). These questions are, of course, rhetorical, and the answer, implicit in the questions, is that mythology, once possible, is now impossible.

Marx says that mythology appears when nature dominates man and promptly disappears when man dominates nature: "All mythology masters and dominates and shapes the forces of nature in and through the imagination; hence it disappears as soon as man gains mastery over the forces of nature" (1971: 45). What is it that enables man to dominate nature? It is technology. When technology advances, Marx says, mythology vanishes. When nature is "technologized," it is demythologized.

In this account, technology does not repress mythology – it simply replaces it. Gods are not only no longer necessary but also no longer possible. Modern technology has rendered ancient mythology redundant. In this respect, what Wolfgang Giegerich says about twentieth- and twenty-first-century technology (the computer and the Internet) – that it has rendered mythology obsolete (1999: 175) – is, in gist, merely a contemporary paraphrase of what Marx says about nineteenth-century technology.

"Greek art," Marx says, "presupposes the existence of Greek mythology." He says that "in any event there had to be a mythology." Greek mythology was a necessary condition for Greek art. "In no event," Marx says, "could

Greek art originate in a society which excludes any mythological explanation of nature, any mythological attitude towards it, or which requires of the artist an imagination free from mythology" (1971: 45).

Greek statues are, of course, Greek art. The statues in this dream are images from Greek mythology – a statue of horses drawing a chariot and a statue of horses and other mythological creatures. Contrary to what Marx says, modern technology – in this instance, the technology of prefabrication and standardization, the technology of cheap, concrete, five-story, Khrushchev-style apartment buildings – does not obviate or obliterate ancient mythology.

Mythology does not disappear, or, if it does, it reappears – as vital as ever, much to the surprise and much to the pleasure of the dreamer. In this event, the dream demonstrates that Greek art can – and does – persist in spite of the efforts of a society, the Soviet Union, to exclude mythological explanations and mythological attitudes or, under the rubric of socialist realism, to require of artists imaginations "free from mythology" – that is, no imagination at all.

From a Marxist perspective, the scene of ancient Greek statues coming out of the top of a Khrushchev-style apartment building is anachronistic and atavistic. From a Jungian perspective, it is archetypal.

Lenin on Dreams

When Lenin asks the question "What is to be done?" he exclaims: "We should dream!" He then says that these words alarmed him when he wrote them. (They induced a spontaneous experience of what Jung calls "active imagination.") Lenin says that he "imagined myself" at a conference opposite editors and contributors from a periodical (1975: 106). These were Social Democrats who opposed attempts to censor political discourse.

In this active imagination, two of the Social Democrats speak sternly to Lenin. One says: "Permit me to ask you, has an autonomous editorial board the right to dream without first soliciting the opinion of the Party committees?" Another says: "I go further. I ask, has a Marxist any right at all to dream?" (1975: 106).

These questions about the right to dream chill Lenin. "The very thought of these stern questions sends a cold shiver down my spine and makes me wish for nothing but a place to hide," he says. "I shall try to hide behind the back of Pisarev" (1975: 106).

D.I. Pisarev was an important Russian literary critic and publicist of the 1860s. Lenin cites an article in which Pisarev discusses what he calls the rift between dreams and reality. He quotes Pisarev at length and with approval:

> My dream may run ahead of the natural march of events or may fly off at a tangent in a direction in which no natural march of events will ever proceed. In the first case my dream will not cause any harm; it may even support and augment the energy of the working men ...

There is nothing in such dreams that would distort or paralyse labour-power. On the contrary, if man were completely deprived of the ability to dream in this way, if he could not from time to time run ahead and mentally conceive, in an entire and completed picture, the product to which his hands are only just beginning to lend shape, then I cannot at all imagine what stimulus there would be to induce man to undertake and complete extensive and strenuous work in the sphere of art, science, and practical endeavour ... The rift between dreams and reality causes no harm if only the person dreaming believes seriously in his dream, if he attentively observes life, compares his observations with his castles in the air, and if, generally speaking, he works conscientiously for the achievement of his fantasies. If there is some connection between dreams and life then all is well.

(1975: 106)

Lenin comments: "Of this kind of dreaming there is unfortunately too little in our movement" (1975: 107).

From a hiding place behind the back of Pisarev, Lenin says to the Social Democrats in this active imagination that Marxists do have a right to dream – but only dreams that cause no harm. Harm to what? The implicit answer to this question is harm to the revolution. Marxists have a right to dream only if those dreams "support and augment the energy of the working men" and only if the dreamer "believes seriously in his dream, attentively observes life, compares his observations with his castles in the air," and "works conscientiously for the achievement of his fantasies."

From this perspective, dreaming is not an inalienable right. Dreaming is a right only in the service of the revolution – or, as Lenin says, the "movement" – and the energy, or libido, of the working men. The implication is that there is no right to dream of the "might be" of pure possibility but only the right to dream of the "must be" of revolutionary inevitability. (Of all "isms," the most extreme is "inevitabilism.")

Lenin is no Freud or Jung. By "dreams," he means not dreams as such, in the strict sense, but, as Pisarev says, "fantasies." Lenin is no psychoanalyst who interprets dreams. He is a politician who represses fantasies that complicate and problematize – or contradict – the revolutionary imperative.

The Futility of Repression

All political states, even democratic ones, are, to a certain extent, repressive. As a totalitarian state, the Soviet Union was infamously so. It attempted to limit or eliminate any activity that it suspected might pose a serious challenge to the absolute authority of the state. By 1930, as Martin A. Miller notes, the Soviet Union effectively repressed psychoanalysis as both a theory and a practice (1998: 92). Why did it do so?

As an activity, psychoanalysis is not public but private – it is strictly confidential. Psychoanalysis serves not the collective but the individual, for whom it is a special opportunity to inquire into and reflect on images that emerge from the unconscious – for example, in dreams.

The purpose of psychoanalysis, as Hillman says, is to "evoke imagination" (1983: 4). As I define the "unconscious," it comprises any and all images of which the ego is unconscious. In this respect, the unconscious is synonymous with the imagination. "I tend to use 'imagination,'" Hillman says, "instead of that word 'unconscious' ... not that there isn't unconsciousness in us all the time" (1983: 32) – and so do I. Ironically, it is not the unconscious that is unconscious. It is the ego that is unconscious, and what it is unconscious of is the imagination – the images that emerge continuously, incessantly from the unconscious.

To repress imagination is to render it unconscious. Ultimately, however, repression is an exercise in futility, for what is repressed – or excluded on any basis – is redressed – or, as Jung says, compensated – by the unconscious. Jung emphasizes what he calls the "compensatory function" of the unconscious. What the unconscious compensates is the partial, prejudicial, or defective attitude of the ego. How does it do so? Images emerge spontaneously and autonomously from the unconscious. These images present alternative perspectives on the attitude of the ego. If the ego is curious and receptive rather than anxious and defensive, it may entertain these alternative perspectives sincerely, evaluate them critically, and engage them effectively.

Compensation does not entail capitulation. It is not a usurpation of the ego by the unconscious. What Jung espouses is not the abdication of the ego but the participation of the ego in conversation with the unconscious. The ego is under no obligation to accept, without demur, the alternative perspectives that the unconscious presents. It has the discretion, or option, to reject them (although not summarily or peremptorily). The only responsibility of the ego is to consider seriously the alternative perspectives that the unconscious presents. What Jung advocates, in both dream interpretation and active imagination, is not a monological dictation by the unconscious to the ego but a dialogical negotiation, on equal terms, between the ego and the unconscious. In this sense, dreams express not what "must be" but what "might be."

It was perfectly prudent for the Soviet Union to repress psychoanalysis. The logic of that repression was impeccable, for psychoanalysis – as a valorization of the unconscious – is a radically subversive activity. (To "subvert" is to "overturn" from "under.") Psychically, the images that emerge from the unconscious subvert the attitudes of the ego. Politically, such images may also subvert the authority of the state. The Soviet Union could repress psychoanalysis – it could, as it did, ban institutes, clinics, private practices, and books – but it could never repress the unconscious, for the unconscious is intrinsically irrepressible. It is ultimately impervious to intimidation. Even the most intrusive totalitarian state cannot censor the unconscious.

Polytheism and monotheism, Hillman notes, epitomize "the psychological alternatives of multiplicity and unity" (1975: 28). Ancient Greece was polytheistic rather than monotheistic. There were many gods and goddesses, not just one god. In contrast, the Soviet Union was atheistic – but only putatively so, for it, too, had a pantheon – what Gleb Prokhorov satirically calls "the gods of the Kremlin Olympus – Lenin and Stalin" (1995: 60). In the "cult of personality," they supplanted and superseded all previous gods and goddesses. Ironically, Lenin and Stalin successively assumed a mythological status that they both, at least officially, opposed. Ideologically, the Soviet Union was atheistic. Mythologically, however, it was monotheistic. Lenin and Stalin were not, of course, gods – they were mere men.

A chauvinistic American might emphasize that the dreamer is no longer a Russian but now a Russian-American, that she is not only an immigrant but also a citizen, and that, although the location of the dream is Moscow, the location of the dreamer is New York, and might argue that what enables her to dream such a dream is the First Amendment to the Constitution – that freedom of expression is what deters both psychic and political repression, that such a dream is possible in the USA but would have been impossible in the USSR. Perhaps freedom of expression does facilitate freedom of imagination. Plausible as that notion may be, it does not address the issue of what is imagined and then expressed in a dream. It does not explain why, in this dream, the mythological unconscious is specifically Greek.

The unconscious is an inexhaustible source of ineradicable images – among them, mythological images. This dream is cogent evidence of that fact. The dreamer is not the only Russian-American for whom Greek mythology is important. A rock and roll band that Manny Theiner (2010) profiles in a newspaper review has a very Jungian name – "Persephone's Dream." The bass player in the band is Roman Propenko, a Russian-American. Rowan Poole, the guitar player in the band, studied ancient history and classical mythology at university – "so," one rather Freudian member of the band says, "he kind of has a jones" – slang for an erect penis – "for Greek myth." As a result, images from Greek mythology thematically dominate the music of the band. For example, the title of a recent album is "Pan: An Urban Pastoral." Whether or not Americans are mythologically literate enough to appreciate these images, Propenko says that Russians are. "Americans often don't know about Greek myths, but in Russia it's a regular thing we study in school," he says. "I studied Marxist economics and philosophy in the Communist era, and you can't think about that without [noticing] that everything is based on Greek philosophy and myth."

Art and the Archetype of Creativity

I assume that the dreamer also studied Greek myths in school, as I did, and that this mythological knowledge remained available to her, although quiescently so, as a potential source of images that, under certain circumstances, might emerge from the unconscious to serve a quite specific compensatory function – for example, as especially apt material for a dream that might energize, or "libidinize," her and motivate her to individuate. The statue of horses drawing a chariot and the statue of horses and other mythological creatures are Greek art. The dreamer describes these statues as "imaginative and inspirational." It should be no surprise that the dreamer aspired to be an artist – although not a sculptor of statues but a writer of poems and plays. In psychoanalysis with me, she proudly shared poems and plays that she had written and that she hoped to publish or produce.

On what Jung calls the "objective level," the husband in the dream is a *person*, an object in the external reality of the dreamer. In contrast, on what Jung calls the "subjective level," the husband in the dream is a *personification*, an image of an aspect of the internal reality of the dreamer as a subject. From this perspective, the husband is an image of what Jung calls the "animus," the archetype of the masculine aspect in the psyche of a woman. More specifically, in the psyche of this woman, the husband is a masculine aspect that would never understand her. This husband is a masculine aspect that has no capacity for empathy. (To "empathize" does not mean to "sympathize" – it merely means to "understand.")

This dream is an archetypal "separation–individuation" dream. The ego has to separate from the husband in order to individuate, for that masculine aspect is incorrigibly unempathic. The dreamer has an animus that would never understand how she feels about what she experiences. What does the dreamer experience, and how does she feel about it? She experiences a revelation. In this respect, the dream is an archetypal "separation–revelation–individuation" dream. In this dream, the unconscious has not only a compensatory function but also what Jung calls a "prospective function." The alternative perspective that the unconscious presents to the ego is a prospect that is a pure possibility. The dreamer feels depressed at what has been repressed but then feels blessed by what is now suddenly expressed. The vision of Greek art – statues of horses drawing a chariot and horses and other mythological creatures – is a revelation that enables the dreamer to envisage who she might be – an artist.

The work that the dreamer did in New York was not art work. It was just a job – not a career and certainly not a vocation. The poems and plays that she wrote she did after work, not at work. Work was realism. Art was imagination. There was an extreme dissociation between work and art, and the decisive issue was how the dreamer might effect a viable reconciliation of these adversarial dimensions – that is, how she might realize what she imagined. (Such a "realization" would mean both to become more conscious of and to become more resolute about the imagination.)

At the end of the dream, the dreamer thinks that her husband will be angry that she is late. (This anger is the "animosity" of an animus with no capacity for empathy.) She tries to call her husband on her cell phone, but the light is flashing red. Her battery is low, so she cannot call him. The attempt does not succeed – it fails.

By the maxim "Stick to the image," what do these images mean? A cell phone is a mechanism for communication. A flashing red light is a warning signal. A battery is a device for the storage of energy. What these images indicate – or intimate – is that the ego does not have enough disposable libido for an effective conversation with the animus. Any effort by the ego to continue to converse with the animus would be in vain – to no avail.

In this dream, there is a radical contrast between the low energy of the battery and the high energy of the horses drawing the chariot and the horses and other mythological creatures. The horses and other creatures are images of a quantum of energy at the disposal of this dreamer. They are images of transformation. The revelatory, compensatory, and prospective function of these images is to evince to the dreamer that there is available to her, in the mythological unconscious, a quite considerable amount of energy that could enable her to attain the artistic ambition that she entertains, if only she would embrace these images. These images could convert – that is, transform – the libido of the dreamer from a lower form into a higher form. (In this respect, to have low energy is to feel exhausted and depressed, and to have high energy is to feel excited and blessed.)

The dreamer had what Marie-Louise von Franz calls a *creative personality*. Von Franz says that the analysis of "creative people is a great problem." Creative people become neurotic, she says, when they "should do something creative" but do not. They have what von Franz calls a "creative task," but they avoid it (1995: 17). She notes that artists often avoid psychoanalysis, even Jungian psychoanalysis, from a concern that "we, in a reductive analytical way, are going to destroy their creativity" (1995: 18). Von Franz says that this apprehension is justifiable "to the extent that not enough analysts know about the creative process in the psyche" (1995: 19).

I consider the most important of all archetypes, not only for artists but also for all people, to be the archetype of creativity. For artists, however, the archetype of creativity is especially important. All people become neurotic if they do not live creatively. This existential creativity is *ars vitae*, the "art of life." For people with creative personalities, there is, in addition, a "life of art." This is the special task of the artist.

Jung says that mythological dreams are "big dreams," and this dream of a Russian-American woman in New York was, for her, a very big dream – an energetic, expansive, explosive, transformative dream. It was a dream that, in the imaginal scene of the mythological unconscious in Moscow, blessed the artistic ambition of the dreamer.

When I arrived in Moscow, a member of the Moscow Association for Analytical Psychology met me at the Sheremetyevo International Airport and accompanied me on the Aeroexpress train to Belorussky Rail Terminal. He then drove me to the hotel where I was to stay. Along the way, he showed me the famous sights of Moscow. I looked out the window of the car – and there, suddenly, was the Bolshoi Theatre.

I had never before visited Moscow. I had never before seen the Bolshoi Theatre, even an image of it. Imagine the surprise I experienced when I saw, coming out of the top of the building, a statue of horses drawing a chariot! The statue, by Peter Clodt von Jürgensburg, the favorite sculptor of Czar Nicholas I, depicts the god Apollo in a *quadriga*, a chariot drawn by four horses.

The Bolshoi Theatre could hardly be more different, in both form and function, from a Khruschev-style apartment building – it is a classical-style arts building for ballet and opera. Although I do not know for certain, it now seems to me probable that the statue of horses drawing a chariot surmounting the portico of the Bolshoi Theatre is the source for the image in the dream of the Russian-American woman in New York. What more apt image could there be, in the mythological unconscious of Moscow, of the archetype of creativity and the artistic ambition of the dreamer?

Figure 12.1 The Bolshoi Theatre, photograph by Michael Vannoy Adams.

References

Adams, M.V. (2010) *The Mythological Unconscious*, 2nd rev. ed., Putnam, CT: Spring Publications.

Atwood, L. (2000) *Gender and Housing in Soviet Russia: Private Life in a Public Space*, Manchester: Manchester University Press.

Casey, E. (1976) *Imagining: A Phenomenological Study*, Bloomington, IN: Indiana University Press.

Giegerich, W. (1999) *The Soul's Logical Life: Towards a Rigorous Notion of Psychology*, 2nd rev. ed., Frankfurt am Main: Peter Lang.

Hillman, J. (1975) *Re-Visioning Psychology*, New York: Harper & Row.

Hillman, J., with Pozzo L. (1983) *Inter Views: Conversations with Laura Pozzo on Psychotherapy, Biography, Love, Soul, Dreams, Work, Imagination, and the State of the Culture*, New York: Harper & Row.

Hillman, J. (2004) *Archetypal Psychology*, *Uniform Edition of the Writings of James Hillman*, vol. 1, Putnam, CT: Spring Publications.

Jones, E. (1955) *The Life and Work of Sigmund Freud: Volume 2, Years of Maturity, 1901–1919*, New York: Basic Books.

Jung, C.G. (1911–12/1952) *Symbols of Transformation: An Analysis of the Prelude to a Case of Schizophrenia*, CW 5.

Jung, C.G. (1934) "The Practical Use of Dream-Analysis," *CW* 16: 139–61.

Jung, C.G. (1935) *The Tavistock Lectures: On the Theory and Practice of Analytical Psychology*, *CW* 18: 1–182.

Jung, C.G. (2008) *Children's Dreams: Notes from the Seminar Given in 1936–1940*, ed. L. Jung and M. Meyer-Grass, trans. E. Falzeder with T. Woolfson, Princeton, NJ: Princeton University Press.

Lakoff, G., and Johnson, M. (1980) *Metaphors We Live By*, Chicago: University of Chicago Press.

Lakoff, G. (2001) "How Metaphor Structures Dreams: The Theory of Conceptual Metaphor Applied to Dream Analysis," in K. Bulkeley (ed.), *Dreams: A Reader on Religious, Cultural, and Psychological Dimensions of Dreaming*, New York: Palgrave: 265–84.

Lenin, V.I. (1975) *What Is to Be Done? Burning Questions of Our Movement*, in *The Lenin Anthology*, ed. R.C. Tucker, New York: W.W. Norton: 12–114.

Marx, K. (1971) *The Grundrisse*, ed. and trans. D. McLellan, New York: Harper & Row.

Miller, M.A. (1998) *Freud and the Bolsheviks: Psychoanalysis in Imperial Russia and the Soviet Union*, New Haven, CT: Yale University Press.

Paris, G. (1986) *Pagan Meditations: The Worlds of Aphrodite, Artemis, and Hestia*, trans. G. Moore, Dallas: Spring Publications.

Prokhorov, G. (1995) *Art under Socialist Realism: Soviet Painting 1930–1950*, Roseville East: Craftsman House.

Raine, K. (1967) *Defending Ancient Springs*, London: Oxford University Press.

Robin, R. (1992) *Socialist Realism: An Impossible Aesthetic*, trans. C. Porter, Stanford, CA: Stanford University Press.

Tannen, D. (1990) *You Just Don't Understand: Women and Men in Conversation*, New York: Morrow.

Theiner, M. (December 2, 2010) "Progressive Rock Band Persephone's Dream Unveils Mythical Epic," *Pittsburgh Post-Gazette*: www.post-gazette.com/pg/10336/1107401-388.stm

Von Franz, M.-L. (1995) *Creation Myths*, Boston: Shambhala.

13

THE METAPHOR OF METAMORPHOSIS

Change in Myth and Psyche

Transformation and the Metamorphoses of Ovid

The topic of this second lecture at the 2011 Conference of the Moscow Association for Analytical Psychology is change in myth and psyche. "To the extent that 'cure' means turning a sick man into a healthy one," Jung says, "cure is change" (1935, *CW* 16: par. 11). Ultimately, however, in Jungian psychoanalysis change is not so much about the cure of illness as it is about the transformation of consciousness. In contrast to Freudians, who emphasize "cure," Jungians emphasize "transformation." In this respect, Jung says that Jungian psychoanalysis comprises "four stages, namely, confession, elucidation, education, and transformation" (1929, *CW* 16: par. 122). The fourth and final stage is not just a transformation of the patient but, Jung says, "a mutual transformation" of both the analyst and the patient (1929, *CW* 16: par. 164).

In Western civilization, the foundational text on change is *The Metamorphoses*. In the very first sentence, as Ovid invokes the gods to inspire him, he says: "Bodies, I have in mind, and how they can change to assume new forms" (1994: 1).

The Metamorphoses is a compendium of Roman myths (which are in derivation, of course, Greek myths). It is a morphology of mythology. The myths that Ovid recounts are myths of change – myths in which gods and goddesses or men and women experience metamorphoses. The number of metamorphoses is impressive. P.M.C. Forbes Irving says that "in Ovid there are about two hundred and fifty" (1990: 19).

A "metamorphosis" is a "transformation" – a change from one form into another form. In *The Metamorphoses*, it is the body that changes. The bodies of gods and goddesses or men and women change to assume new forms. They "morph." These bodies change from divine or human forms into animal, vegetable, and mineral forms. In Ovid, the bodies of men and women also live and die and change in that ultimate respect.

Toward the end of *The Metamorphoses*, Ovid introduces as a character Pythagoras, who says: "Things change." Pythagoras goes on at length about change. "As long as I'm going on this way," he says, "I may as well do the

196

whole paradoxical notion of change as the only constant, for all things change" (1994: 312). Then he says that we, too, change: "Our bodies are also changing" (1994: 313). Pythagoras offers advice about change: "Think of it not as progress or regress but merely process" (1994: 314). He says that change is perfectly natural: "Nothing in Nature is constant but continual change and process, which seem to be Nature's nature" (1994: 316). For Pythagoras, the paradox is not, as the aphorism says, "The more things change, the more they remain the same." It is that the only constant is inconstancy, or change. The only thing that remains the same is that things change. For Pythagoras, all change is inevitable.

For Ovid, however, most change is not at all inevitable. In *The Metamorphoses*, some gods and goddesses have the capacity, by choice, to change bodily form. For most gods and goddesses or men and women, however, the function of bodily change is either to reward or to punish. Either the change tends to be the bestowing of a favor, the granting of an appeal, or the answering of a prayer, or, alternatively, the change tends to be the imposing of a penalty. As a result of bodily change, gods and goddesses or men and women either escape from some situation that is intolerable or suffer for some action that is offensive.

In *The Metamorphoses*, change is mythological, not psychological. Ancient people, James Hillman says, "had no psychology, properly speaking." They had mythological stories about men and women in relation to "more-than-human forces" that they called gods and goddesses (1979: 23–24). Modern people, Hillman says, "have no mythology, properly speaking." They have psychological theories about men and women in relation to "more-than-human forces" that they call instincts and complexes (1979: 24). The more-than-human forces have changed to assume new forms. There and then, they were concrete mythological images. Here and now, they are abstract psychological concepts.

Ovid emphasizes bodily change, not psychic change. When gods and goddesses or men and women experience a bodily change, they also, often if not always, experience a psychic change. In *The Metamorphoses*, however, psychic change is merely an incidentally contingent, epiphenomenal concomitant of bodily change.

In addition, for Ovid, metamorphosis is not a metaphor – or, more accurately, bodily change is not a metaphor for psychic change. For a psychic change to occur, a bodily change has to occur, quite literally. In *The Metamorphoses*, when mythic figures change, they do not do so figuratively, or metaphorically. For Ovid, the body is a body is a body – it is not a metaphor for the psyche. Ovid is a mythologist, not a psychologist.

Stones and Rocks

The Metamorphoses includes many myths in which gods and goddesses or men and women change into stone. Bodies change from divine or human form into mineral form. That is, one variety of transformation is petrification. Forbes Irving identifies "a number of obvious common features in the stories of petrification." The stones in these myths, he says, are inanimate objects with a permanent fixity, and the purpose they serve is most often to grimly remind, to warn, or to punish (1990: 139). Although bodily change in Ovid is not a metaphor for psychic change, Forbes Irving notes that it is possible to regard "stones as metaphors" (1990: 140). He says that petrification may function, as it does in the myth of Medusa, as a correlative of an emotional state – for example, "horror and fear" (1990: 142). Forbes Irving says that in most of the myths "petrification reflects human qualities." He remarks that just as "animal and plant metaphors tell us something about the meaning of transformation into an animal or plant," so, too, do stone metaphors tell us something about the meaning of transformation into a stone. "Stone metaphors," Forbes Irving says, "often suggest an inhuman or cruel quality in an attitude" (1990: 143). Metaphorically, to be "stony" means to be emotionally insensitive, indifferent, unresponsive, rigid, inert, inexpressive, or cruel.

Martin Heidegger argues that, ontologically, mineral forms are radically different from human and animal forms. "The stone," he says, "is worldless, it is without world, it has no world." He declares: "Worldlessness is constitutive of the stone" (1995: 196). What Heidegger means is that stones have no access to the world around them:

> The stone is without world. The stone is lying on the ground, for example. We can say that the stone is exerting a certain pressure upon the surface of the earth. It is 'touching' the earth. But what we call 'touching' here is not a form of touching at all in the stronger sense of the word ... Returning to the stone: it lies upon the earth but does not touch it ... Nor of course can the stone ever sense this earth as such.
>
> (1995: 196–7)

That is, stones are utterly insentient. Heidegger says of the stone that "everything present around it remains essentially *inaccessible* to the stone itself" (1995: 197).

Charles Hartshorne, one of the most important proponents of panpsychism, also says that stones are insentient. Hartshorne provides this definition: "Panpsychism (from the Greek for 'all' and 'soul') is the doctrine that everything is psychic or, at least, has a psychic aspect" (1950: 442). (In this respect, panpsychism is a contemporary version of animism, which asserts that all material reality is animate – that all material objects have souls.) Although from the perspective of panpsychism, everything has a psychic aspect, not every kind of thing is psychic to the same degree. All things are, at least to a certain extent, psychic, but only some things are truly sentient. Hartshorne differentiates between "individual" things (which are psychic and sentient) and "aggregative" things (which are psychic but insentient). A person is an example of an individual, sentient thing, while a stone is an example of an aggregative, insentient thing. To be sentient is to have the capacity to feel sensations (that is, to experience sense impressions). Just as Heidegger says that stones do not touch (in the sense of "feel") the earth on which they lie, Hartshorne says that "stones do not feel." He says that stones "furnish no evidence" that they have the capacity for such an experience (1937: 165).

David Ray Griffin emphasizes that panpsychism (or what he prefers to call panexperientialism) "does *not*, in spite of a host of detractors wishing to be able to dismiss it in a phrase as obviously ludicrous, necessarily imply (for example) that 'rocks have feelings'" (1998: 78n.). Lynn White, Jr., an advocate of a contemporary version of animism as a component of environmental ethics, does not say that rocks have feelings, but he does pose a question that might imply as much. "Do people," he asks, "have ethical obligations toward rocks?" White says that to most Americans the question is nonsense. He says that "when to any considerable group of us such a question is no longer ridiculous," it may then be possible to adopt measures to address the current ecological crisis (1973: 63).

"We know," Hartshorne says, "what it is like to be a person studying rocks," but "we do not know what it is like to be a rock." He says that, "with a rock, all that we seem to have are our human perceptions of it, these perceptions being how the rock influences our psychophysical being under certain conditions." For humans, what a rock is like is a question that is, epistemologically, out of the question. Humans are external to the rock – they are never internal to it. "We know the rock 'from the outside,'" Hartshorne says, "ourselves 'from the inside'" (1978: 90).

Heidegger says that "we cannot transpose ourselves into a stone." Such a transposition is impossible, he says, not just in practice – that is, "because we lack the appropriate means to accomplish something that is possible in principle" – rather, it is impossible in principle. Heidegger admits that a person never regards objects such as stones as "purely material" but "rather 'animates' them" (although such a description, he says, is deceptive). In effect, he concedes that animism is among the varieties of human experience – for example, in "myth." He says that it would be an error "to dismiss such animation as an exception or even as a purely metaphorical procedure" with a basis in "imagination" (1995: 206). Heidegger insists, however: "With respect to the stone, the question: Can we transpose ourselves into a stone?, is impossible in principle" (1995: 207).

As a boy, Jung had a very personal experience with a particular stone. He wondered whether he was the stone:

> In front of this wall was a slope in which was embedded a stone that
> jutted out – my stone. Often, when I was alone, I sat down on this
> stone, and then began an imaginary game that went something like

this: "I am sitting on top of this stone and it is underneath." But the stone also could say "I" and think: "I am lying here on this slope and he is sitting on top of me." The question then arose: "Am I the one who is sitting on the stone, or am I the stone on which *he* is sitting?" This question always perplexed me, and I would stand up, wondering who was what now.

(1963: 20)

Thirty years later, Jung stood on the same slope and again "sat down on a stone without knowing whether it was I or I was it" (1963: 20).

For Jung as a boy, to be interchangeable with the stone – to "be" the stone – was an opportunity to be as unchangeable as the stone:

At such times it was strangely reassuring and calming to sit on my stone. Somehow it would free me of all my doubts. Whenever I thought that I was the stone, the conflict ceased. "The stone has no uncertainties, no urge to communicate, and is eternally the same for thousands of years," I would think, "while I am only a passing phenomenon which bursts into all kinds of emotions" ... I was but the sum of my emotions, and the Other in me was the timeless, imperishable stone.

(1963: 42)

This anecdote is an example of the animistic perspective on objects that are putatively purely material. Hillman says that "everything has soul in some way or another," and he wonders "what kind of soul" various objects have. Among these objects, he explicitly mentions "a stone" (1983: 132).

Although Jung does not explicitly say that this particular stone has a "soul," he imagines that it has an "ego" and a "voice" – it, too, he says, could "say 'I'." The experience is not psychopathological. It is neither a delusion in which Jung seriously believes that he is a stone nor a hallucination in which he hears a stone speak. Rather, as Jung says, it is an imaginary game that a boy plays and that affords him an opportunity for reflection on what is permanent and what is temporary. In this respect, Mircea Eliade defines a stone as "that which man is not." In contrast to a man (or, in this instance, a boy), a stone is durable. Eliade says: "It resists time; its reality is coupled with perenniality" (1956: 4).

In imagination, Jung accomplishes what Heidegger insists is impossible in principle – he transposes himself into a stone. In this instance, transformation is transposition. What purpose does this transposition serve? It functions as an effective defense against emotional experience. For Jung, the stone is a metaphor in a very personal myth. If he could "be" a stone, perhaps he, too, could endure. Eventually, when Jung identifies alchemy as a historical precursor of psychoanalysis, the stone also assumes theoretical significance for him. Jung quotes with approval the injunction of the alchemist Gerhard Dorn: "Transform yourselves from dead stones into living philosophical stones!" (1937, *CW* 12: par. 378) – or, as a contemporary Jungian psychoanalyst might say, "psychological stones."

Petrification

In the *Motif Index of Folk-Literature*, Stith Thompson presents a number of types of transformation by petrification. Among these are type "A974. *Rocks from transformation of people to stone*" (1955, 1: 179), type "D230. *Transformation: man to a mineral form*," and type "D231. *Transformation: man to stone*" (1955, 2: 28).

Thompson also includes type "D.581. *Petrification by glance*" (1955, 2: 65), of which the myth of Medusa is perhaps the most important example. In *The Metamorphoses*, Ovid notes that men are "changed by a glimpse of Medusa's face to a lithic likeness" (1994: 84). In *The Mythological Unconscious*, I mention a 19-year-old Japanese woman who adopted "Medusa" as a name. The name accurately reflected the fact that, in terms of human qualities, she was not an emotionally warm person. "I'm not saying I'm evil," she says, "but I'm a bit cold." The name empowered her – it implied that she had the power (not literally, of course, but metaphorically) to petrify people – or, as she says, "the power to change people into stone" (Adams 2010: 40). In this instance, petrification is a conscious decision.

Although "petrification" is not among the technical terms in the psychoanalytic jargon of defenses, it might well be. R.D. Laing defines what "petrification" means psychologically. It is, he says:

1 A particular form of terror, whereby one is petrified, i.e. turned to stone.

2 The dread of this happening: the dread, that is, of the possibility of turning, or being turned, from a live person into a dead thing, into a stone ...

3 The "magical" act whereby one may attempt to turn someone else into stone, by "petrifying" him.

(1969: 48)

Rather than say that one petrifies another person, Laing says that it might be preferable to say that "one depersonalizes him, or reifies him" (1969: 48). (To depersonalize, or reify, a person is to turn him or her from a "being" into a "thing.")

Laing presents an example of petrification that is not a conscious decision but an unconscious occurrence. He recounts a dream in which "petrification of others occurs, anticipating the dreamer's own petrification" (1969: 53). The dreamer was a 25-year-old woman. In the dream, she cooked and served dinner and called her family, but no one replied. Laing describes what the dreamer then did:

She rushed upstairs to look for her family. In the first bedroom, she could see her two sisters sitting on two beds. In spite of her impatient calls they remained in an unnaturally rigid position and did not even answer her. She went up to her sisters and wanted to shake them. Suddenly she noticed that they were stone statues. She escaped in horror and rushed into her mother's room. Her mother too had turned into stone and was sitting inertly in her armchair and staring into the air with glazed eyes. The dreamer escaped into the room of her father. He stood in the middle of it. In her despair she rushed up to him and, desiring his protection, she threw her arms round his neck. But he too was made of stone and, to her utter horror, he turned into sand when she embraced him. She awoke in absolute terror, and was so stunned by the dream experience that she could not move for some minutes.

(1969: 53–4)

The experience temporarily immobilized the dreamer – but that was not the only effect.

This dream was a recurrent dream. Laing says that the woman dreamed it "on four successive occasions within a few days" (1969: 54). As Laing interprets the dream, it presaged an imminent psychotic episode. He says of the dreamer:

At that time she was apparently the picture of mental and physical health. Her parents used to call her the sunshine of the whole family. Ten days after the fourth repetition of the dream, the patient was taken ill with an acute form of schizophrenia displaying severe catatonic symptoms. She fell into a state which was remarkably similar to the physical petrification of her family that she had dreamt about.

(1969: 54)

Among the catatonic symptoms that Karl Jaspers mentions are *immobility* and *statuesque postures* identical with the ones in the dream. Jaspers says that catatonic patients "remain totally inexpressive, as if turned to stone" (1963: 181). Silvano Arieti describes a catatonic patient with fear "so intense as to inhibit any movement." The immobility of this patient was another example of petrification. "He was almost literally petrified," Arieti says. "To use his own words, he 'saw himself solidifying, assuming statuesque positions.'" Arieti reports that after a suicide attempt, the patient "could not move at all." The patient, he says, "was like a statue of stone" (1974: 157). If there is such a condition as a vegetative state, there is an even more extreme condition – a "minerative" state.

Metaphors in Psychoanalysis

Harold F. Searles also mentions a paranoid schizophrenic who experienced petrification – or at least anxiously anticipated it. "In my notes concerning one of our earliest hours I described her facial expression as one of 'stony hopelessness,'" Searles says, "and I was reminded of this phrase when, months later in therapy, she revealed her anxiety lest she be 'turned into a rock'" (1965: 193). He continues: "Her massive repression did indeed tend to render her rocklike – figuratively so to the observer, literally so in her own subjective experience" (1965: 193–4). To this woman, to be "turned into a rock" was neither a simile nor a metaphor. In this respect, she was one of those schizophrenics whom Eugen Bleuler says take (that is, mistake) "metaphors in a literal sense" (1950: 429).

In a discussion of metaphor, Searles describes an extreme example of metamorphosis – the comprehensive delusion of a schizophrenic for whom "practically everything in the world which we would call non-human" had once been "a human being who had been turned, through the greatest sort of *violence*, into something non-human and was waiting desperately to be liberated into a human form again." From previous experience with this particular patient, Searles concludes that "it was repressed hostility towards various individuals which in part accounted for his experiencing of them, on different occasions, as metamorphosing" into, among other forms, "a rock" (1960: 570). Such metaphors, Searles says, "do violence to human beings by transforming" a person into a non-human form – for example, turning "an unyielding one into a rock" (1960: 572).

As I have previously argued, metaphors are extremely important in psychoanalysis (Adams 1997). Jung says: "An archetypal content expresses itself, first and foremost, in metaphors" (1940, *CW* 9, 1: par. 267). Hillman says: "Nothing is literal; all is metaphor" (1975: 175). What is a metaphor? A simile asserts that one thing is, in some respect, comparable to some other thing. In contrast, a metaphor asserts that one thing is, in all respects (or at least in all essential respects), identical with some other thing. As Jacques Lacan says, "There's not a comparison but an identification" (1993: 218). In a metaphor, the one thing is not "like" or "as" the other thing – it "is" that thing. I might say that when a metaphor identifies one thing with another thing, it takes that identification not literally but seriously. "Taking it seriously," Jung says, "does not mean taking it literally" ([1916]/1957, *CW* 8: par. 184). A metaphor is a subjunctive assertion. It is not to be a rock literally (as it is) but to be a rock metaphorically (as it were).

Philip Wheelwright (1954: 345) notes that the rock is a prominent metaphor in the Bible – for example, God is "the rock of my salvation" (Psalms 89: 26) and "the rock of thy strength" (Isaiah 17: 10). When Jesus says, "Thou art Peter, and upon this rock, I will build my church" (Matthew 16: 18), he employs a pun – "Petros" means "rock."

The rock or stone metaphor (or, in this instance, simile) manifested to a 52-year-old man in analysis with me. He recounted a dream in which his brother, now dead for many years, had appeared. While his brother was alive, relations between them had been fraught with conflict. The dreamer informed me that, after the dream, he had conducted a conversation with his brother in "active imagination." This is the transcript of that exchange:

DREAMER: Why are you here?
BROTHER: To bother you.
DREAMER: I'm angry! Go to hell! *(The dreamer had then beaten his brother with his fists.)*
BROTHER: Stop!
DREAMER: You ruined my life!
BROTHER: No, I didn't. This is just your life. I didn't ruin it. Stop complaining. Stop using me as an excuse. I'm just what you have to contend with.
DREAMER: You're such a dolt. You're like a rock that I have to contend with. *(The dreamer had then pictured a huge, smooth, life-size black rock.)*
BROTHER: Well, that's true.
DREAMER: You're like a rock.
BROTHER: That's right, and what are you going to do with the rock?

The dreamer then offered some comments. By a "dolt" (which means a "stupid person"), he said that he meant a person as "immovable as a rock" – a person who would "not make any effort to change." The active imagination posed a question and presented the dreamer with an opportunity to ponder an answer. What was he going to do with the rock? He mentioned a number of possibilities. "I could walk away and leave it, or I could chisel it and make it into a statue, or I could make it into a jewel, polish it, and wear it – or," he said, "I could worship it." These possibilities meant, he said, "It isn't set in stone."

I then asked the dreamer what he meant when he said that he could worship the rock. On the night of the dream, he had been reading a biography of Muhammad. (Although the dreamer was a Christian, he had a personal interest in Islam – he had an important Turkish friend, a Muslim.) "It's profound – and funny – that all of Islam is still," he remarked, "worshipping a rock." (He meant the black stone in the Ka'ba at Mecca. On the *hajj*, Muslims circumambulate the Ka'ba and kiss the black stone.) He laughed and exclaimed, with a sense of irony, "For saying that, I could be stoned!"

In *The Book of Idols*, Hishām ibn-al-Kalbī describes how, before Islam, the Arabs did worship rocks or stones:

> The Arabs were passionately fond of worshipping idols. Some of them took unto themselves a temple around which they centered their worship, while others adopted an idol to which they offered their

adoration. The person who was unable to build himself a temple or adopt an idol would erect a stone in front of the Sacred House or in front of any other temple which he might prefer, and then circumambulate it in the same manner in which he would circumambulate the Sacred House. The Arabs called these stones baetyls (*ansāb*). Whenever these stones resembled a living form they called them idols (*asnām*) and images (*awthān*).

Whenever a traveler stopped at a place or station [in order to rest or spend the night] he would select for himself four stones, pick out the finest among them and adopt it as his god, and use the remaining three as supports for his cooking-pot. On his departure he would leave them behind, and would do the same on his other stops.

The Arabs were wont to offer sacrifices before all these idols, baetyls, and stones.

(1952: 28–9)

Among the gods that the Arabs worshipped in the form of stones were Hubal, "red agate" (ibn-al-Kalbī 1952: 23), dhu-al-Khalaṣah, "white quartz" (1952: 29), Saʿd, "a long rock" (1952: 32), and al-Fals, "a [red] rock" (1952: 51). When Muhammad entered Mecca, he immediately destroyed the 360 idols – among them, stones – that surrounded the Ka'ba. When Muhammad rebuilt the Ka'ba, he installed the black stone in the southeastern corner. Apparently, the black stone is a semicircular rock approximately six inches high and eight inches wide. Although Muslims kiss the black stone, they would deny that they worship it – that is, that they conflate the black stone with Allah. To do so would be to commit the sin of idolatry.

Were Ovid still alive, he might include this "myth" from a psychoanalytic session in a contemporary version of *The Metamorphoses*. Stone and rock metaphors are cogent evidence of the existence – and the persistence – of what I call the *mythological unconscious*. They confirm that we moderns, however psychological we may be, are just as mythological as the ancients were. The unconscious continues to be just as mythological as it has ever been.

To Change or Not to Change

In the spring of 1994, Ginette Paris taught a course on Jungian psychotherapy at Pacifica Graduate Institute. Paris recounts that in class one day a colleague chalked a question on the blackboard for the students: "What are the people who pay you paying you for?" That is, what do people in psychotherapy expect in return for the money they spend on it? Among the answers from the students was "To change" (1998: 172). Change is not the only expectation of people in psychotherapy, but it is a frequent one.

Some people desire or love change. It is, however, a notorious fact that some (many, most, all?) people in psychotherapy, even if they expect change, also at least occasionally resist it. In this sense, "resistance" is a synonym for "defense." The relevant "ism" is "misoneism" (Walton 1968: 15). A misoneist is a person who fears or hates change – or, as Jung says, "novelty" (1911–12/1952, *CW* 5: par. 653). Such a person enters psychotherapy not to change but to preserve the *status quo*. For example, Searles mentions a borderline psychotic patient who "manifested an almost rocklike resistance to analysis" (1979: 147).

What does "change" mean in psychoanalysis? It does not mean, as it does for Ovid, bodily change – it means, for both Freud and Jung, psychic change. What people who pay psychoanalysts pay them for, Freud and Jung say, is a *transformation of consciousness*. Freud says that psychoanalysis "works by transforming what is unconscious into what is conscious, and it works only in so far as it is in a position to effect that transformation" (1916–1917, *SE* 16: 280). The very first word in the title of one of the most important books by Jung – *Wandlungen und Symbole der Libido* (*Transformations and Symbols of the Libido*), originally published in 1911–12 and subsequently revised and republished in 1952 as *Symbols of Transformation* – is "transformations."

Hillman disputes – or at least complicates – the notion that the purpose of psychotherapy is psychic change. "Sameness," he emphasizes, "is a very important part of life – to be consistently the same in certain areas that don't change." Hillman employs the rock metaphor (or at least a rock simile): "Some things stay the same. They're like rocks. There's rocks in the psyche" (Hillman and Ventura 1992: 9). Just as rocks do not change, so some things in the psyche do not change. "The job in therapy is, not to try and make the changeless change," Hillman says, "but how to separate the two." That is, for Hillman, the purpose of psychotherapy is not to change the psyche but to differentiate what is changing from what is unchanging in the psyche, so that people are then in a position to consider whether to change (if they will) and what to change (if they can) – not to mention how to change – and, perhaps more important, to appreciate that, as Hillman says, "there are parts of the psyche that are changeless" (1992: 10). What is so valuable about the rocks in the psyche is that they are characterological. It is those rocks, Hillman says, that "make for character, for the peculiar idiosyncrasy that you are" (1992: 30).

Psychoanalysts, whether Freudian or Jungian, should neither hope to nor attempt to change the psyche. To change or not to change is the question, and the answer, if there is one, is that if psychoanalysts arrogate that responsibility, they deny it to the people in analysis with them. That is, they deprive them of the opportunity to experience all the ambiguity and all the ambivalence that change invariably presents. Ultimately, it should be all the same to psychoanalysts whether the psyche changes or remains the same.

References

Adams, M.V. (1997) "Metaphors in Psychoanalytic Theory and Therapy," *Clinical Social Work Journal*, 25,1: 27–39.

Adams, M.V. (2010) *The Mythological Unconscious*, 2nd rev. ed., Putnam, CT: Spring Publications.

Arieti, S. (1974) *Interpretation of Schizophrenia*, 2nd rev. ed., New York: Basic Books.

Bleuler, E. (1950) *Dementia Praecox; or The Group of Schizophrenias*, trans. J. Zinkin, New York: International Universities Press.

Eliade, M. (1956) *The Myth of the Eternal Return; or, Cosmos and History*, trans. W.R. Trask, Princeton, NJ: Princeton University Press.

Forbes Irving, P.M.C. (1990) *Metamorphosis in Greek Myths*, Oxford: Clarendon Press.

Freud, S. (1916–1917) *Introductory Lectures on Psycho-Analysis*, SE 16.

Griffin, D.R. (1998) *Unsnarling the World-Knot: Consciousness, Freedom, and the Mind–Body Problem*, Berkeley, CA: University of California Press.

Hartshorne, C. (1937) *Beyond Humanism: Essays in the New Philosophy of Nature*, Chicago: Willett, Clark & Company.

Hartshorne, C. (1950) "Panpsychism," in V. Ferm (ed.), *A History of Philosophical Systems*, New York: The Philosophical Library: 442–53.

Hartshorne, C. (1978) "Physics and Psychics: The Place of Mind in Nature," in J.B. Cobb and D.R. Griffin (eds.), *Mind in Nature: Essays on the Interface of Science and Philosophy*, Washington, DC: University Press of America: 89–95.

Heidegger, M. (1995) *The Fundamental Concepts of Metaphysics: World, Finitude, Solitude*, trans. W. McNeill and N. Walker, Bloomington, IN: Indiana University Press.

Hillman, J. (1975) *Re-Visioning Psychology*, New York: Harper & Row.

Hillman, J. (1979) *The Dream and the Underworld*, New York: Harper & Row.

Hillman, J., with Pozzo, L. (1983) *Inter Views: Conversations with Laura Pozzo on Psychotherapy, Biography, Love, Soul, Dreams, Work, Imagination, and the State of the Culture*, New York: Harper & Row.

Hillman, J., and Ventura, M. (1992) *We've Had a Hundred Years of Psychotherapy – And the World's Getting Worse*, San Francisco: HarperSanFrancisco.

Ibn-al-Kalbī, H. (1952) *The Book of Idols, Being a Translation from the Arabic of the Kitāb al-Aṣnām*, trans. N.A. Faris, Princeton, NJ: Princeton University Press.

Jaspers, K. (1963) *General Psychopathology*, trans. J. Hoenig and M.W. Hamilton, Manchester: Manchester University Press and Chicago: University of Chicago Press.

Jung, C.G. (1911–12/1952) *Symbols of Transformation: An Analysis of the Prelude to a Case of Schizophrenia*, CW 5.

Jung, C.G. ([1916]/1957) "The Transcendent Function," CW 8: 67–91.

Jung, C.G. (1929) "Problems of Modern Psychotherapy," CW 16: 53–75.

Jung, C.G. (1935) "Principles of Practical Psychotherapy," CW 16: 3–20.

Jung, C.G. (1937) "Religious Ideas in Alchemy: An Historical Survey of Alchemical Ideas," CW 12: 225–483.

Jung, C.G. (1940) "The Psychology of the Child Archetype," CW 9, 1: 151–81.

Jung, C.G. (1963) *Memories, Dreams, Reflections*, ed. A. Jaffé, trans. R. and C. Winston, New York: Pantheon Books.

Lacan, J. (1993) *The Seminar of Jacques Lacan: Book III: The Psychoses, 1955–1956*, ed. J.-A. Miller, trans. R. Grigg, New York: W.W. Norton.

Laing, R.D. (1969) *The Divided Self*, New York: Pantheon Books.

Ovid (1994) *The Metamorphoses of Ovid*, trans. D.R. Slavitt, Baltimore: Johns Hopkins University Press.

Paris, G. (1998) "Broken Promises," *Spring: A Journal of Archetype and Culture*, 64: 171–84.

Searles, H.F. (1960) *The Nonhuman Environment in Normal Development and in Schizophrenia*, Madison, CT: International Universities Press.

Searles, H.F. (1965) "The Differentiation between Concrete and Metaphorical Thinking in the Recovering Schizophrenic Patient," in *Collected Papers on Schizophrenia and Related Subjects*, New York: International Universities Press: 560–83.

Searles, H.F. (1979) "Pathologic Symbiosis and Autism," in *Countertransference and Related Subjects: Selected Papers*, Madison, CT: International Universities Press: 132–48.

Thompson, S. (1955) *Motif Index of Folk-Literature*, Bloomington, IN: Indiana University Press, 6 vols.

Walton, M. (1968) *'Isms: A Dictionary of Words Ending in -Ism, -Ology, and -Phobia*, 2nd rev. ed., Sheffield: Corporation of Sheffield.

Wheelwright, J. (1954) *The Burning Fountain: A Study in the Language of Symbolism*, Bloomington, IN: Indiana University Press.

White, L., Jr. (1973) "Continuing the Conversation," in I.G. Barbour (ed.), *Western Man and Environmental Ethics: Attitudes Toward Nature and Technology*, Reading, MA: Addison-Wesley Publishing Company: 55–64.

14

O BAAL, HEAR US

Active Imagination and the Mythological Unconscious

The Method of Active Imagination

The topic of this third lecture at the 2011 Conference of the Moscow Association for Analytical Psychology is active imagination and the mythological unconscious. What does Jung say about active imagination? He says that, as a method, it is the "most important auxiliary" for evoking and engaging images that are the most immediately accessible and the most probable to "irrupt spontaneously" from the unconscious. Jung also, however, cautions that active imagination may, "in certain circumstances," be a dangerous method. He says that the images that emerge from the unconscious may induce "a condition which – temporarily, at least – cannot easily be distinguished from schizophrenia, and may even lead to a genuine 'psychotic interval'" ([1916]/1957, *CW* 8: 68).

Although I would not dispute what Jung says, the opinion that I have of active imagination is rather different – and more positive. I regard the concern that Jung expresses about the danger of active imagination as an exaggeration. Any authentic confrontation with the unconscious is, of course, an encounter that entails surprise and an element of risk. No person in analysis with me, however, has ever had, in active imagination, any experience even remotely similar to a psychotic episode. I conclude that, if such incidents do indeed occur, they are very rare – anomalous in the extreme. In addition, I do not regard active imagination as a mere auxiliary (however important) to other Jungian methods. I consider dream interpretation and active imagination to be the most valuable methods in Jungian psychoanalysis. I might argue that active imagination is even more valuable than dream interpretation – that it is, in fact, the method of all methods.

What is the special merit of active imagination? As an experiential method, it engages images from the unconscious more immediately, more intimately, and more mutually than any interpretative method does. The impact of such direct contact with the unconscious is often profound. Also, active imagination is a solitary activity, a very private, interior experience that entails a rather splendid isolation and, ultimately, a grand independence. In contrast to other methods, in active imagination the participation of the psychoanalyst as an interlocutor – even the very presence of the psychoanalyst – is utterly unnecessary, even positively detrimental to the process. I have had four psychoanalysts, three of them Jungian. One of them very much impressed me when she remarked that mastery of the method of active imagination renders the psychoanalyst redundant. For her, the answer to the question whether analysis is terminable or interminable was that proficiency in active imagination is a sufficient (although not a necessary) condition for termination. The psychoanalyst is perfectly dispensable if a person is adept at active imagination.

What does the word "active" in active imagination mean? The method "activates" the images that emerge from the unconscious, and then the ego "actively" engages these images. That is, in this process, the ego actively participates rather than merely passively observes. It might, however, have been even more apposite had Jung called the method "interactive imagination," for the ego and the unconscious mutually interact. Active imagination is a reciprocal exchange. It is a conversation between the ego and the unconscious. Édouard Dujardin invented the "interior monologue," but Jung invented the "interior dialogue."

Jung did not write much about the method of active imagination. Joan Chodorow has compiled, in one convenient volume, most of what Jung did write about it (1997). Sonu Shamdasani has edited *The Red Book*, in which Jung transcribed and illustrated the active imaginations that he conducted (2009). In addition, Marie-Louise von Franz has written important articles about the method (1993a; 1993b). The most valuable – I might say, the only really valuable – book about active imagination is *Invisible Guests: The Development of Imaginal Dialogues* by Mary Watkins (1986). These are, if I may say so, the most important primary and secondary sources. A few Jungian psychoanalysts have published accounts of the process of active imagination, with psychological commentaries on excerpts from transcripts of dialogues, but when I have read those accounts, they have disappointed me. They have not seemed to me to demonstrate at all adequately just how marvelous, just how magnificent, a method active imagination actually is.

This lecture is an effort to rectify that deficiency. The material that I shall present comprises the complete, verbatim transcripts of two active imaginations that a 32-year-old woman recounted to me in analytic sessions. The woman had known about active imagination before she began analysis with me. On a number of occasions over a six-year period, I had mentioned to her that she might consider active imagination, but she had declined to do so – not from any anxiety but from skepticism about the method. She was dubious that active imagination was at all efficacious. Then, one day, the woman informed me that she had finally attempted an active imagination. She then proceeded to describe it. She had discovered, as Jung says he did, that "there are things in the psyche which I do not produce, but which produce themselves" – that "there is something in me which can say things that I do not know and do not intend" (1963: 183). She had experienced what Jung calls the "autonomy of the unconscious."

Baal in the Bible

The title "O Baal, Hear Us" is from the Tanakh, or "Old Testament." Ahab reigns as king of the Israelites in Samaria for twenty-two years. Although Yahweh is the god of the Israelites, Ahab "went and served Baal, and worshipped him" (I Kings 16: 31) and "reared up an altar for Baal in the house of Baal" (I Kings 16: 32). The prophet Elijah rebukes Ahab for worshipping other gods besides Yahweh. He says to Ahab that "ye have forsaken the commandments of the Lord, and thou hast followed Baalim" (I Kings 18: 18). ("Baalim" is the plural of the singular "Baal.") As a prophet of Yahweh, Elijah is a minority of one. In contrast, the prophets of Baal are vastly more numerous. Elijah says that "I, even I only, remain a prophet of the Lord; but Baal's prophets are four hundred and fifty men" (I Kings 18: 22). To demonstrate that Yahweh is a more efficacious god than Baal, Elijah challenges those prophets to "call on the name of your gods" (I Kings 18: 25), and the prophets "called on the name of Baal from morning even until noon, saying O Baal, hear us" (I Kings 18: 26).

Baal, however, is unresponsive. The silence of Baal speaks volumes: "But there was no voice, nor any that answered" (I Kings 18: 26). Elijah mocks the prophets of Baal. He insinuates that Baal must be too busy with some other activity to reply to them: "Cry aloud: for he is a god; either he is talking, or he is pursuing, or he is in a journey, or peradventure he sleepeth, and must be awaked" (I Kings 18: 27). Although the prophets call on Baal from midday until evening, "there was neither voice, nor any to answer, nor any that regarded" (I Kings 18: 29).

Elijah then summons all the Israelites, and "he repaired the altar of the Lord that was broken down" (I Kings 18: 30). With twelve stones, the same number as the twelve tribes of Israel, he "built an altar in the name of the Lord" (I Kings 18: 31). Then Elijah orders the Israelites to kill all the prophets of Baal. He says to them: "Take all the prophets of Baal; let none escape." The Israelites then capture the prophets, and "Elijah brought them down to the brook Kishon, and slew them there" (I Kings 18: 40).

In the very first of the Ten Commandments, Yahweh says: "Thou shalt have no other gods before me" (Genesis 20: 3). The Tanakh includes many accounts of how the Israelites periodically violate this commandment – how they revert to the worship of false gods and how prophets then appear to restore them to the worship of Yahweh, the one true god. This passage is one of those accounts. From a psychoanalytic perspective, the tendency of the Israelites to relapse is a "repression" (of the one true god) and a "regression" (to false gods).

Why is the title of this lecture "O Baal, Hear Us"? When the woman initially attempted an active imagination, "Baal" was the name of the very first figure that appeared to her. I should emphasize that, when she began the active imagination, she did not summon Baal by name. A figure simply appeared spontaneously to her. Only much later, more than two-thirds of the way through the active imagination, did she call the figure by name. When the prophets of Baal called him ("O Baal, hear us"), he did not hear them, and he did not come. In contrast, when the woman called him ("Baal!"), he heard her, and he came.

After the active imagination, the woman had researched the name. What she learned about Baal had astonished her:

> It's the craziest thing. I looked up the name "Baal." I thought that it might be something from the Bible. I'd heard it before. It *is* from the Bible. It's a name that was co-opted – turned into the name of a demon. Actually, it's the name of a god who's been around for centuries, for civilizations, the entirety of written human history. Ancient cultures wrote about Baal. They made sculptures of Baal. And that freaked me the fuck out! Honestly!

Although the woman had previously heard the name "Baal," she had had no idea who Baal was.

Who was Baal? "Baal" was an honorific title that ancient Semites applied to any number of local gods in the Middle East and that the Israelites regarded as false gods. In Hebrew, "Baal" means "lord," "master," "owner," "keeper," or "husband." Christian tradition associates Baal with Beelzebub (more accurately, "Baalzebub") – "Lord of the Flies" (in Hebrew, "zebub" means "fly") – and identifies Beelzebub as a demon or devil or even as Satan. In the New Testament, some people say that when Jesus performs exorcisms, "He casteth out devils through Beelzebub the chief of the devils" (Luke 11: 15).

Transcript of the First Active Imagination

> I immediately sense a presence. I think: "That's there. Let me talk to that." I ask: "Who's there?" The face of an old woman flashes before me, then the face of a young woman. I ask: "Why do you change faces?" A deep, rich, resonant voice – the voice of a man – replies: "So that I don't frighten you. You're skittish. I'm showing you the face that's not going to scare you away."
>
> The voice is coming out of a cave. I say to the man: "Well, maybe I don't have to see you for a while. Maybe we could just sit in the dark together." I ask: "May I come in and sit with you in the cave?" The man says: "Yes." I go into the cave. I say: "I can't see you. Will you

come out of the cave into the light?" The man says: "No, not yet, you're still too afraid." I ask: "May I go out of the cave?" He says: "Yes, but come back." I ask: "Will you still be here?" He replies: "Yes, I will be here."

I go out and then come back into the cave. I say: "You sound beautiful." The man says: "I am beautiful." I say: "I wish that I were beautiful, but most of the time I feel small. You're big, and, next to you, I feel small. I'm envious of your beauty, and that makes me feel bad." He replies: "It's the flaw that makes the diamond sparkle." The man exudes a kind, calm acceptance of me. At some point, I begin getting comfortable with the idea that this thing is going to be bigger and more beautiful than me – and that that's just the way it is.

I say: "I feel naked." The man says: "I like you that way." I say: "Will you also be naked?" He laughs and says: "Why is everything always about sex with you?" I shrug and say: "I don't know – I like sex." I ask again: "Will you also be naked?" He replies: "No, that's not what I do. You are naked, and I am clothed."

I begin to see beautiful, glittering, shimmering colors coming from the corners of the cave. The man is now a great blue and gold, bejeweled creature, androgynous but masculine. Every so often, he looks to me like a majestic peacock. I feel tremendous love and strength emanate from him. I say: "I humble myself in front of you." He says: "You are right to do so."

I sense that the man knows that he is majestic, that he is a greater creature than I am. I begin to get a little freaked out. I ask: "How is it that we can talk so openly? We just met, and this is all so new. How can you tell me all this so fast? Don't we have to establish a relationship before we can talk?" He replies: "Well, I've been waiting for you a long time."

Suddenly, I sense another presence. From a corner of the cave, I see smoke and the glowing red tip of a cigarette. I think, with a sense of recognition: "Oh, it's the critic. I know who this is." The critic says: "That's right, darling, I'm here too."

For a moment, I vacillate over whether to pay attention to the critic or to the peacock. I look at the big, beautiful creature, but he doesn't say anything, doesn't try to influence me either way. So I think: "I'll just talk to the other voice for a while and see what it says." The peacock doesn't seem to mind, so I focus all my attention on the critic. I look at the critic, and he says: "That's right, look at me. I'm not afraid of you. You're afraid, but I'm not. Look at my face. I'll turn on the lights." Suddenly, all these floodlights come on, and I see the critic in clear detail. He's a middle-aged white man with blondish hair, long, elegant hands, and tortoise-shell eyeglasses, impeccably dressed in a tailored, pinstriped suit. When he was younger, he was probably gorgeous. He's still rather dashing, but now he looks so mean. He speaks with an upper-class English accent. The critic says: "Well, here you are. I am not going away."

I look around and see that I'm in a metal room, all stainless steel. The critic is sitting on a metal chair, close to me. The room becomes clearer, and I see that it's an operating theater. It's a room made for surgery – made for people to be cut open. The floodlights are all in my eyes, so I can't see whether people are in the stadium seats around the room, but I don't think so. I think it's just me and the critic. The room is metal so that when they cut people open, they can take out the viscera and then just wash the blood away and not leave any stains.

I know what's going to be done to me in this room. My stomach is going to be cut open, I'm going to be eviscerated, and I'm going to bleed. I feel panic. The critic is just sitting there, smoking, waiting for me. He has a scalpel in his hand, and I don't have anything. It's just slaughter, a sacrificial sport. It's as if it's just fun for this person to cut me up, watch my guts spill out everywhere, wash the blood away, and then do it again – to me or to someone else. The critic is very clever. I wonder whether he specifically chose this space because he knows that I'm going to study medicine.

The critic says: "So here we are." I say to him: "I realize something. You can't initiate anything. All you can do is to rip apart what I give you. You're totally reactive. You're sitting there, and you're so mean, but you can't do anything on your own. You have to wait for me to give you something to work with. You have no agency. You can't act. You have to wait for me to speak and then react to what I say. On your own, you have nothing to say."

I basically call him a vampire. He bares his teeth and gives me a flash of huge fangs and a hiss. He laughs and says: "Well, that's a bit melodramatic, isn't it, sweetheart? Did you enjoy my little display?" He's making fun of me. He does this little vampire act for a second to show me how ridiculous I am, but on some level what I've said is true – he's just taking what I give him.

The critic says: "It's a pity you're not better. I just want you to be better, just wish you could be better." He says this to me in this amazing, amazing voice. The tiny portion of him that can stand to focus on me is just utterly disgusted. It's a combination of his being appalled and not really caring. It hurts! I'm not important enough for him really to care, but, if he has to look at me, well, I really sicken him. I ask him: "Well, all right, what would make me better? How can I be better?" He just looks at me for a second, aghast. I ask: "Are you going to tell me? If you want me to get better, tell me what would make me better." He replies: "No, I certainly will *not!*" Suddenly, the floodlights go out. He's done talking to me. It's a big "Fuck you!" I've pushed him, but he won't be backed into a corner. He won't be nice to me. He's going to take what he wants when he wants it. He wants me hurt and cut open. He's not interested in a feel-good talk about how I could feel better – or how I could be better. As soon as I'm not afraid of him, the conversation is over as far as he's concerned.

The lights are out, and I don't know where I am, and I'm terrified. So I call for the peacock – except now I know his name. Suddenly, somehow, I just know his name. It just comes out of my mouth. I call him in terror. I yell: "Baal! Please help me! Come and get me!" And he *does*! Can you imagine? It's so sweet! He comes to me and wraps his arms around me. This creature is really, really old, really, really big. This is a majestic creature, but I'm safe with him. I say: "Baal, I wish that you were my father." He says: "I am better than that. I am *you*."

I'm struck by how loving Baal is. I ask: "Why do you love me, Baal?" He says: "Because I *am* love." I ask: "But is there anything specific to me that you like, anything in particular about me that's worth your love?" He replies: "Yes, I like it that you are small and pink and strange and vulnerable. I think that you are cute and funny."

Then I begin to think about how I have to go to band practice tonight. I say: "I have to sing these new songs, and I'm not entirely done with them." I want very much to ask Baal to help me with my music, but I don't know how. I doubly want to ask him for help because now I know that the critic is also there. Finally, I say: "Baal, I have to sing tonight." He says: "I will be there with you."

I thank Baal and then ask: "Are you going to be here again? May I come and visit you again?" He says: "Yes, of course, whenever you want." I ask: "What will you do when I'm not here with you?" He replies: "*Do*? I don't do. I just am. I will *be*." He says: "I've been here for centuries, long, long before you. I will be here long, long after you." What was I thinking when I asked him, "What will you do when I'm not here with you?" Did I think he'd say, "I'll make myself a cup of coffee and maybe walk the dog?" I say: "Baal, I'm done. For now, that's as much as I can take." He says: "All right. You can go now – we're cool." That's what one of my friends famously says when she dismisses someone: "You can go." Baal ended the conversation with a joke that was a humorous reference to someone I know, and that was exactly what I needed.

Transcript of the Second Active Imagination

I say to Baal: "I'm tired." He puts me into an egg full of peacock feathers. It's *so* nice. It's awesome. *He* is the egg somehow, but he's also *inside* the egg with me. I feel that I can relax. Then I feel ready to come out of the egg, so I come out. Baal and I are sitting around a fire. I'm sitting "Indian style," and he is too, with the fire between us. I say: "Baal, I came for help." He says: "I know."

Somehow Baal's "in my face." He's more or less human, but his eyes turn into snake eyes. He blinks. The little film of skin on his eyes is gold. He becomes this beautiful, big, gold snake, a constrictor. He's upright in front of me like a "snake-charmer" snake. I think that's funny. Those snakes are supposed to be hypnotized, and I wonder which of us – Baal or me – is hypnotized.

Baal puts his head down onto the arch of my foot. He coils up my leg, around my back to the base of my spine, and then coils up my spine to the top of my head. Baal's tail is by my foot. I can't see his head, but it's by my left ear, and he begins talking into it. My left ear is where my in-ear monitor goes when I'm singing in musical performances with my band. My in-ear monitor enables me to hear my own voice. It's smart of Baal to talk into my left ear, because I'm used to hearing a voice in my left ear and I'm used to its being my own voice. I'm comfortable with his talking into my left ear. I can relax and trust the voice.

Baal says: "Tell me what you want to tell me." I explain the problem. I'm in an emergency vehicle, and I'm both the patient and the medic. I have the skills to deal with the emergency. I can *do* it, but I don't know what's wrong, so I don't know how to heal the patient. I ask Baal: "Do you have any thoughts?" It's hilarious that I would ask such a majestic creature whether he has any thoughts.

Baal is still coiled around my body. Suddenly, he constricts. For a second, I wonder: "Is he going to kill me?" Then I think: "No, this is Baal. I'm safe." He constricts just enough so that I can feel my muscles becoming tense, my breathing becoming shallow, my heart palpitating, and my throat constricting. I have all this anxiety, and the anxiety's right *here*, like a fucking knot, right *here* in the area of my lungs, heart, and throat. I have this feeling that there's an emergency – that there are things that I have to do – but I don't know what they are.

Baal flicks his tongue into my ear. He says into my ear: "Shhhh. Do you feel that?" I say: "Yes." Then he puts the end of his tail inside me – into my vagina. He doesn't move. It's erotic. It feels good. It feels sexy. It focuses my whole attention. It's the fastest shift in mood that I've ever experienced. It's, like, "BAM!" One second I'm there with a knot in my throat, constricted, and the next second my whole attention drops to the base of my spine, and my whole body opens up with light. It's instantaneous.

Baal says: "Do you feel that?" I say: "Yes, I do." He asks: "Is that all right?" Baal wants to make sure that I don't feel violated, worried, or upset. I say: "Yes, this is great. I love this." Then Baal says:

> You're made for union.
> You're made for communion.
> You're a link between the earth and the sky.
> You're made for divining.
> You're marked for me.
> You're marked for love.

When Baal says this, he brings my attention to the shift in mood, the moment of focus that I've just experienced. He says: "Seek that out. Seek out the edge of the precipice, the moment of greatest clarity. You're a lightning rod."

Psychological Commentary

The woman recounted to me other active imaginations – among them, other conversations with Baal. In all of these active imaginations, she did exactly what Jung says that a person should do with figures that spontaneously emerge from the unconscious. Jung says that "if it is a speaking figure at all then say what you have to say to that figure and listen to what he or she has to say" (1973: 460). He says that a person must "compel the figures to give you an answer." This woman did just that, and the result was what Jung calls "a dialogue between yourself and the unconscious figures" (1973: 561).

Roy Schafer notes that such figures can be extremely influential. (As an example, he mentions the figure of the critic.) He says that these figures are "essentially a product of the imagination" (1968: 82). Schafer asks: "How can an unreal figure apparently acquire influence that equals or exceeds that of external objects?" (1968: 82–3). He says that all too frequently, such figures "are written about (and discussed in the clinic) as if they are actual persons carrying on lives of their own, with energies of their own, and with independent intentions directed toward the subject." Schafer says: "This is how patients often experience them and describe them, but is it good metapsychology?" (1968: 83).

From a Jungian perspective, I would reply: "It is not just good metapsychology – it is excellent metapsychology." In this respect, James Hillman says that "the primary activity of the psyche is imagining." He says that "we humans are primarily acts of imagination, images" (Hillman and Ventura 1992: 62). This primacy of the imagination is what I call the *fantasy principle* (Adams 2004).

Although Schafer criticizes the tendency to regard the figures that emerge from the unconscious "as if they are actual persons," Jung says that when he began to employ the method of active imagination, he did exactly that: "I summoned up my courage and approached them as though they were real people, and listened attentively to what they told me" (1963: 181). The metapsychological assumption of an "as if" (or "as though") ontology is indispensable to active imagination – Hans Vaihinger systematically addresses the reality of the imagination in *The Philosophy of "As If"* (1924). The alternative is to disparage the image, as Schafer does, as an "unreal figure." The imagination, however, is a reality just as real as any other reality.

By what criteria did I select these two active imaginations? They seemed to me especially impressive examples of the process. To me, they vividly epitomize what active imagination is. They cogently demonstrate the efficacy of the method.

In these active imaginations, the woman introverts, or turns inward, where she encounters Baal, one of the many images of what Jung calls the archetype of the *God within* (1939/1940, *CW* 11: par. 101). Jung says that "'God' can just as well mean Yahweh, Allah, Zeus, Shiva, or Huitzilopochtli" (1952, *CW* 11: par. 454) – or, in this instance, Baal. As Baal appears in these active imaginations, he is not at all demonic, devilish, or satanic. He is not a false god. He is a true god – responsive (not silent but very vocal), efficacious, and benevolent.

In contrast, the critic who appears in the first active imagination is malevolent. The critic is mean, and at every opportunity he demeans the woman. He is sardonic, sarcastic, and sadistic. He is demonic, devilish, and satanic. The smoke and the glowing red tip of the cigarette are, in this respect, images with a quite sinister insinuation. The critic was a figure that the woman had mentioned to me two years before the first active imagination. She had described him as "malicious," "nasty," and "cruel." He was, she said, a "bully," who had "a talent for immediately finding a person's insecurity." The woman had drawn two charcoal-and-pastel pictures of the critic as he first appeared to her in the cave. The color was black, except for the red tip and white smoke of the cigarette (Figures 14.1 and 14.2).

Active imagination is an experience on what Jung calls the "subjective level." The figures that appear in active imagination (as well as dreams) are personifications of aspects of the psyche of the subject – in this instance, the woman. As Baal says to her, "I am *you*." In this respect, Baal is a personification of an aspect of the psyche of the woman, and so is the critic. What Jung calls personifications, John Rowan calls subpersonalities. Among the many subpersonalities that Rowan mentions, one of the most prominent is the critic. He describes the critic as the subpersonality that "tells us we have got it wrong," that "notices everything which could make us feel rotten about ourselves" (1990: 91). Rowan says that the critic is a "standard" subpersonality that exists "in all people at all times." Such subpersonalities, he says, appear

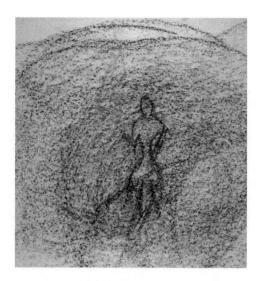

Figure 14.1 The Critic.

Figure 14.2 The Critic.

"so often that they may be universal" (1990: 107). W.R.D. Fairbairn mentions a woman who "tended to personify various aspects of her psyche." One of the most conspicuous and "persistent of these personifications," he says, was a figure that she called "the critic" (1990: 216). Fairbairn describes "'the critic' as a characteristic personification in the dreamlife of the patient" (1990: 219).

A capacity for criticism is a vitally important competence. Criticism may, of course, be either constructive or destructive. In this respect, the motivation of the critic who appears to the woman in the first active imagination is utterly to destroy her. In psychoanalysis, Freud says that the method of free association is dependent on the capacity to suspend what he calls the "critical faculty" (1900, *SE* 4: 102) – and this is equally true of the method of active imagination. Criticism that is too strict and severe prevents the spontaneous emergence of images from the unconscious, whether in free association or in active imagination.

In the first active imagination, the woman enters a cave, where she encounters Baal and the critic. The cave, Jung says, is one of the most important images of the archetype of the "unconscious":

> Anyone who gets into that cave, that is to say into the cave which everyone has within himself, or into the darkness that lies behind consciousness, will find himself involved in an – at first – unconscious process of transformation. By penetrating into the unconscious he makes a connection with his unconscious contents. This may result in a momentous change of personality in the positive or negative sense.
>
> (1940/1950, *CW* 9, 1: par. 241)

The cave is where images of transformation spontaneously emerge from the unconscious.

In addition, in this first active imagination, there is a room in the cave. This room serves a quite specific purpose. It is a theater for operations, a space for surgeries – for dissections as vivisections. It is where the critic cuts people open with a scalpel. It is where he disembowels them – that is, discourages them. (To "have guts" is to "have courage," and to be "gutless" is to be "cowardly.") The intestines are a vital organ. In this respect, evisceration is an even more radical procedure than castration, the favorite atrocity of Freudian psychoanalysts. It is, in fact, invariably fatal. The critic is a captious, censorious aspect of the psyche of this woman. The criticism that he utters is utterly pernicious. It is lethal. Ultimately, however, the woman proves too gutsy for the critic. She refuses to give him what he wants, denies him the opportunity to cut her up and watch her guts spill out.

Baal is an image of the archetype of the "shape-shifter." In the first active imagination, he appears in the shape of an old woman, then shifts into the shapes, successively, of a young woman, a man, and a peacock. In Greek mythology, Proteus is the very epitome of the shape-shifter. He is a very slippery character. He has the capacity to shift into an infinite variety of shapes. The motivation of these shifts in shape is for Proteus to escape the grasp of anyone who might wrestle him, hold him, and force him to speak. "Proteus," Jung says, "is evidently a personification of the unconscious" (1951, *CW* 9, 2: par. 338). That is, the unconscious is just as mutable and just as elusive as Proteus.

Baal, who also shifts shape, has a different motivation – in fact, a number of different motivations. Evidently, the purpose of these shifts in shape is to exhibit to the woman various aspects of the psyche. In the first active imagination, Baal appears as a woman – old, then young – so as not to scare the woman away. Then Baal shifts shape into a man (masculine but also, paradoxically, androgynous). Finally, Baal shifts shape into a peacock.

What is the peacock as an aspect of the psyche of this woman? Peacocks are fabulously proud, beautifully exhibitionistic creatures when they strut and display the majestic fan of iridescent blue and gold tail feathers for which they are so justifiably famous. The peacock is one of the most important images of transformation in alchemy. The alchemists call the peacock's tail the *cauda pavonis*. Jung says that "the peacock stands for 'all colours' (i.e., the integration of all qualities)" (1955–56, *CW* 14: par. 391). He says that the *cauda pavonis* "announces the end of the work." That is, the peacock's tail is an image of the culmination of the transformative process. "The exquisite display of colours in the peacock's fan," Jung says, "heralds the imminent synthesis of all qualities and all elements" (1955–56, *CW* 14: par. 397).

In the second active imagination, Baal puts the woman into an egg full of peacock feathers. She is inside the egg with Baal, and also, paradoxically, Baal is the egg. Eventually, the woman emerges from the egg. The peacock's egg is another important image in alchemy. Jung says that "the peacock's egg is synonymous with the *sperma mundi*." He says that it "contains the 'fullness of colours,' 365 of them" (1934/1950, *CW* 9, 1: par. 580n.). Jung interprets a dream that includes the images of "a peacock, fanning its tail" and "an egg, presumably the peacock's." He mentions "the important role which the peacock and the peacock's egg together play in alchemy." He says that when these images manifest, "we may expect the miracle of the *cauda pavonis*, the appearance of 'all Colours'," which he interprets as "the unfolding and realization of wholeness" (1950, *CW* 9,1: par. 685). Jung remarks that the peacock is an image of "rebirth and resurrection." He says that "the colours of the *cauda pavonis* appear, as a sign that the transformation process is nearing its goal" (1950, *CW* 9, 1: par. 686). From this perspective, the emergence of the woman from the egg full of peacock feathers is an experience of rebirth and resurrection – or, in Jungian terminology, a transformation of the psyche.

Then Baal shifts shape again – from a peacock into a snake. In this active imagination, the snake engages the woman in both verbal and sexual intercourse. The snake is penetrative, and the woman is receptive (rather than defensive, or resistant). This active imagination is an example of what Edward C. Whitmont calls "orificial dynamics" (1969: 239). In this instance, the

221

specific orifices are the ear and the vagina of the woman. The snake penetrates both orifices – the one verbally, the other sexually.

A strict Freudian interpretation of this active imagination would be exclusively sexual. It would emphasize the tail of the snake and the penetration of it into the vagina of the woman. When Freudian psychoanalysts interpret such an image, they assume that, as a result of repression, the image of a penis *per se* does not appear explicitly. What appears, as an alternative, is some other image (in this instance, a snake – or, more specifically, the tail of a snake) that, on the basis of a commonality in form or function, is an allusion to and a euphemism for the penis. Ernest Jones says that what make the snake an especially apt image of the penis are "the objective attributes common to both" – for example, "shape, erectibility, habits" (1948: 123). A Freudian psychoanalyst would interpret the tail of the snake in this active imagination as a "manifest content" that belies a "latent content," a penis, and would regard the image as evidence of sexual repression.

I should note, however, that, while in analysis with me, this woman was very sexually active, audaciously so, and invariably orgasmic. There was no indication of sexual repression. (In the first active imagination, Baal asks her: "Why is everything always about sex with you?" and she replies: "I don't know – I like sex.") The second active imagination does include a quite explicit image of sexual intercourse – in fact, an image of perverse, bestial intercourse, sexual intercourse between an animal and a human, a snake and a woman. Jung says of snakes that they "could, after all, come to you, and the strange and uncanny could penetrate you" (2008: 213). What, however, does this image mean? As I would interpret the image of sexual intercourse, it is a metaphor for "psychic intercourse." That is, it is a metaphor for an especially intimate relation between the conscious and the unconscious – or, more specifically, between the woman and a "snake-like" aspect of the psyche. In this instance, the experience of psychic intercourse is an instantaneous, erotic mood shift, orgasmic with a "BAM!" This is the "pleasure principle" in capital letters with a climactic exclamation mark.

The snake in this second active imagination coils around the body of the woman. The head of the snake is at the foot of the woman. The snake coils up her leg, around her back to the base of her spine, and up her spine to the top of her head, until the head of the snake is by her ear. Then the snake speaks into her ear. The snake asks the woman to tell him what she wants to tell him. When she does, the snake does not speak into her ear, but suddenly constricts around her body. The woman wonders: "Is he going to kill me?" In this respect, Jung notes that sexuality may appear as a scary snake that "squeezes its victims to death" (1927/1931, *CW* 8: par. 332). Rather than speak words into her ear, the snake flicks its tongue into her ear. Then the snake inserts its tail into her vagina. This double penetration of tongue and tail immediately focuses her attention away from her anxiety and drops her attention to the base of her spine – where, she says, "my whole body opens up with light."

It is as if the woman is an expert at Kundalini yoga. In Sanskrit, *Kuṇḍalinī* is energy that is both sexual and psychic. It is the equivalent, in psychoanalytic terminology, of "libido," which Freud defines as sexual energy in particular and Jung defines as psychic energy in general. In Kundalini yoga, the snake is the image of this energy. The snake coils around the base of the spine, where it sleeps. When it wakes, it rises up the spine, through all the chakras, to the top of the head, where the result is "enlightenment." In Kundalini yoga, the image of this ultimate state is sexual–psychic intercourse between Śiva, the masculine principle, and Śakti, the feminine principle. From a psychoanalytic perspective, the libido begins in an utterly unconscious state and ends in a supremely conscious state.

It is then that the snake speaks words of wisdom to the woman. "A snake," Jung says, "in one case may mean something favourable, 'the wisdom of the depths,' in another something unfavourable." The image of the snake has not one but many meanings. "A snake," Jung says, "may have seven thousand meanings" (1984: 251). In this case, the snake means something very favorable. Jung says that the snake, "as the collective unconscious and as instinct, seems to possess a peculiar wisdom of its own" (1951, *CW* 9, 2: par. 370). In this second active imagination, the snake speaks "a word to the wise" (in Latin, *verbum sat sapienti*). In English, the expression is an idiom that means "an intelligent person can take a hint, draw his own conclusions without a lot of explanation" (Cowie, Mackin, and McCaig 1983: 597) or "just a slight suggestion is enough for a clever person" (Long 1979: 373). The phrase means "good advice" that a person "would do well to heed," and is the equivalent of the expression *words of wisdom* (Ammer 1992: 413). The snake says to the woman that she is made for "union" and "communion," that she is "a link between the earth and the sky," that she is made for "divining," that she is marked for "me" and for "love." Then the snake says for her to seek out "the edge of the experience, the moment of greatest clarity." Finally, the snake says to the woman: "You're a lightning rod."

What is so wise about these words? What do these images mean? All of these images have to do with what Jung calls the "problem of opposites." For Jung, the most important of the opposites is the conscious and the unconscious. The solution to the problem of opposites, he says, is the "union of opposites." In this respect, the snake explicitly says that the woman is made not only for union but also for communion and then immediately says that she is a link between the earth and the sky. The earth and the sky are, of course, opposites – and, from a psychoanalytic perspective, images of the conscious and the unconscious. This woman is made for divining – that is, for interpreting what these images mean. She is also marked for the snake and for love – that is, for sexual–psychic intercourse. Man and woman (in this instance, snake and woman) are sexual–psychic opposites. Intercourse is the union of these opposites. The sexual–psychic intercourse between the woman and the snake is an example of what Jung calls the *coniunctio* – the conjunction of the conscious and the unconscious. Although Jung says that the snake is an image of the "cerebrospinal nervous system," he emphasizes that the snake "is not just a natural animal, but also a mythological animal" (2008: 215). That is, it is an image from what I call the *mythological unconscious* (Adams 2010). In this respect, the snake is one of the most important images of transformation. It is, Jung says, an image of "the transformative act as well as the transformative substance itself" (1911–12/1952, *CW* 5: par. 676).

The woman, the snake says, is a lightning rod. A lightning rod is a rod that grounds lightning when it strikes. Like the woman, a lightning rod is a link between the earth and the sky, the conscious and the unconscious. "Lightning," Jung says, "signifies a sudden, unexpected, and overpowering change of psychic condition" (1934/1950, *CW* 9, 1: par. 533). I might say that, metaphorically, lightning is "enlightening." A lightning rod is a device that renders safe what is dangerous – electricity that, from a Jungian perspective, is an image of libido, or psychic energy. That this woman is a lightning rod indicates that she has the capacity effectively to ground any transformation, or "change of psychic condition."

A few days before I completed this lecture, I telephoned the Archive for Research in Archetypal Symbolism in New York to inquire whether they had any images of Baal. They informed me that there was an excellent image of Baal in *The Book of Symbols: Reflections on Archetypal Images*, which they had just published. Although I did not own a copy, a friend did. I telephoned him to ask whether he would loan the book to me. I completed this lecture late that night, and the next morning he brought the book to me. I immediately checked the index, and there it was – an entry for "Baal." I located the page, and – surprise of surprises – the image of Baal was an illustration for a chapter with the title "Lightning." The image was a limestone stele from 1600–1400 BCE (Figure 14.3). It depicted Baal in profile. The descriptive note that accompanied the image said: "He holds the lightning spear, or 'thunderbolt,' with his left hand" (Ronnberg and Martin 2010: 71).

Imagine the shock that I experienced! With a flash, the image electrified me. I had no idea that Baal was a lightning god.

In these active imaginations, Baal (in the successive shapes into which he shifts – an old woman, a young woman, a man, a peacock, and a snake) hears the woman. He listens to her, and he speaks to her. She speaks to him, and she listens to him. These interior dialogues demonstrate just how marvelous, just how magnificent, the method of active imagination is. When we call the unconscious, "Baal" (by that or any other name) will hear us – and the result will be an impressive psychic transformation.

Figure 14.3 Baal with lightning spear.

References

Adams, M.V. (2004) *The Fantasy Principle: Psychoanalysis of the Imagination*, Hove: Brunner-Routledge.

Adams, M.V. (2010) *The Mythological Unconscious*, 2nd rev. ed., Putnam, CT: Spring Publications.

Ammer, C. (1992) *Have a Nice Day – No Problem! A Dictionary of Clichés*, New York: Dutton.

Cowie, A.P., Mackin, R., and McCaig, I.R. (1983) *Oxford Dictionary of Current Idiomatic English: Volume 2: Phrase, Clause and Sentence Idioms*, Oxford: Oxford University Press.

Fairbairn, W.R.D. (1990) "Features in the Analysis of a Patient with a Physical Genital Abnormality," in *Psychoanalytic Studies of the Personality*, London: Tavistock/Routledge: 197–222.

Freud, S. (1900) *The Interpretation of Dreams*, SE 4.

Hillman, J., and Ventura, M. (1992) *We've Had a Hundred Years of Psychotherapy – And the World's Getting Worse*, San Francisco: HarperSanFrancisco.

Jones, E. (1948) "The Theory of Symbolism," in *Papers on Psycho-Analysis*, Baltimore: Williams and Wilkins: 87–144.

Jung, C.G. (1911–12/1952) *Symbols of Transformation: An Analysis of the Prelude to a Case of Schizophrenia*, CW 5.

Jung, C.G. ([1916]/1957) "The Transcendent Function," CW 8: 67–91.

Jung, C.G. (1927/1931) "The Structure of the Psyche," CW 8: 139–58.

Jung, C.G. (1934/1950) "A Study in the Process of Individuation," CW 9, 1: 290–354.

Jung, C.G. (1939/1940) *Psychology and Religion (The Terry Lectures)*, CW 11: 3–105.

Jung, C.G. (1940/1950) "Concerning Rebirth," CW 9, 1: 111–47.

Jung, C.G. (1950) "Concerning Mandala Symbolism," CW 9, 1: 355–90.

Jung, C.G. (1951) *Aion: Researches into the Phenomenology of the Self*, CW 9, 2.

Jung, C.G. (1952) *Answer to Job*, CW 11: 355–470.

Jung, C.G. (1955–56) *Mysterium Coniunctionis: An Inquiry into the Separation and Synthesis of Psychic Opposites in Alchemy*, CW 14.

Jung, C.G. (1963) *Memories, Dreams, Reflections*, ed. A. Jaffé, trans. R. and C. Winston, New York: Pantheon Books.

Jung, C.G. (1973) *Letters 1: 1906–1950*, ed. G. Adler with A. Jaffé, trans. R.F.C. Hull, Princeton, NJ: Princeton University Press.

Jung, C.G. (1984) *Dream Analysis: Notes of the Seminar Given in 1928–1930*, ed. W. McGuire, Princeton, NJ: Princeton University Press.

Jung, C.G. (1997) *Jung on Active Imagination*, ed. J. Chodorow, Princeton, NJ: Princeton University Press.

Jung, C.G. (2008) *Children's Dreams: Notes from the Seminar Given in 1936–1940*, ed. L. Jung and M. Meyer-Grass, trans. E. Falzeder with T. Woolfson, Princeton, NJ: Princeton University Press.

Jung, C.G. (2009) *The Red Book: Liber Novus*, ed. S. Shamdasani, trans. M. Kyburz, J. Peck, and S. Shamdasani, New York: W.W. Norton.

Long, T.H. (ed.) (1979) *Longman Dictionary of English Idioms*, Harlow: Longman.

Ronnberg, A., and Martin, K. (eds.) (2010) *The Book of Symbols: Reflections on Archetypal Images*, Cologne: Taschen.

Rowan, J. (1990) *Subpersonalities: The People Inside Us*, London: Routledge.

Schafer, R. (1968) *Aspects of Internalization*, New York: International Universities Press.

Vaihinger, H. (1924) *The Philosophy of "As If": A System of the Theoretical, Practical, and Religious Fictions of Mankind*, trans. C.K. Ogden, London: Routledge, Kegan Paul, Trench, Trubner & Co. and New York: Harcourt, Brace & Company.

Von Franz, M.-L. (1993a) "Active Imagination in the Psychology of C.G. Jung," trans. M.H. Kohn, in *Psychotherapy*, Boston: Shambhala: 146–62.

Von Franz, M.-L. (1993b) "On Active Imagination," trans. M.H. Kohn, in *Psychotherapy*, Boston and London: Shambhala: 163–76.

Watkins, M. (1986) *Invisible Guests: The Development of Imaginal Dialogues*, Hillsdale, NJ: The Analytic Press.

Whitmont, E.C. (1969) *The Symbolic Quest: Basic Concepts of Analytical Psychology*, New York: G.P. Putnam's Sons.

NAME INDEX

Aaron 79
Abernathy, R.D. 117
Abraham 89–90
Adams, M.V. 3–4, 11, 14, 23, 28, 34, 48,
    73–4, 78, 84, 118, 120, 124, 183,
    201, 203, 217, 224
Adler, A. 158–60, 164–5
Ahab (in the Bible) 211
Akbar 92
Al-Akili, M.M. 90
Allah 89, 93–4, 205, 218
Allen, J. 21
Ammer, C. 28, 122, 132, 150, 223
Amos 87
Apollo 124, 135–6, 173, 193
Aquarion 50
Ariadne 123
Arieti, S. 202
Arion 62–3
Arnold, T.W. 112–13
Athena 10, 168–9, 173, 175
Atherton, C. 18
Atropos 171
Atwood, L. 185
Augustine 108
Austin, J.L. 59
Axelrod, D. 121

Baal 211–12, 215–18, 220–2, 224–5
Baartman, S. 98–9
Bacchus 109–10
Bachelard, G. 4, 127
Bajaj, V. 131
Balint, M. 132
Bateson, G. 16, 19, 78
Baudrillard, J. 33
Baumol, W.J. 110
Beardsley, M.C. 107, 151

Beelzebub 212
Bell, D. 133
Bennet, E.A. 159
Beowulf 22
Bernanke, B.S. 121
Blake, W. 3, 7–9, 74, 136, 167–76
Bleuler, E. 203
Boas, G. 41
Boatner, M.T. 132
Bohm, D. 10, 58
Bonime, W. 44, 46
Booker, C. 19
Boss, M. 52
Botticelli 100
Brann, E.T.H. 36
Brown, N.O. 5, 8
Bunger 51, 151
Burton, B. 131
Bush, G.H.W. xiii, 119
Bush, G.W. 19, 22, 108, 120

Campbell, J. 22, 98, 119, 121–2, 174
Captain Ahab 6, 20, 22, 24, 29, 51,
    141–8, 150–2
Captain Boomer 51
Captain Hook 51
Captain Quint 51
Casey, E.S. 185
Ceres 109–10
Cespedes, R. 63
Chapman, G. 168
Chapman, R.L. 129
Chodorow, J. 210
Clinton, B. 119–20
Clinton, H. 25, 120
Clotho 171
Cohen, D. 4
Commandini, F. de L. 53

SUBJECT INDEX

abstract: concepts 16–18, 57, 64, 77, 79, 197; generalizations 18, 31, 57–8, 77
action capacity(-ies) 33, 39, 43, 46; distinctive 32, 37–8, 57–8, 62, 64; and interaction capacities 32
action language 33
active imagination: as an auxiliary 209; as a conversation xi, 24, 204, 217; as a dangerous method 209; as a dialogue xi, 24, 217, with God or the universal unconscious 92; not a dictation xi, 24, 189; as diplomacy 24; as an experiential method xi, 209; as interactive imagination 24, 210; as an Islamic method 91; as the method of all methods 209; as a mutual transformation 24; and the mythological unconscious 209; as a negotiation xi, 24, 189
actual world 38–9
aesthetic: form versus psychological content 174; of realism 184; socialist realism as an impossible 184
affective-attitudinal psychology 130
agent(s): as an entity with a capacity to act 39; images as 32–3
ālam al-mithāl 91–2; as an imaginal, not imaginary, dimension 92
alchemy 221; as a historical precursor of psychoanalysis 200
amplification: as a comparative and contrastive method xi, 118, 182; as an interpretative method xi; mythological 102–3, 109
anima: exotic, erotic 102; as the guide of the ego on the journey of individuation 175; as a psychopomp 175
animal(s): helpful 61–2; imaginal 53

animism: definition of 198; and environmental ethics 199; panpsychism as a contemporary version of 198
animus: as the archetype of the masculine aspect in the psyche of a woman 191
anxiety: ego as seat of 14; neurosis 14
Apollonian: ego 135; maxims 135
app(s) xi–xii
application(s): clinical xii, interdisciplinary xi–xiii
applied: psychoanalysis xii; science xii
archetypal: content as metaphors 146, 203; image of capitalism 108; image of communism 108; images 4, 84, 174–5; psychology 3
archetype(s): as abstract generalizations 58; and archetypal images 84; animus 191; cave 220; of the collective unconscious 29; as concepts 58; creativity 192–3; descent to the underworld 65; fool as wise man 147; helpful animal 61–2; high-flying hero 135; journey 66, 96, 98, 174; libido 123; monster 49, 148; monster-slaying hero 50–2, 148; monster-slaying monster 53; perfect man 91; rescuer 62–3; rite of passage 65; sea monster 50–1; shape-shifter 220; as standard pattern 118; terrible mother 65; as a theme with many variations 122; treasure hard to attain 150; trickster 46; of the unconscious 220; value 146
Archive for Research in Archetypal Symbolism 224
art: Greek and mythology 186–7, 191; prejudice of Jung against 174; visionary 173–6

233